DIVING INTO THE VOLCANO!

"[O]ne of the gifts of a well-handled Pluto transit involves reclaiming lost but valuable parts of ourselves that we've managed to suppress or deny in the past. These inner qualities have been battered and bruised from years of rejection, and have almost been snuffed out, yet now they can be restored to their original creative power."

—from Chapter Two

"During a frictional Pluto/Mars transit, some of us may fear that we'll blow our top and physically hurt someone else, or ourselves, although most often any harm done is psychological. Mars doesn't willingly turn its forces inward, especially when more stimulating, external targets are available. Our temper can surface more vividly than usual, with an extra dose of Plutonian fury that erupts quickly and inexplicably. What triggers us may seem minor, but nonetheless is symbolic of unfinished business regarding frustrated attempts at self-assertion."

—from Chapter Six

"Pluto is on familiar turf here [in the Eighth House] and knows how to navigate its way around this shadowy labyrinth. There's very little about our Eighth House that scares Pluto. Actually, Pluto admits to no fears whatsoever, which is a way to deny having secret vulnerabilities . . . this is a house where we are to get in touch with an entirely different underground realm, an area we guard closely and are unwilling to share with others."

—from A Plutonian Tour of Our Natal Houses

"[A] few of us probably haven't done so hot in coping with life's daily rituals thus far—we've made far too many stupid mistakes already, leaving our life at loose ends and vulnerable to failure. . . . If this sounds like us (we claim we can't even boil water), Pluto will probably force us to dissect the hidden reasons behind our consistent incompetence, and ask why nothing seems to work right in our lives."

—from Chapter Eleven

ABOUT THE AUTHOR

Bil Tierney has been involved with astrology for over thirty-two years. As a full-time professional, he has lectured and given workshops at major astrological conferences throughout the United States and in Canada since the mid-1970s. He has a special interest in studying the birthchart from a practical, psychological level that also encourages spiritual growth. He is a longtime member of the Metropolitan Atlanta Astrological Society (MAAS), and has served as its newsletter/journal editor several times. Bil's work has also been published in astrological publications such as *Aspects* and *The Mercury Hour*. Other books he has written are *Dynamics of Aspect Analysis*, and the Llewellyn publications: *Twelve Faces of Saturn*, *Alive and Well with Neptune,* and *Alive and Well with Uranus.*

When Bil is not busy with client consultations, lecturing, tutoring, and writing articles and books, his other big passion is computers. Clients enjoy Bil's animated, warm, and easy-going style, and they are impressed with his skillful blend of the intuitive and the analytical. His humorous slant on life is appreciated as well. Readers enjoy his thorough, insightful approach to astrological topics.

TO CONTACT THE AUTHOR

If you would like to contact the author or would like more information about this book, please write to him in care of Llewellyn Worldwide. All mail addressed to the author is forwarded, but the publisher cannot, unless specifically instructed by the author, give out an address or phone number. Please write to:

Bil Tierney
c/o Llewellyn Publications
P.O. Box 64383, Dept. K714–5
St. Paul, MN 55164–0383, U.S.A.

Please enclose a self-addressed, stamped envelope for reply or $1.00 to cover costs. If ordering from outside the U.S.A., please enclose an international postal reply coupon.

Llewellyn Worldwide does not participate in, endorse, or have any authority or responsibility concerning private business transactions between our authors and the public.

Alive and Well with PLUTO

Transits of Power and Renewal

Bil Tierney

1999
Llewellyn Publications
St. Paul, MN 55164–0833 U.S.A.

FIRST EDITION
First Printing 1999

Cover design by William Merlin Cannon
Book design by Ken Schubert
Editing by Marguerite Krause
Project Management by Eila Savela

Library of Congress Cataloging-in-Publication Data
Tierney, Bil.
    Alive & well with Pluto : transits of power and renewal / Bil Tierney. —
    1st ed.
       p.   cm.
    Includes bibliographical references (p.   ).
    ISBN 1-56718-714-5
    1. Astrology. 2. Pluto (Planet) — Miscellanea. I. Title.
II. Title : Alive and well with Pluto.
BF1724.2.P4T54   1999
133.5'392—dc21   99-35402
                                                     CIP

Llewellyn Publications
A Division of Llewellyn Worldwide, Ltd.
P.O. Box 64383, Dept. K714-5
St. Paul, MN 55164-0383, U.S.A.
www.llewellyn.com

Printed in the United States of America

DEDICATION

I dedicate this book to Donna Cunningham, a
fearless astrologer who has dared to look Pluto
straight in the eye without flinching.

ACKNOWLEDGEMENTS

A thanks goes to Llewellyn's Acquisitions Manager Nancy Mostad for accepting my Pluto manuscript for publication. I'm also very appreciative of Ken Schubert for his fine book design, William Merlin Cannon for the striking cover he created, and hard-working Marguerite Krause for her fine editing skills and for keeping my book's offbeat humor intact. I also applaud the efforts of Project Manager and Astrology Editor, Eila Savela (thanks, Eila, for smoothly handling last-minute details). My thanks also goes to Jerry Rogers (Publicity), Wendy Crowe (Marketing), and everyone else who helped in the production of this book.

And last, I wish to express my gratitude to my colleagues Angel Thompson and Kim Rogers-Gallagher, who read pre-publication copies of *Alive and Well With Pluto* and submitted their comments for the back cover.

Oh, and thanks, Pluto, for permitting me to descend into your darkened realm, with my trusty torch in hand, to shed a little light on your hidden wealth that awaits us below life's surface. You enabled me to brag about what a dynamic force of vibrant soul-power and renewal you really are!

OTHER BOOKS BY BIL TIERNEY

Twelve Faces of Saturn
Alive and Well with Uranus
Alive and Well with Neptune

TABLE OF CONTENTS

Chapter Eight

Chapter Nine

Chapter Ten

Chapter Eleven

Chapter Twelve

Chapter Thirteen

Chapter Fourteen

Chapter Fifteen

Chapter Sixteen

Chapter Seventeen

INTRODUCTION

TALES FROM THE UNDERWORLD

We know him in astrology as Pluto, thanks to Roman mythology. This, of course, was also the name agreed on by astronomers shortly after the planet was physically discovered in the Arizona sky on the night of February 18, 1930.[1] The Greeks, however, called him Hades. This grim god dwelt in the underground realm of the dead, which was also named Hades. If you've already read volume two of this Outer Planet trilogy—*Alive and Well with Neptune*[2]—you'll recall that Hades and Poseidon (Neptune) were brothers who shared an identical fate immediately after birth: both were swallowed by their paranoid father, Cronus (Saturn). Both were unhappily entombed for a while in Cronus' dark belly and thereby deprived of the early emotional bonding so necessary between mother and child.

The damage incurred by this post-natal trauma was later evident: Poseidon grew up to be a periodic rage-aholic and a bit of a mindless sex addict, known for his destructive, infantile blow-up scenes whenever thwarted in action or desire. Hades had his own share of inner conflicts and personality disturbances. After ousting their father from his seat of power, Hades and his brothers,

1

Poseidon and Zeus, drew lots to determine which realm of the world each would govern. Old "Dark Face"[3] ended up with the Underworld as his ruling domain. Fate ensures that there are no accidents in life.

Hades promptly withdrew from the social scene altogether and transformed into a powerful, hidden force—remote, icy, unyielding, and unwilling or unable to show mercy. Parts of him were fully shut down. He was completely unmoved by the emotions of others. However, probably due to this god's basic loner streak, Hades was comfortable living in his cold, dark dominion, deep below Earth's surface. He was also unapproachable and forbidding in his demeanor, which explains why he was never invited to join the company of the other gods, who were probably uneasy with his line of work: keeper of the dead and supreme ruler of all aspects of the afterlife. No god or goddess on Mount Olympus wanted to get Hades too interested in him or her. Some were even afraid to whisper his name and risk evoking his intimidating presence. He was the Invisible One, and none dared to directly confront him. I'd say that much of this stems from the repercussions of his early childhood trauma.

All in all, he was feared for his power and avoided because of his spooky personality. In today's psychological jargon, withdrawn Hades would be diagnosed as a borderline schizoid, with all the anti-social traits that underscore such a personality disorder. He was also a rapist, a crime fueled by deep rage against (mostly) women. Did a subconsciously furious Hades hold his weak and passive mother, Rhea, accountable for not intervening on his behalf at birth to prevent his father from consuming him? Why didn't Rhea put up a big fight and just say no (while giving Cronus' Saturn-ruled kneecaps a few real hard kicks)? Why did she chicken out and let the despot have his way—was this a sign of battered-wife syndrome on a psychological level?

Hades' mom eventually did wise up, however, and showed a little courage by the time she gave birth to lucky Zeus (Jupiter), who escaped being swallowed. In Hades' case, however, it's obvious that his unprocessed childhood wounds were never adequately addressed and resolved, wounds caused by a father who gobbled up his identity and made him disappear, and by a mother who abandoned him during his moment of greatest peril—how do you ever learn to trust anyone after that?

WHAT HADES DESIRED MOST

A complicating event that really put the Hades myth on the map was when this dark god forced himself on the virginal, sunny-natured Kore, kidnapped her, and later coerced her to co-rule the shadowy Underworld as his eternal bride. Thereafter, she was known as Persephone. Was this abduction his twisted attempt to reach out and share something of himself with another? Didn't he realize that no one could really love and honor him under such manipulative conditions? Even today, forceful Plutonians who compulsively insist on owning and controlling people still have trouble being truly loved, much less respected.

Hades was protective of his underground existence and only surfaced into the world of fresh air and bright light a few times. Even then, he preferred to travel unseen, and wore a special helmet that made him invisible. Similarly, Plutonians and Scorpio Rising folk wear their trademark sunglasses almost everywhere as their way to symbolically hide from the world, as well as create an air of mystery. Hades' invisibility is probably what made the others gods the most nervous—he could theoretically be anywhere, nosing in on private conversations, and nobody would know it. Plutonians make excellent spies and undercover agents.

Myths told by different ancient writers and by modern translators are dissimilar in certain details, and in Hades' case, we have at least two versions of how he ended up kidnapping the sweet and ingenuous daughter of the grain-and-harvest goddess, Demeter (Ceres). The young maiden Kore personified the lightness, gaiety, and beauty of Spring.

In one account, the often naughty-but-nice Aphrodite (Venus) observed Hades making the rounds in his underground world, literally inspecting for cracks that might allow unwanted intruders or even a little sunlight to enter. (I guess everyone was supposed to remain deathly pale in the Underworld.) In a mischievously match-making mood, Aphrodite told her son, Cupid, to shoot lonesome Dark Face in the heart with one of the little cherub's arrows of desire. Hades soon had a burning, overwhelming urge to go above ground and, as fate would have it, Kore was the first sweet, young thing he laid eyes on. He was hopelessly mad for her, almost dangerously smitten, and had to "have" her right then, exclusively as his own. Apparently, Aphrodite wasn't much into the true spirit of sisterhood in those days, because she thought nothing of pitting such an innocent soul, a devoted momma's girl, against this power-house recluse god, eager to ravish such a tender, delicate prize—gosh, what was that crazy Aphrodite thinking? As the earth yawned opened, Hades swept his "love" captive away in his roaring, flaming chariot and headed down toward his favorite theme park!

The other account offered is even more disturbing because it smacks of shady collusion and betrayal. By today's standards, this tale would definitely be considered unsavory in a particularly Plutonian way—the tabloids would love it! Supposedly, Kore's father Zeus (Jupiter) helped to get the whole abduction plan going—incredible, since he was her daddy! These male sky gods—think of Uranus—can be quite insensitive when it comes to how they treat females.

Zeus once mated with Demeter, and darling Kore was their offspring. Then Zeus took off for new adventures in sexual conquest, while leaving Demeter to play the devoted single-mom role, which she did to the nth degree. Mother and daughter were very tight, very bonded, and didn't need anyone else to butt in and ruin their excellent, conflict-free relationship. This wise earth-mom knew that there were other lusty "love-'em-and-leave-'em" Jupiter-types out there, waiting to take advantage of the virtues of young maidens everywhere, and good old mom was going to make darn sure that her precious daughter would not end up a victim of any smooth-talking cad.

Zeus certainly didn't go for this cozy mother-daughter alliance, viewing it as unnatural because, obviously, no male was involved. It just happened that Hades somehow caught a sneak glimpse of Kore and fell hard for her. He pleaded with Zeus to let him have her as his mate and, together, these brothers—who normally weren't that close—hatched a devious plan to kidnap the young virgin (although it was mostly Hades' scheme). Hades even planted a seductive narcissus flower in the meadow where Kore would romp with her friends, because he was certain that she would be hypnotically drawn to it. This sounds as if he knew her daily routine well, as any good stalker would. Sure enough, Kore wandered away by herself, saw the narcissus in full bloom, picked it, inhaled (hmmm, big mistake!), and that was all it took: the earth roared open and an overpowering Hades came forth in his chariot to snatch Kore up, rape her, and then pretty much "swallow" her by making her an unwilling captive of his dark chambers as he vanished with her down below. In some ways, this echoed his own wounding childhood trauma with his dad—a case of the abused become the abuser.

This long tale continues with a few Plutonian plot twists, but let's just say that Zeus felt partly justified in allowing this match, because Hades was also known as the Rich One. Jupiterians are typically impressed by prosperity. Hades ruled all of the hidden wealth buried in the ground, such as metals and gemstones. His realm had an impressive gross worth. Demeter, meanwhile, felt betrayed to the bone when she discovered that Zeus had played a key role in what was, for her, a devastating tragedy. Her resultant rage and deep grief almost ended life on the planet, which really shook up Zeus and made him have second thoughts. He eventually conceded that a daughter needs her mother—and, even more important, Earth needed a thriving plant kingdom so that the human race would survive and be able to continue happily worshipping the gods.

Kore was in complete depression while imprisoned during her year in Hades, but that's probably how Hades liked his women—emotionally shut down and almost catatonic! Yet she did "spring" back to life on that glorious day when Hermes (Mercury) descended into Hades to deliver the message that she was to immediately return to her mother on orders of the king of the gods, Zeus. However, Kore evidently snapped out of her stupor a little too excitedly on hearing the good news, because crafty Hades was able to offer her a parting snack consisting of a few pomegranate seeds, which, in her elation, she ate—probably just to get back into being her old sweet, accommodating self. Apparently, sharp-eyed Hermes must have been staring at Hades' long, dirty toenails or something at the time, because he missed this little ploy altogether. It was well known among the gods that, when visiting Down Below, you never ate the food offered unless you planned to make Hades your permanent abode. Tricky Hades knew that he would soon have his way—so why not let Kore spend a little time with Mom if that would help to put her in a better mood?

Upon hearing from Kore about the pomegranate ruse and realizing it sealed her daughter's fate, Demeter pitched another climatological fit, while Zeus freaked out again about the dim future awaiting the planet. Exasperated, he demanded a final compromise: Kore was to spend half of each year in Hades as Persephone,[4] the Queen of the Underworld, and a bitter Demeter in mourning was allowed to go on strike, thereby creating the non-vegetative seasons of autumn and winter. Afterward, Persephone was free to reunite with her mother for the remaining half of every year—although never quite again as her innocent Kore persona. Meanwhile, obsessive-compulsive Dark Face completely focused all of his energies on running the increasingly populated Underworld, with souls of the newly dead and the damned lining up to enter its gates every day—business as usual!

Now, let's switch to a few present-day matters involving our Pluto transits.

HOW TO BEST USE THIS BOOK

Let's say that transiting Pluto is just starting to move into your Eleventh House and that it will be there for over a decade. Read Chapter Sixteen to find out what special challenges may await you. It's likely that you'll have a radically different outlook about many matters of this house by the time this transit is finished. For additional insights, you also can read in that same chapter about transiting Pluto aspecting your natal Uranus. Although Uranus and the Eleventh House do not exactly symbolize the same kind of energy, they certainly share several themes in common. Still, keep in mind that a house transit is about how we outwardly structure our life more than how we inwardly process ourselves, even though our inner world plays a critical role in determining the external frameworks that we attract. The theme of exercising the freedom to completely be ourselves within our social environment is highlighted by Pluto transiting our Eleventh or our Uranus. Therefore, read the entire chapter pertaining to any transited house and associated planet that is stimulated by Pluto's energies.

It may also prove valuable to apply parts of any transiting interpretation to your natal delineation. If you were born with Pluto in the Second House, then read the transit of Pluto in the Second for any insights to be had about your natal situation. Realize that Pluto's house at birth is a permanent condition throughout your lifetime which slowly works on a level of character development as well as of circumstantial unfoldment. That same house, during Pluto's transit, stimulates events of a temporal nature—which include new people entering our life—and may or may not have a lasting impact on our psyche. Therefore, modify the transit report to suggest patterns at work manifesting on a more long-term basis. Likewise, any Pluto transit to a natal planet can be interpreted, when modified, to define those same planets when found in a natal aspect (transiting Pluto/Moon is thus similar to our natal Pluto/Moon). Using my book in this manner will help to make your reading experience more informative and enjoyable.

MERCURY AND VENUS: LIVING A DOUBLE LIFE

Mercury rules two signs—Gemini and Virgo. This means that it has an airy side to its nature and an earthier side. In two separate chapters, I refer to this dual-personality as "air Mercury" and "earth Mercury." Many of the more stereotypical traits we ascribe to Mercury belong to its airy, Geminian nature. The less obvious, atypical earthy qualities belong to Virgo. I'll cover Pluto's transit to both facets of the Mercury experience in Chapter Eight (air Mercury) and in Chapter Eleven (earth Mercury). It makes no difference what actual sign our natal Mercury occupies—sometimes we approach life using our air Mercury resources, while at other times our earth Mercury sensibilities come into play. In many instances, we are quickly processing both sides of the Mercury principle when trying to handle our environment.

All of the above also applies to Venus, who also lives a double life by ruling earthy Taurus and airy Libra. Read Chapter Seven to see how Pluto impacts our earthy Venus awareness, and Chapter Twelve to find out how our airy Venusian side interacts with Pluto. Activating both sides of Venus helps us to better experience this planet's principles. It's not easy to look at someone's chart and instantly know if his or her Pluto transit will trigger an air Venus versus an earth Venus response. The same goes for air Mercury versus earth Mercury. However, Pluto is very thorough in how it uncovers what's not working well within us. Therefore, we can expect that both sides of our Mercury or Venus consciousness will get a demanding but well-needed workout during our Pluto transit.

GALLOWS HUMOR

Astrology becomes an even more enjoyable study when we inject a little lightness in the form of humor. If we do it while offering insight and a bit of wisdom, we get to learn more regarding the human condition while we also laugh about it. At first glance, there seems to be absolutely nothing funny about sometimes morbid Pluto. If anything, this planet is associated with "sick jokes" that often revolt rather than amuse us—nothing is taboo in the name of Plutonian humor.

Still, I prefer to assume that the Cosmos enjoys a good laugh now and then, which explains why, even after we die and our flesh rots away, we each are undeniably left with a maniacal-looking skull flashing its outrageous smile—a grin made to look even goofier if some of us didn't have all of our teeth when we kicked the bucket. This probably is one of those cosmic, Plutonian "inside" jokes—sort of an archetypal victory sign conveying Death's smug sense of, "Ha-ha—gotcha at last, sucker!" That demented smile eventually will be found inside every coffin, once time devours all traces of our familiar human form. Think of all those skeletons smirking in the dark throughout the centuries, as if getting the last laugh on mortals who dare to dream of immortality!

Actually, Pluto invites astrological humor because of the extremism of its reactions and behavior. What often makes humor work is how well it exaggerates the foibles of human nature in ways that unexpectedly tickle our funny bone. Nonetheless, portraying a Pluto transit as something we can occasionally chuckle about is a hard sell. I tried my best to do so in this book, but still, transiting Pluto is a weighty topic to cover. Please take my "comic relief" in the spirit in which it was intended. Let's not get too sanctimonious and straight-faced when using astrology, especially those of us who have no time for frivolity because we're too busy seriously "burning off *all* our karma" in this lifetime. Pluto knows otherwise.

Thank goodness that other astrologers have been zeroing in on our vital need for astro-humor. Kim Rogers-Gallagher is one gal who's been galloping way ahead of the pack for years now. You have to be one smart and perceptive astrologer to consistently pull off astro-humor, and that's why Kim shines here. Treat yourself to her witty insights in her entertaining *Astrology for the Light Side of the Brain* and her equally fun *Astrology for the Light Side of the Future.*[5] With Neptune and Uranus passing through formality-defying Aquarius, these upcoming years (1999–2012) could very well be the "Golden Age" of astrological humor. In fact, for the mass market, there is available *The Complete Idiot's Guide to Astrology,*[6] a title that already confirms my feelings!

NOTES

1. Read Jeff Jawer's "The Discovery of the Outer Planets," pp. 13–29, in the anthology *How to Personalize the Outer Planets,* edited by Noel Tyl, Llewellyn Publications, 1992. Interestingly, on the night of this planet's discovery, the Moon "just happened" to be in Pluto's ruling sign Scorpio and Pluto itself was near the Midheaven in the event chart.

2. Bil Tierney, *Alive and Well with Neptune,* Llewellyn Publications, St. Paul, MN, 1999.

3. "Dark Face" is my personal nickname for Hades-Pluto.

4. After her transformation in Hades, Kore was known as Persephone. In *The Astrology of Fate,* Samuel Weiser, Inc., York Beach, Maine, 1984, Liz Greene says that Persephone means "bringer of destruction." It is thus a Plutonian-sounding name that wouldn't have made as much sense before her abduction, when everything about her was all sweetness and light.

5. Kim Rogers-Gallagher, *Astrology for the Light Side of the Brain,* ACS Publications, San Diego, CA, 1995. Also by the same publisher, *Astrology for the Light Side of the Future,* 1998.

6. Madeline Gerwick-Brodeur and Lisa Lenard, *The Complete Idiot's Guide to Astrology,* Macmillan General Reference: Alpha Books, 1997.

PART ONE

IGNITING OUR INNER FIRE

CHAPTER ONE

NOWHERE TO HIDE

PROBING PLUTO'S MYTH

In the Introduction, I presented a less in-depth interpretation of mythological Hades, especially regarding his abduction of Kore. Taken at face value, this story doesn't make this god look very evolved in matters of the heart. As a mythic figure, he seems tremendously insensitive, even brutal. Some would call him a dirty rat for conspiring to snatch Kore away from her mom and from the only loving, protected environment she had known. Besides, kidnapping is a criminal act. When strictly analyzed on the surface, Hades seems like a disturbed isolationist who had trouble controlling his obsessive desire once he surfaced in the world. He treated Kore as an object that he could grab, own, and control. Everything about his actions here was covert—the unsuspecting maiden was ambushed!

However, to approach Hades in only this way—and from now on, I'll just call him Pluto—overlooks the more profound meaning of his archetypal profile. He represents more than just some devious, power-crazed bully suffering from psychological defects. Astro-mythologists, such as astrologer Liz Greene,[1] have already figured out a lot about this god's role in our psyche's development.

Even Pluto's underground realm Hades is itself ripe with psycho-dynamic meaning for us.[2]

All who have taken time to decode the mythos of Pluto arrive at the same conclusion: he represents powerful primal forces that dwell in the depths of our personal unconscious, which itself acts as our own symbolic Hades. In myth, the Underworld was considered to exist far below the surface of Earth. Anything above ground becomes an apt symbol of our waking consciousness. Hades was not an easy place for any soul to enter, living or dead. Caves, deep cracks in the ground, fissures in remote areas, and lakes were typical entry points—as were all fairly inaccessible places, for the most part. Once a soul arrived at the gates of Hades—after crossing any of the five rivers that surrounded it, especially the River Styx—a monstrous, three-headed, dragon-tailed dog named Cerberus imposingly guarded the official entrance. By some accounts, he also had the heads of snakes protruding from his back and a dragon's head at the tip of his reptilian tail—giving him a particularly intimidating Plutonian look.

Except in a few cases, no mortal was able to enter those gates without provoking a barking incident: only the dead were quietly admitted—but this "hound of Hades" would turn particularly ferocious and vicious when anyone later attempted to exit the Underworld. This symbolizes the power of our unconscious to trap and retain psychological material that is not easily released to the surface. We must struggle to break free of whatever intimidatingly oppresses us in our private underworld.

One of the most disturbing elements of the Hades-Persephone story is the initial rape of defenseless Kore. Astro-mythologists explain that this is often how Pluto (especially a Pluto transit) feels to us at first—like a violation from a dark, external element in the environment or from some overpowering and unrelenting inner complex that we never knew existed. Strange and troubling forces can rise up from our personal underground when transiting Pluto activates our chart. Any natal planet seized by Pluto is seldom a willing captive—in contrast to what happens when a planet is transited by intoxicatingly seductive Neptune. Our instinct is to resist being overtaken by hidden Plutonian factors within us or by those operating in the outer world. We struggle to release ourselves from this planet's invisible, tight grip. By the way, it seems that Pluto wore his helmet of invisibility when he attacked Kore—imagine how terrifying that must have been for her. However, transiting Pluto insists on penetrating those parts of us that can no longer afford to remain innocent and unaware.

Once Kore was in the depths of Hades, she began a transformative process that was to result in the development of her more empowered persona—Persephone. You'll recall that Kore was tricked into eating the seeds of the pomegranate, and yet that simple act was profoundly life-altering for her, for now she was a permanent part of Pluto's inner world. Analysts of astro-myth wonder if this meant that some unconscious part of Kore felt compelled to eat those seeds, knowing that this action would irrevocably break her seamless tie to her mother; and that, as Persephone, she could no longer remain the eternal child sheltered by an over-protective parent. She'd be forced to shed that underdeveloped identity. Thus, something deep inside Kore's unconscious probably knew that she was destined to play the role of Persephone, given the right Plutonian trigger. After all, no one forced her to eat or drink anything in Hades, although Pluto, in offering the pomegranate, was powerfully persuasive and devious enough to manipulate Kore at a particularly vulnerable moment of distraction.

The innocent Kore fulfilled her evolutionary fate by metamorphosing into the more capable Persephone, a regent powerful in her own right as well as an equal partner in Pluto's eyes. That's one good thing to be said about Dark Face—he didn't keep his mate in a powerless state once she surrendered to inhabiting and co-ruling his vast realm. Actually, Persephone got so good at taking on this power-role that she developed a reputation as fearsome as Pluto's—well, we all overcompensate now and then, don't we?

What this myth implies is that Pluto transits seem to intrude and take over our normal behavioral patterns and our life routines, often against our conscious desire and will. When Pluto transits in hard angle, any planet feels violated at first—especially when the environment introduces elements of change that are forceful and unyielding. Plutonian changes can be drastic and final. A part of us may fear that we are being denied the safe comfort of protective securities that we've held on to for much of our lives. Depending on the aspects involved, these transits can feel as if we've been yanked away from familiar support and thrown into a pit of psychological or situational darkness, where no one can immediately come to our rescue. We are forced to slowly adjust to new, inner realms that won't allow us to regress to previous behaviors that we've already unconsciously outgrown. Let's look at this process further.

PLUTO RISING

Transiting Pluto moves very slowly, yet purposefully, as it entrenches itself in our transited natal house long enough for us to get this message: our complete acceptance of a needed internal overhaul will help us to deeply revolutionize our future approach to the house matters in question. We can't continue to mindlessly go along with certain chronic patterns in this life department. A crisis may impose on us the demand to self-transform. This is typically a slow-building crisis that can get more complicated as time goes on, until the issues we must deal with finally erupt. Remember that Kore, miserable and despondent, spent about a year in Hades, which for her was more like doing time in Hell. She desperately wanted to return to her home, not remain imprisoned in this dark, alien world deep below the sunlit surface.

We, too, may feel trapped in darkness as overpowering conditions slowly reshape the total direction of our life, often in ways that bring up old, unresolved fears. As a consequence of the long-lasting transformations that occur, we're not allowed to revert to old defenses and emotional resistances that once worked for us, but that kept us from dynamic inner growth. When descending into Pluto's realm, we are stripped of anything we've formally used to cover up our hidden flaws and hang-ups, as well as our less obvious strengths and untapped powers. Kore felt the strange impulse to eat those juicy pomegranate seeds. Similarly, a mysterious urge within us desires to partake of this depth-provoking experience in ways that ensure—when this transit is over—that we cannot return to what we once were.

FEELING CURSED?

If our hidden strengths and latent powers could quickly surface after about a week or so of internalized and intensified Pluto transit activity, then this period in our life wouldn't feel so bad—a piece of (devil's food) cake. Some astrologers put a rosy spin on a word that gets casually tossed about—"transformation"—thinking of it mainly in terms of the inspiring caterpillar-to-butterfly motif, but never the frightening human-to-werewolf scenario. However, if the transformative process was all that simple and clear-cut, Pluto wouldn't really be Pluto.

Pluto doesn't do simple things in simple ways. Even the mythic god himself, grappling with a few childhood fears involving rejection, couldn't just flat-out ask Zeus or Aphrodite to set him up on a normal blind date with a willing goddess—although it would probably have to be a date where he was not allowed to wear his helmet so that he could be clearly visible in the light! Interestingly, Pluto rules vampires, and vampires don't do well in broad daylight. Pluto was a bit of a tortured soul fighting his own transformational challenges; therefore, he never took the uncomplicated, honest approach to obtaining love and intimacy. Likewise, this is a planet that does not make our rebirths easy experiences. We can go into prolonged periods of labor first. It seems Pluto doesn't believe in effortless activity. The magical "wish it and it shall be yours" routine belongs to Jupiter and Neptune.

Therefore, when undergoing a major tensional Pluto transit, we are likely to feel that we have upset the gods or the cosmic powers that be for some obscure reason. We don't understand why life takes a heavier turn for us, and perplexingly so. The path we are on becomes a more complex obstacle course, and a suspicious attitude about the whole thing certainly won't help us feel at ease with what's unfolding. That's primarily because we resent not being able to control the entire situation. This is the overall feeling that some of us may have when transiting Pluto conjuncts, squares, quincunxes, or opposes our natal planets— although similar serious, inner issues needing our attention can also be part of the sextile or the trine phase. Pluto never stops being Pluto no matter what aspect it forms.

The theme of this book is about learning to be "alive and well" with Pluto transits. Therefore, we are going to have to stop feeling cursed by the Universe whenever Dark Face pays us a visit, although he mainly comes to audit us. He also comes bearing powerful gifts that we may not appreciate just yet—but we will, once we've shed enough of our illusions about ourselves and about life itself. To make sense of any Pluto transit, however, means that we will need to penetrate the heart of our internal conflicts, and that may involve digging up the "dirt" on our psychological past. It's time to play detective and track down a few critical leads that can help us to solve our own mystery as to why we are not finding fulfillment in our life, according to the house or planet Pluto's transiting. Pluto typically forces us to focus on our wounded parts, maybe a little too obsessively at times. However, if we persist in feeling only victimized or persecuted by the world, while never seeing how much we help create this unwelcome experience, we become our own worst enemy—the one who betrays our soul the most.

Self-destruction is a legitimate Plutonian urge. Pluto is one of our "terminator" planets (Saturn, the other). Mythic Pluto never allowed the shades of the dead to leave Hades and return to the upper world, probably because he didn't want that which was properly buried and then put to rest to ever come back to life again and problematically resurface. No one dead could even enter the gates of Hades unless they were properly interred (certain burial rituals were to be observed). We feel a struggle during our Pluto periods to kill off parts of ourselves that have caused us much torment or that have led to our alienation from others. Pluto has no problem annihilating that which can no longer empower us, or that which has always tried to thwart our self-empowerment. Those self-defeating facets within us have to die, but they must be buried (resolved) the right way to satisfy

Pluto! They must be dealt with in a manner that enlightens us and helps us to let go of such conflicts while also bringing us inner peace. We'll need to carefully and responsibly handle any toxic material that we bury in this process. Pluto certainly doesn't want us to further contaminate ourselves or others.

BATTLING INVISIBLE FORCES

It does seem that, if we are on a conscious path of self-realization, and if we have read all of the deepest astro-mythic material available about Pluto and attended workshops on transpersonal astrology, we still typically find our understanding of this planet to be more intellectual than emotional—we're too detached to allow for intense gut responses. The god of the intellect, Hermes (Mercury), had no problem descending into Pluto's netherworld to both deliver and receive messages. This helped clinch his role as a skilled "go-between" and savvy negotiator. In the upper world, Hermes had a reputation for being clever with words, bordering on hype and little white lies at times. Yet whenever he descended into Hades, he had to be on his best behavior, no doubt, because Pluto certainly wouldn't tolerate this vocal god's glib, sales-pitch approach. Similarly, Plutonians don't trust those who talk too much, especially when they say so little. Hermes had to ditch his flighty, restless persona while visiting down under; he was forced to deepen his perceptions and focus his attention.

Sometimes, with our Pluto transits, we can feel as if we're battling invisible forces that play dirty with us. Primal Pluto, after all, doesn't abide by civilized rules. Although our intellect is pressured to be more sharp and alert during our Pluto transits, we can feel as if we're straining our brain to come up with smart, clear-cut solutions to any dilemma at hand—solutions that "should" work but often, mysteriously, do not. It will take more than just intellectual prowess to appease Pluto. When Hermes convinced Pluto to surrender Kore to the upper world, he had to speak gently rather than aggressively to get results, using persuasion, not threats, fiery rhetoric, clever put-downs, or brilliant arguments. This suggests that our intellectual side won't get much accomplished by vigorously applying logic and reason, as if sheer brain power alone will solve our Plutonian conflicts. In addition, Pluto's agenda is much too unfathomable for Mercury to ever figure out, unless Mercury is willing to suspend its expectations of reasonability. These transits are times when we need to deeply listen and observe more than talk and analyze. That's a hard task for any over-stimulated, undisciplined mind to achieve.

In the long run, we'll just have to drop our defenses and let ourselves more fully feel what we're going through without fearing that to do so will destroy us. It will only destroy parts of us, those parts that have been silently sabotaging our real needs for a long while. By the way, when Hermes made his journeys to the Underworld, he was allowed to wear Pluto's helmet—symbolically helping him to view life from Pluto's perspective—and he used torches to light the way on these dark journeys into and out of the depths. Our mind can also help to bring light to our darker Plutonian experiences, but we mentally need to be more receptive and absorptive than active and projective during these irrational, yet profoundly meaningful, periods.

Some of what I've said in this chapter might make impressionable readers feel that Pluto transits probably should come with clear warning labels, emphasized by little skull-and-crossbones symbols. This planet does sound like poison to those who worship a life of little change. In the next chapter, we'll explore what makes a rousing Pluto transit so fabulous. What are the Pluto perks we can look forward to? What rewards are ours for working constructively and bravely with these intensive passages of our life? Do any of us really survive a lengthy Pluto transit with a gleam in our eye and a song in our heart?

NOTES

1. Especially read "Chapter Two: Fate and Pluto" from Liz Greene's *The Astrology of Fate*, Samuel Weiser, Inc., York Beach, Maine, 1984.

2. Astrologer Brian Clark has written the best account I've read so far of the Underworld—its inhabitants and its territories—in his work

Hades as Place: The Underworld in Myth and Antiquity, Astro*Synthesis Publications, 1998. Brian uses every opportunity he can to connect all aspects of Hades' actual environment with what goes on in the depths of our unconscious. This analysis was printed in Australia and may be hard to get. The address given in *Hades as Place* as of 1998 is: Astro*Synthesis, Chiron Centre, 407 Johnston Street, Abbotsford, Victoria 3067, Australia.

CHAPTER TWO

GIFTS FROM THE RICH ONE

MINING FOR GOLD

When Pluto (as Hades) drew lots with his brothers Zeus and Poseidon, after overthrowing their father Cronus (Saturn), and when fate allotted him the Underworld as his slice of the pie, I bet the other two gods were silently congratulating themselves, thinking, "Thank God, not me!" Yet Pluto didn't bat an eyelash as he quietly accepted his inheritance—the cold, dark, gloomy depths of Earth. "At least it will forever remain a quieter place," he probably realized, "compared to Mount Olympus with its socially busy comings and goings." Actually, Hades grew increasingly populated each day by the spirits of the dead in the form of semi-transparent, gauzy shades—washed-out versions of their former earthly selves; thus, it was busy in a different way.

What was not so apparent at that fateful moment when the world was divvied up was that Pluto's realm would also be the one blessed with buried treasure—all of the subterranean riches of the planet. No wonder Plutonians today sense that valuable things lie below life's surface, waiting to be found. This will require focused probing—and it's no wonder that archeologists and psychotherapists are Pluto-ruled.

At some stage in Greek mythology, this god was dubbed Plouton, "the Rich One,"[1] suggesting that his private turf, Hades, was more than the abode of the dead—it was Fort Knox as well! The vast, unseen resources below the ground were under Pluto's control. By the time he made a name for himself in Roman mythology, this aspect of Pluto was even more emphasized. He became known as a wealthy—if greedy—god, determined to stockpile and keep what was his. Even the souls of the dead became his permanent property once they passed his gates. I suspect that he was compelled to amass a large quantity of things of great value to compensate for his wounded self-image. He never quite got over the devaluing experience of being swallowed by Saturn and made to seem non-existent.

During our Pluto transits, there is hidden gold to be mined for those of us willing to make the tremendous efforts required to uncover precious, inner resources buried in those less accessible places of our psyche. They cannot be summoned to surface and unveil themselves at the demand of our ego-directed will. Such treasures are the assets of our personal unconscious, our internalized Hades, and therefore are not easily released. However, if we think about how freely Hermes was allowed to come and go in Pluto's world, we realize that possessing a flexible mind that adapts well to change helps us greatly in our search for what is carefully hidden in our psyche's underground.

Thus, one of the gifts of a well-managed Pluto transit involves reclaiming lost but valuable parts of ourselves that we've suppressed or denied in the past. These inner qualities have been battered and bruised from years of rejection, and have almost been snuffed out, yet now they can be restored to their original creative power. However, anyone who works in an actual underground mine knows how perilous the conditions can be. The gold nuggets and the precious gems of our psyche, not easily reached, will require our utmost skill and persistence if they are to be dislodged from their tricky hiding spots, assuming we approach unearthing them gingerly to ensure that the secret passageways leading to them do not collapse all around us and leave us trapped.

Finding hidden inner treasure sounds like a marvelous and exciting thing to look forward to—but our success will not be achieved in any classically Jupiterian manner, where we innocently stumble upon pots of gold that instantly enrich our soul and enable us to live happily ever after! Some measure of blood, sweat, and tears will instead be required—which means that you can count Jupiter out of the deal. Before we can gain a valued Plutonian resource that can transfigure our life, we often must first shed something that we've held on to with an iron grip, something which now is no longer of any use to us, whether we realize it or not. Pluto especially demands that we release anything in its last stages of decay before such an attachment becomes so toxic that it's downright lethal. Applying the clear-headed adaptability of Mercury is critical during these periods. Without it, we can't expect long-buried Plutonian treasures to surface and reward us in the upper realms of our conscious world.

AUTHENTIC LIVING

The Outer Planets have absolutely no interest in supporting those authorized social masks that we've been programmed to wear in order to ensure society's approval. However, feeling included as an accepted part of mainstream culture is usually preferred to feeling flat-out like an outcast or a social reject. The established Saturn-Jupiter foundations of most cultures demand that we follow set social customs and manners that grant us practical collective benefits, as long as we fundamentally hide who are really as individuals. Those who unknowingly suffer most under this set-up are the ones who believe "one size fits all" regarding the appropriate public mask to be worn—make that a blandly-colored mask with a frozen smile, one that falsely signals to the world that everything inside us is just doing fine and dandy—*no problemo!* The sad truth is that too many people are terrified to release their full potential to the world, because they fear that society won't warmly support such individualistic self-expression. And they're right.

Uranus, Neptune, and Pluto realize that the attainment of secure levels of social respectability comes at a heavy cost, because our soul is then chained to the concrete wall of conformity. Each of these planets believes in using revolutionary methods to free us from spirit-deadening self-concepts foisted on us by society, concepts that keep us stuck in limited realities not of our own choosing. Uranus seems to come closer to Pluto in its energy-tone than does Neptune. Both Uranus and Pluto believe in the direct, forceful approach to tearing down walls. They will blast away our illusions and leave us shattered for a while before we rebuild ourselves. The more insidious, slow-erosion technique employed by Neptune to enforce change is not appealing to these other two planets because it takes too long and is just too subtle and silent to feel like a full-fledged upheaval. Uranus and Pluto go for more dramatic, extreme, noisier options.

Pluto, unlike Uranus, which can suddenly drop out of the game, is keenly determined to never end up a quitter or a loser once it embarks on a purposeful enterprise. It's even willing to fight dirty, if necessary, to attain its goals against all odds. Pluto is forever the survivalist, willing to use guerrilla tactics in the name of a great evolutionary cause. Little detachment is shown in its strategy, especially once it gets its meat hooks into our emotional system. When infused with Plutonian energy, we can become obsessed about getting rid of anyone or anything that impedes our progress.

Of course, these surges of emotion-fed power are also what frightens us about the Plutonian energy currents coursing through our psyche's circuitry, because we can feel a compulsion to demolish anything foolish enough to stubbornly stand in our way—yes, beware our death ray! One of the special gifts with which the Rich One arms us during our moments of internal and external crises is an unrelenting will to overcome obstacles by exercising powerful primal instincts—the stuff that is immune to social indoctrination. It's during such arduous times that Plutonian fortitude really gets to shine.

Okay, so we get tough with ourselves during our Pluto transits and we refuse to let the world push as around anymore. That firm core of resolve sounds self-empowering, for sure. Lo and behold, we literally witness ourselves being motivated to clean up our act by taking a load of our dysfunctions to the garbage dump. "This transiting Pluto is great stuff," we claim at first as our psychological muscles start to bulge, until we realize the price we pay for living out an authentic life: we might no longer be labeled "normal" in society's book. We should brace ourselves for some degree of alienation, because we now are confirmed outsiders who have earned our social-outlaw status—I don't mean a life of criminality, but an unconventional, self-enriching existence that some Saturnians in the world think should be against the law (no one should get away with flaunting *that* much courageous self-acceptance). What threatens the Mighty Saturnians, who excel at playing hardball, is that we've now lost our innocent, childlike sense of blind social obedience, so much so that some of us now will no longer render anything unto Caesar!

Still, to arrive at this milestone, psychological passage is a blessing, as we get to finally toss old, well-worn masks into the blazing fire. We can become a vital part of the world which now, ironically, may feel compelled to seek out and exploit our creative power, even if it won't directly embrace us. However, we are clear about one thing: such a world won't ever again own our mind, will, and soul. Hopefully, we've become self-assured enough to no longer waste vital Plutonian energy despising that world for still trying to swallow us whole!

ALONE AND LOVING IT

Those who emotionally survive a series of life-intensifying Pluto transits realize that they must credit themselves most for getting through any challenging ordeals along the way, thanks to their previously untapped, underground resources finally coming to the fore. It's doubtful if anyone can really help us during our more stressful Pluto passages until we show the will and the desire to totally renew ourselves—we simply need to devise a custom-tailored way to do it. Although there are Plutonian guides out there who can assist us, our personal Plutonian dilemmas are complex puzzles that require individualistic solutions. That's why nobody seems to have ready answers that appeal to us. Our journey to our uncharted depths can be a lonely one, and yet this is a reflective time when the one trusty guide that can light our path is a quiet, observant, discerning mind that won't miss a trick along the way.

Unlike Neptune, where we learn to let benevolent strangers teach us to trust a helping hand, our Pluto transits make us wiser about the blessings of being utterly self-sufficient. We can't expect to appreciate the value of being alone, for example, while we're caught up in the thick of addictive, co-dependent relationships. Too many needy people may want us for a host of reasons—they count on us to deliver the goods. There's no inner stillness to be realized under these demanding and draining conditions. Pluto's dimension is a much different inner experience, one that tells us that the fewer people involved in our act right now, the better.

Note that even when the god Pluto secured a mate, she eventually proved to be as autonomous as he was. There are no mythic reports that insinuate his interference in her underworld functions, once her Kore persona was killed off and replaced by her more mature, self-possessed Persephone identity. Plutonian periods in our life are times when unhealthy relationships are abolished, and when being left alone in a greater state of inner equilibrium is often our reward for an inside job well done.

Of course, heavily Lunar or Venusian types may think that being left alone too much is a form of punishment. Pluto transiting these connection-seeking planets may have its work cut out for itself, yet it's not an impossible mission. It's one thing to be all alone and to feel hollow and empty inside. It's another to be by ourselves and yet feel full and satisfied by the depth our own being. The latter possibility is what a well-managed Pluto transit offers. This doesn't mean that Pluto insists that we remain in an isolated state forever. Even Dark Face didn't go for that. Pluto just wants us to be clear that when we typically feel we *must* have a partner, we're also refusing to marry parts of ourselves first. Once those rejected parts are re-owned and embraced, having a relationship is as much a conscious choice as ordering chicken salad on rye at the deli! Our unconscious is not forcing anything unwanted on us at this point.

FEARLESS SOUL

Another gift bestowed by transiting Pluto is soul-courage, a steely sort of bravery that is deeper and more self-affirming when facing life than anything gutsy Mars can muster. Martian courage often mixes in a little bravado with its boldness, and is thus ego-vulnerable. Consciously living an authentic life qualifies as an act of utmost Plutonian courage, because it often requires that we willingly defy social dictates that most people seldom feel driven to rebel against, much less question. Many people fit smoothly into tradition-based cultural systems without much ado, and probably so did we for the bulk of our lives—that is, until transiting Pluto decided it was time to snatch us up and take us for a wild ride down into our private, inner world for some needed deprogramming.

When we reemerge—assuming that our tour of our interior affairs went well and that we freely ate of the forbidden fruit of insight offered by Pluto—we can radiate a self-possessed power that even our ego can't manage to sabotage. When we arrive at such a psycho-spiritual state, not much can frighten us about living on this planet from that point onward. Even our own shadow parts aren't as dark and mysterious as they once were. This doesn't mean that we are now invincible, and immune to the pain caused by life's slings and arrows. Some degree of vulnerability will always be an essential part of our inner journey.

Although some of us may think that we're getting a handle on Plutonian consciousness by becoming human icebergs who show to the world a cool, diamond-hard exterior—that's right, we're tough as nails and nothing's gonna make us feel powerless anymore!—we're still missing the boat if we don't remedy that image with a fiery passion for being fully alive and willing to invigorate all those we psychologically touch with the healing strength of our self-reclaimed power. However, let's not overwhelm anyone in the process with our intensity. Maybe we're starting to feel a bit super-human regarding our capacity to deeply experience life, but that doesn't mean that the rest of the world can deal with it. One sign that we are not empowering ourselves effectively is when intolerance for the character weaknesses of others rears its ugly head and ignites destructive Plutonian urges to wipe out all such human foibles, including those that still lurk within us. When we start to act like a bully driving a bulldozer, something's very wrong with our pattern of unfoldment.

FACING DEATH

A major gift from Pluto is our ability to bravely look Death in the face. What does Death look like to us? Grim and pale? Fierce and smug? Grotesque and seething? Many of us haven't wanted to explore this heavy realm consciously and willingly—after all, we're dealing with the final extinction of consciousness as we know it. And what if the grave is truly the last stop on life's long, hard road? Typically, it's only when a loved one dies that we have our sad and unwelcome close encounters with the reality of physical non-existence. While we can read newspaper accounts about people around the globe dying each day, it doesn't have the same immediate impact as when one's child or even one's cherished pet is killed by a speeding car. Even knowing that thousands perished in a major catastrophe seems too unreal to cause an emotional ripple inside many of us. What makes death seem so deadly real and so vividly assaulting to our sensibilities is when this Pluto experience is right at our doorstep and is about to knock.

Pluto transits almost always carry with them underlying themes of death. Maybe the death of a loved one won't be the private pain we wrestle with during a major Pluto passage, because we can instead use up a good amount of this transit's energy by undergoing the psychological death of a few secret, inner hang-ups that we've battled. When Pluto's running the show, anything that's in a state of increasing decay must come to an inevitable end, because such decay blocks the life-force within, which is something that Pluto fiercely protects. Pluto demands that this vital force be released and recycled as germinating power. Something to which we've been attached for a long time, usually for all the wrong reasons, may leave us during a major Pluto transit. It will die on some level so that we have a better chance of being reborn. Yet our fear-based instinct is to use our defenses to thwart this transitional stage and to deny that we need this soul-baring experience. Well, that's one not-so-smart way to prolong our misery. In the end, we are to come around and see life the way that Pluto does, whereby dynamic inner change opens the door to tremendous future possibilities. Why wouldn't we wish for the death of all that impedes our path to such fulfillment?

VITALITY PLUS

If you observe natal Plutonians (and those with Scorpio emphasis as well), some of them begin their journey after birth by having to endure a life-threatening physical crisis or two. The unconscious message that the infant or the young child picks up is that life will involve a struggle to exist, a fierce fight to stay alive. The flame within must be protected from being put out, because outer forces we run up against can be hostile. The little Plutonian never seems to give up the battle, but instead pushes hard to survive and overcome what sometimes appear to be impossible odds.

Maybe the physical crisis comes a bit later on. Those who do make it to full-fledged adulthood—perhaps around their first Saturn Return—are unlikely to forget any early or previous trauma experienced, at least subconsciously. They will feel driven to go on convincing the world: "I am here to stay and I am not easily done in. I have incredible powers of endurance and the emotional stamina it takes to carry on no matter how rough the going gets. And I dare you to prove otherwise!" Sure enough, life makes certain that the going does get rough now and then to keep many a Plutonian powerhouse on his or her toes! Much vitality is required to always keep them a jump or two ahead of the game.

With transiting Pluto, each of us will have opportunities to feel strongly alive and alert in our chosen or fated approach to success, wherever that may lead us. Our physical vitality allows us to do much more while in a state of rousing passion than ever before. Our drive to accomplish can be awesome. Still, it's good to spread some of that vitality-plus around to energize a variety of life matters rather than to over-concentrate in just one area of burning interest, whereby we're tempted to shut out everything else. Typically, when Pluto is red hot and ready to turn on our engines, we'll find ourselves animated by a magnificent obsession that captures our total being. Our goals are tackled in a very purposeful manner, and usually we won't allow others to step in and take over. We want to be in charge of it all. Depending on the aspect and the natal house or planet involved, this could be too taxing on our physical system. Our efforts smack of maniacal zeal at times, to the point that loved ones wish they could pull us away from our fixations long enough so that we get some needed rest and relaxation. But no luck!

People mean well when they wish to intervene and get us to take a break, but those of us enthralled by the inner Plutonian power that is now coming alive for us do not want our energy surges to be interrupted. We look at the anxious concerns of others as unnecessary interference. Imagine having transiting Pluto conjunct our Sun or our Mars—it's doubtful that we'd currently have the objectivity needed to evaluate the pros and cons of our intensely driven nature and of our urge to strike out at those who dare get in our way and try to sidetrack us. Even if we are over-taxing ourselves physically—really burning rubber—it feels like a perfectly natural, Plutonian thing to do at this time. Our gut feeling is that we don't want to stop using up our seemingly inexhaustible supply of Solar or Martian energy, especially if we are on a roll and are getting the results we so greatly desire! Well, if that's truly the case, then everyone else needs to back off and watch in amazement at what a dedicated human dynamo can do under an invigorating Pluto transit. This super-charged energy is apparently here to be exploited, so let's see how far we can go with it!

NOTE

1. Refer to Brian Clark's *Hades as Place: The Underworld in Myth and Antiquity;* also read Jean Shinoda Bolen's *Gods in Everyman* for more about Pluto's association with wealth. See the bibliography at the end of this book.

CHAPTER THREE

A PLUTONIAN TOUR OF OUR NATAL PLANETS

THE BIG SWITCH

Before delving deeper into the life-altering potentials of Pluto's transits to our natal planets, let's first explore an unusual astronomical phenomenon involving Pluto and Neptune. Pluto is the slowest-moving of the known planets, because it's the most distant from the Sun (and from us). What makes Pluto particularly fascinating in a generational sense is that its highly elliptical orbital path, steeply inclined to the ecliptic, allows it to speed up its passage through certain signs the closer it gets to the Sun (most notably from Leo through Capricorn). As it moves at top speed during its 248-year cycle, it trades places at a certain stage with Neptune, which then becomes our outermost planet for a while. However, Pluto's orbit is not on the same plane as Neptune's, so there's no chance of a catastrophic planetary collision at the points of orbital intersection. This little switch-a-roo lasts about twenty years. The most recent cosmic switch—lasting about twenty years—began on February 7, 1979 (with Pluto at 19° Libra), and ended on February 11, 1999 (with Pluto at 10° Sagittarius).[1]

As Pluto moves farther away from the Sun, it slows down as it passes through certain signs (notably Aquarius through Cancer). It takes more than twice as long for Pluto to move through Taurus and Gemini as it does through Scorpio and Sagittarius. It also moves slowly in Aries (over twenty-nine years), which explains why the Ram has been increasingly testy ever since Pluto's discovery—Aries doesn't want any visiting planet to hang around that long! Pluto is one guest whose forceful, take-over personality can really rub Aries the wrong way. It's also no surprise that Taurus—the sign most resistant to change—gets Pluto quite worked up and determined to stick around the longest, just to experience the ultimate challenge of revolutionizing such firmly entrenched, earthbound consciousness. Pluto knows better than to hurry through Taurus, a sign that will stubbornly freeze in its tracks when it senses it's getting a rush job—never get pushy with the Bull if you want cooperation!

What the big switch means, astrologically, is that Pluto moving through the "fast" signs will make aspects to itself much earlier in life than when it passes through the "slow" signs. Most people born in the twentieth century who are alive are enjoying (?) relatively fast Plutos, compared to folks of the nineteenth century, when a slower-paced Pluto trudged along (in Pisces by 1800 and in Gemini by 1899). Those of us born after the birth of the Atomic Age will have transiting Pluto opposing our natal Pluto while we're in our mid-to-late eighties, assuming we continue to eat right and stay fit (Pluto supports all high-vitality preserving efforts). Our fast Pluto also will pass through more of our natal houses, although the limit is usually six houses from the one where natal Pluto resides.

Someone born in 1880 would have had to live to the overripe age of 113 to experience that same Pluto/Pluto opposition (hardly anyone with teeth experienced it). Anyone born in 1800 couldn't undergo this opposition until around the "you gotta be kidding" age of 153—so forget that! What's very interesting, especially beginning with the Pluto-in-Leo generation, is that more and more Pluto/Pluto oppositions will be happening only about a few years after our Uranus Returns, which happen just a year or so after our Neptune/Neptune oppositions! Each Outer Planet is thus in high focus. This is a characteristic pattern of old age during any century when Pluto is mainly moving through more fast than slow signs.

Therefore, all of the Outer Planets are really cooking for us throughout our eighties. Save those bell-bottoms, love beads, head-bands, tie-dyed shirts, and Grateful Dead albums, because apparently a potential renaissance awaits us in our golden years. However, we can forego the platform shoes—why risk falling, breaking a hip, and ending up in a nursing home? This certainly wasn't the cosmic pattern experienced in the nineteenth century for the few oldsters who made it to such an advanced age. I don't know exactly what this means, but let's make a personal vow to live through it and find out first hand. Who knows, this could be the most psychically tuned-in decade of our entire lives (as long as we're not relying on heavy medication by then).

THE USUAL SUSPECTS

It's time to preview the various planets in our chart from Pluto's critical perspective. Pluto is a no-nonsense analyst with a talent for easily spotting hidden strengths as well as less obvious weaknesses. You can bet that, since our birth, Pluto has been silently scrutinizing every natal planet's performance with a degree of sharp, eagle-eyed clarity. Don't be surprised if many existing traits of each planet fail to make the final cut in Pluto's book, which explains why such transits feel compelled to revamp how the planet in question responds to life. Pluto is always looking for something it can enliven with a little fiery passion and revolutionary zeal. Every planet actually has desirable material with which resourceful Pluto can work.

THE SUN

The Sun symbolizes our ego as the central seat of our conscious awareness, from which springs forth our sense of "I am." Perhaps the strongest statement made by our inner Sun is the confirmation that our ego's alive and awake, and that it undeniably exists and has an unalienable right to be. The astrological Sun thinks that it's hot stuff in more ways than one. Its impassioned affirmation of life intrigues Pluto, who's always interested in estimating another planet's level of strength and determination. The Sun never seems to want to turn itself off and probably hates it when we fall asleep and involuntarily surrender our ego-control over to Neptune, but Neptune knows better than to keep us awake forever and thereby deprived of the nightly soul-nourishment and psychological benefits that a dip into our unconscious provides. However, even while we're deep in dreams, our Sun is ever on the alert and ready to awaken us when we've had enough sleep or too much surrealistic cinema for one night.

While in the physical realm, the Sun is in charge of organizing our life's overall orientation. It symbolizes the vital power-to-be that defines our human experience. We're conscious, sentient beings eager to activate our energy and directly control our environment. The Sun also rules our heartbeat, which is one sure-fire way to gauge if we're dead or alive. Without that steady pumping rhythm—our soul's own drum beat—we're not an existing part of this physical world. Assuming that we do have a heartbeat and a pulse, our will to move out into life (helped by the thrusting desire of Mars) is associated with the Sun—as is the eternal life-force itself, the animating principle.

Pluto seems to be especially drawn to the fire planets, because Pluto itself relates to the deep fiery core—the internal furnace—of Earth itself. If Pluto's basic intention is to transform us by burning off whatever impedes our real growth (Pluto transits are often purifying trials by fire), then each fire planet already understands and appreciates the benefits of burning away gross matter in order to further liberate the spirit. Although very active and dynamic in the world, fire planets and fire signs don't instinctively attach themselves to anything that might weigh them down or threaten to put out their flame. They instead seek to remain unburdened by gravity and unfettered by time, two signs of their affinity to matters of the spirit.

Still, one big problem that Pluto has with the Sun (and with the other fire planets) is that, while Pluto teaches us about preserving the life-force so that we conserve our inner flame to ensure its availability when most needed—often during crises when superhuman strength and courage are a must—an over-confident Sun feels that it has endless fuel to burn. Our natal Sun believes that it's inextinguishable and feels as if it can afford to squander its energy at will (it's like leaving every house light on *all* the time). Pluto knows that such a waste of energy keeps us from being focused enough to make the best use of our ego-power and our physical vitality. Pluto prefers to keep energy in reserve where it can quietly grow stronger. Such internal storage of power is alien to the Sun's psychology—the Sun, a very extroverted planet, would rather have everything about itself rise to the surface and flame out.

However, during our Pluto/Sun transits, we'll find that life demands that we harness this solar power and redirect it—with dramatic intensity if need be—in order to burn up much of the psychological crud that stands in the way of our deep self-fulfillment. In general, the Sun has the courage and the guts to be what it wants to be, and that's something Pluto respects. Knowing that the Sun also has a strong sense of self-honor, transiting Pluto is willing to roll up its sleeves and work hard to transform our ordinary, ego-absorbed solar drives into something more transcendent and universal in scope. We can feel reborn when we realize how far-reaching our capabilities are, once we open ourselves to a more dynamically enhanced life-perspective.

THE MOON

Pluto realizes that the Moon represents a much more powerful human factor than solar-dominated, ego-worshipping societies have assumed. The development of lunar consciousness predates the Sun's orientation to life for a good reason: gut instinct helps to best shepherd our will in ways that result in greater inner attunement. We first must honor our "insides" for the protective wisdom they provide to us, for their innate knowledge of human tides and rhythms, for their sensitivity to inner and outer fertility cycles, and for their ability to instinctively cooperate with the knowing, maternal spirit of Nature. Our body's reflexes provide built-in, instinctive knowledge of how to best stay alive in the world. Such survival techniques are not something we actually learn from the Sun (who indiscriminately expends vital energy and takes adventurous risks). Therefore, Pluto respects the Moon for patiently collecting deeper body-and-soul experiences throughout life's long process of evolution. And yet Pluto despises how devalued the Moon and its related feminine principles have become in modern times. Remember, mythic Pluto never wanted Persephone to remain forever as the obedient, childlike, highly dependent Kore. Even if his initial methods of introducing her to his transformational realm were raw and coercive, his intention was for Kore to learn to renew her identity by revealing her own depth and maturity as the more self-possessed, capable Persephone.

Transiting Pluto will look at any out-of-touch natal Moon as if it's another clueless Kore who knows little about her real inner strengths and has never felt the power of her true depths. Our natal Moon, in response to feeling deprived of the power of will in action, develops unconscious defenses that shield its vulnerabilities. It tries to avoid direct attack by staying adaptable and submissive, but perhaps it's a little too willing to accommodate the demands of more selfishly assertive planets and people. Transiting Pluto decides that it's time for a little "tough love" therapy—no more soothing baby-talk, comfort food, or hiding under the covers! This Moon needs to do a lot of growing up if it's ever going to truly feel secure from within and self-sufficient in the outer world. Therefore, transiting Pluto/Moon periods can be times when we feel as if life won't allow us to perpetuate emotional patterns of immaturity that may have worked so well for us in the past, during times when securing "peace and quiet" in our relationships was more important to us than an honest presentation of our sometimes injured, hostile feelings.

The Moon's active emotionality is something self-controlled Pluto must adjust to (Pluto has a talent for hiding or repressing its own feelings). But even the Moon can be reluctant to review its storehouse of memories, because it knows that this can prove to be painful. However, Pluto realizes such pain and psychological discomfort can be cathartic. Those emotions and feelings that strengthen us are further fortified by Pluto's transit, but those that keep us fear-based and psychologically impotent will need to be wiped from the slate. The problem is that our possessive Moon holds on very tightly to all emotional baggage and will resist even allowing for the ultimate destruction of our hang-ups. In contrast, Pluto doesn't believe in clinging to the past, especially when doing so only reinforces unhealthy, habitual responses to life in the here-and-now. Still, these two water planets have an uncanny sense of the subtleties of human nature. Together, they sharpen our perceptions of people and help us to tune in to the hidden motivations of others. A strong detective streak arises. Transiting Pluto enjoys the fact that, after the dust has cleared, our transformed Moon has changed its psychology for the better—plus it will likely collect and retain all those valuable, in-depth insights gained by its exposure to Pluto's underground realm of consciousness. It'll be hard to continue any innocent, helpless approach to life once Pluto has renovated our emotional framework. See Chapter Nine for more on this.

MERCURY

You'll recall from Chapter One that Mercury (Hermes) was the only god detached enough and curious enough to descend into the Underworld to deliver messages from Mount Olympus. He was also a guide for special visitors in Hades and even accompanied the souls of the dead to the banks of the River Styx, where the ferryman Charon would await them. Mercury wasn't afraid to visit Pluto's neighborhood then, and isn't scared of facing up to Pluto now! Astrological Mercury likes to be able to travel freely throughout various levels of consciousness and unconsciousness, as long as a quick escape hatch from anything too stifling or boring is guaranteed. Transiting Pluto is hoping that, while on its assignments, it will get to interact with a few adaptable, resilient planets, of which Mercury is certainly one. Pluto seeks in another planet a mix of strength and power along with a capacity for intelligent flexibility (just to ensure that planet doesn't waste energy fighting Pluto's reformative measures tooth-and-nail). Mercury is the perfect guinea pig for undergoing Pluto's radical transmutations in awareness. Luckily, Mercury will try out any planet at least once, especially if that means it will gain a new slant on interpreting life.

Mercury likes to study life's details and learn first hand how things work. Transiting Pluto instills mental powers of investigation that result in marvelous researching skills and incisive communication ability. Pluto teaches Mercury the value of concentration and even of body/mind stillness and control. As long as Mercury doesn't overdo its logical but skeptical side, it can learn to stay enthralled by Plutonian explorations of life, even when the subject matter turns a little dark and unsettling—and when doesn't it, with Pluto? This can be a time for Mercury to be at its introspective best—ain't nothing superficial going on here!

By employing a little imagination, we can assume that the god Hermes was alert enough to notice practically everything going on in Hades, and even took mental notes. Although not reported in actual myths, Hermes probably asked Pluto plenty of nosy questions and then made clever, amusing commentary regarding his own quickie observations of the Big H. In fact, someone should write a new tale about that little known day when wise-cracking Hermes made Pluto laugh so hard that ole Dark Face dramatically came alive and performed his finger-snapping "If I Were a Sky God" song-and-dance routine—about secretly wanting to trade places with brother Zeus—all while accompanied by a knee-slappin' Hermes spontaneously playing a mean kazoo! Not surprisingly, a disgusted Persephone immediately got on the hotline to complain to her Ma about this silly spectacle, while also whining again about how rotten—literally— the food is in the Underworld. Of course, in real life, Pluto/Mercury transits probably won't seem anywhere near as lighthearted as this mythic fantasy scenario.

We will only benefit ourselves by using the powers of our mind to translate as clearly as possible—without censorship or exaggeration—the ongoing influx of Plutonian impulses and mental images. Our mind perceives buried material—maybe hidden memories—that is now freely erupting to the surface. By changing our perspective and by establishing a little emotional distance (detachment), we can learn to view all that more fully emerges with greater self-understanding. It's best not to overreact to anything we're experiencing. Pluto often works in various stages of release (as do newly awakened volcanoes). We'll need to apply patience and greater self-composure if we are to successfully withstand this sometimes painstaking process. It's vital to remain pliable and open to change.

Mercury in its purely observational state views everything thrown at it by Pluto as just compellingly fascinating data to delve into, although Plutonian material can actually be seductively mind-altering stuff. Still, there's little need to suffer a devastating mental collapse regarding any disturbing information received, thinks Mercury—just fly away in your head somewhere else when things get too weird and scary. Don't remain fixated. Of course, infamous "no one can hide from me" Pluto will become a tireless bloodhound when tracking down any planet on the run from stark reality. It's best to stay mentally focused while in the thick of our transiting Pluto/Mercury experiences and simply face the educational life-exams that come. Pluto will make sure that dedicated truth-seekers won't get failing grades! For more, read Chapters Eight and Eleven.

Venus

At first glance, you'd think that sweet and delicate Venus—imaged almost as another flower-loving Kore type, only wearing lots of make-up—would be overwhelmed by the dark sensuality of passionate Pluto. We generally assume that the Venus archetype is gentle, wholesome, and truly at home with tender matters of the heart. Had Walt Disney ever put the pantheon of gods on the silver screen, that's how he'd portray this fair and lovely goddess (Snow White in a toga). However, before Venus went to charm school in Rome, she was first that lusty Greek gal, Aphrodite, who miraculously manifested from the foaming, mutilated sexual organs of Uranus—whoops, there goes that PG rating! Mighty

Aphrodite reclaimed her animus early on in life and never, ever felt like a member of the weaker sex. She would play no tradition-bound feminine roles, but was instead very Martian in many of her impulses—especially her overtly sexual ones. She was also a bit of a troublemaker when it came to pairing couples. Plus her secret "weapon" to assure successful sexual conquest was her magic girdle, which made her irresistibly enticing. This here's a cocksure, robust Venus with attitude!

Pluto appreciates a feisty planet, because such a planet has guts and will take risks—Pluto's transits often involve tremendous risks for the ego. Pluto doesn't tolerate wimpy archetypes and is tempted to run over them like a steamroller. However, if we have learned to consciously cultivate Aphrodite's more assertive traits (although society still considers such behavior a bit naughty, especially if we are women), expect Pluto to show us a little more respect when it transits our Venus. At some particular point in its archetypal history, astrological Pluto became quite interested in sexuality, even in those areas that cultures have always deemed taboo. Nothing is truly unspeakable or sinful in Pluto's amoral dimension. However, Pluto is behind many of the relational complications we attract when it interacts with Venus.

Both planets, able to feel and instill passion, can generate strongly magnetic attractions. Each enjoys vivid sensory stimulation. As long as Venus doesn't act in too refined or cultivated a manner or become caught up in shallow social niceties, it'll get along well with Pluto, a planet that loathes and seeks to destroy phony behavior. Venus has a talent for swaying people's emotions. This is a powerful asset that Pluto will want to exploit. Plutonians can be hypnotically persuasive, although they lack the Venusian charm that others find so appealing. The magnetizing of material comfort is another facet of the Venus experience that interests Pluto. Pluto's mythic realm held underground wealth in the form of Earth's natural resources. Venus also has an ability to protectively hold on to what's valuable, and the earthy side of Venus appreciates Nature's resources. Both planets coming together can stimulate powerful worldly appetites, although Pluto doesn't want us to stagnate due to our worldly self-indulgences.

Pluto/Venus transits can be times when we may attempt to amass material objects that fortify our standing in the world—that is, if our power drives are solely focused on tangible gains. However, if we are primarily motivated by greed and if we believe our self-worth is based solely on what we own, Pluto has other plans for us that will rattle our foundation, because our value system is apparently too messed up to help us to transform and grow. If we are that greedy, then we're obviously better at taking rather than giving. Pluto doesn't want to waste its precious energy on this kind of selfish enterprise. Therefore, things begin to break down for us materially, and our losses can be great if we refuse to get the message.

Sensuality is of common interest to both planets. Pluto's energy makes us curious about what turns us on and what gratifies those we love or find attractive. When a Pluto/Venus transit heats up, it can act like "Love Potion Number Nine" or any other mysterious elixir that rejuvenates our erotic potential and enables us to enjoy our sex-appeal. We may be the first to recognize that we have something hot going for us here. Feeling truly sexy is not easily achieved in our culture, because while some may regard such feelings as sinful, others accuse us of being vain or preoccupied with external appearances. Why do we wish to look so provocative and tempting to others? Why must we send out those sultry vibes? Pluto wisely knows that our sexual self-image is the key to our physical and emotional vitality. The more confident we are here, the more we know how to go for all the gusto we can out of love and life. Yet let's not devour another whole as we give pleasure to ourselves. Read more on this in Chapters Seven and Twelve.

MARS

It wouldn't be uncommon for astrologers to look at a transiting Pluto square or opposition to Mars and wonder how bumpy will be the ride that awaits the unsuspecting client. Of course, Jupiterian-type astrologers will immediately want to focus on (and stay focused on) the invigorating possibilities that libido-arousing Pluto can offer to a high-energy planet like Mars. Under this transit, our body is ready to energetically come alive. We'll have to determine whether that means we'll have an impulse for vigorous physical activity or just suffer from a stubborn case of dermatitis. Such a body rash could be telling us that we're in an angry, inner state due to a thwarted readiness to take dynamic action. Pluto allows our body to erupt a little frustrated Martian fury for us here and there. The more indirect we are about our need to self-assert and make independent moves, the greater the chance that Pluto will manifest in unwanted ways that eventually make us feel agitated or physically out of sorts.

Pluto has a special regard for Mars—after all, they co-rule Scorpio. It respects this red planet for being capable of much bravery when facing life's obstacles and challenges. By temperament, Mars is an undaunted survivor. It never gives up and it certainly would fight to protect its own life-force whenever possible. Pluto, finding these traits tailored to its own needs, will make an extra effort to harness the surging energies of Mars by fine-tuning our aggressive impulses. Still, as long as Mars is only taking orders from the Sun (ego)—sometimes reluctantly so—it's not going to easily submit to Pluto's agenda. Mars relishes self-will, which wouldn't bother Pluto so much if self-will always led to smart moves. Often, it doesn't. We can easily get in hot water when we fail to think things through before acting. It's that irritable, hair-trigger side of Mars that strategy-expert Pluto can do without.

Pluto will want to recycle pumped-up Martian energy and apply it toward clearing out fears and doubts that have stopped us from making constructive changes in the past. One of the problems with this combo, however, is that our Martian impulse is to take quick action once we're convinced we're on the right track. Pluto will slow down the pace and wait for an optimum time to make its move. Pluto wants Mars to deeply ponder the workings of cause-and-effect. It's determined to turn Mars into a more reflective planet, so that we learn to mobilize our energy for new experiences only after we've gauged our strengths—we don't blindly push our way into life in hopes that we'll automatically get our desires met through sheer, brute force.

Of course, if we've been passive and indecisive in how we've directed our self-will throughout life, transiting Pluto may have no choice but to trigger an explosion in order to catapult us into fresh cycles of courage-reinforced awareness. Maybe we have to act alone to get what we need during this time—fortunately, both planets are good at being independent. Whether this transit is enlivening for us or simply stormy depends a lot on how well we've cultivated true autonomy. Read Chapter Six for more.

JUPITER

Unlike the Sun, Moon, Mercury, Venus, and Mars—collectively considered to be "personal" planets, willing to support our need for ego-fulfillment—Jupiter and Saturn fall into the category of "social" planets, motivated to support society's long-term objectives. In their case, Pluto doesn't have to piddle around with subjective and sometimes small-minded human issues (those most often driven by a self-absorbed ego that wants exclusive attention). Jupiter is especially eager to have us branch out into a socially connected Universe of grand possibilities and ideal community relationships. Jupiter wants us to seek greater intellectual breathing space and stretch our human potential in hopes of improving our earthly experiences. It also gives us hope about collective progress and helps us to trust the brighter world of tomorrow. Jupiter is a fire planet with a strongly mental orientation—although in a warmly philosophical sense—and has a taste for the theoretical.

However, as industrialized nations expand and grow in typically Jupiterian ways, their societies becomes harder to organize and manage. Bigger does not always mean better, and quantity doesn't guarantee quality. Social progress, especially of a profit-motivated, materialistic nature, may come at a human cost. We end up overloaded with too many daily decisions based on too many options. Although that sounds like one benefit of social freedom, in actual practice it's not easy to juggle so many choices—our life becomes unduly complex and fragmented. When Jupiter focuses on

surface cultural improvements and glosses over the hidden weaknesses of a bloated, overindulged society, we may collectively end
up seeing far and wide, but not very deeply. Here's where Pluto
comes in to offer this buoyant planet of "up and away" a better feel
for how things really are "deep down below."

Mythic Jupiter (as Zeus) never made the descent into Hades
(probably because he heard there were no windows, no birds, and
no celebratory feasts in the Underworld). He always sent someone
in his place whenever he had to conduct business with Pluto (the
old Jupiterian "pass-the-buck" routine). Perhaps Hades was too
dark of a place for him, too distressing, and too much of a reminder
of human loss and pain (only humans were mortal and subject to
death). However, Pluto is naturally right at home with all of this.

When Pluto transits our natal Jupiter, we might feel that we
need to look at the bigger picture of life and its ultimate purpose,
because both planets have vast perspectives. It's time for a
reemergence of our spiritual values or a reexamination of our religious beliefs. Are such values and beliefs real to us, or do we just
pay lip service to them? We are in need of a renewed sense of
trust in the Universe and in humankind. Jupiter must have a
vision in order to bring out its best (and sometimes its worst).
Pluto wants that vision to represent our deeper, more authentic
self. Transiting Pluto is also intent on having us face up to how
and when we engage in hypocrisy—those times when we openly
promote Jupiterian ideals or moralistic social values even though
we fail to live up to them ourselves. Pluto wants us to truly practice what we preach, or else get off the pulpit and stop with the
phony, self-righteous act!

While Pluto can intensify the nature of any planet it contacts,
it demands that we use our Jupiterian energies discriminatingly,
or else suffer the consequences—such as poor judgment that gets
us in financial or legal trouble. Maybe our ethics are questioned by
social authority. However, Pluto admires Jupiter's optimistic willingness to dream big, take mind-expanding risks, and look forward
to a fruitful future. Transiting Pluto alone requires varying
degrees of risk-taking to help us to bury our unredeemed past and
usher in a totally new life pattern in its place. Our potency is based

on how well we let go of limiting here-and-now securities, in favor of the greater things that can be ours when we allow for a leap of faith. Jupiter intuits that there is so much more about the Cosmos that we just don't know, while Pluto instills in us a burning curiosity to find out what the Universe is really all about. This transit is great for making progress along those spiritual paths that deeply enthuse us, as long as we don't succumb to ideological fanaticism or become dictatorial and arrogant in our dogmatic assumptions about Truth. For more on this, read Chapter Fourteen.

SATURN

In Greek mythology, Pluto (Hades)—one of the sons of Saturn (Cronus)—was victimized shortly after birth by being swallowed by his fearful, power-obsessed father. From the moment of his emergence, Pluto was forced into an interior realm of darkness. Although dwelling in underground realms of experience later played a major role in his destiny as an adult, Pluto probably saw everything that Saturn stood for as disturbingly confining and harshly authoritarian. Astrological Pluto therefore vows to be Saturn's worst nightmare, especially a Saturn that is unresponsive to change and unable to share power or control. Pluto has a better time working with Jupiter, because Jupiter is open to new experiences and will try to make the best of any situation, even when that approach smacks of opportunism. In addition, Jupiter has its sights set on bigger and better worlds of future promise. Pluto realizes that, after its phase of destruction, it must rebuild from the ground up; Jupiter gets excited about the possibilities offered by such a new lease on life.

With Saturn, however, Pluto is keenly aware that it's dealing with a brick wall of built-in resistance and fear. Pluto knows, right off the bat, that Saturn is paranoid about losing ground and about being overpowered. In addition, its rigidity often forces it to learn things the hard way, especially when it refuses to adapt to Outer Planet progress. There's also an ancient mutual animosity at work whose dynamics probably concern Pluto more than they do Saturn, because Pluto is a natural psychoanalyst.

In fact, there is something about Saturn that makes each Outer Planet wary. Uranus, Neptune, and Pluto were all involved in a troubling mythological father-son relationship involving the planet. Saturn is not as deep or as penetrating as Pluto. Although it can be subtle in operation, earthy Saturn is not sly or devious. It's not known for tricky maneuvers. However, Saturn correctly senses that Pluto can be a relentless force bent on covertly undermining structure, violently if need be. Pluto's primal fury frightens cool, reserved Saturn, who'd rather think of itself as a pragmatist acting on common sense, not on raw emotion.

Actually, both planets can be serious, somewhat depressive, anti-social, and humorless, but certainly not naive about the world. These two heavies are aware that things must come to an end once they no longer serve a legitimate purpose, especially once they start to drag us down instead of raising our consciousness. Pluto's endings can be quite dramatic and tumultuous, whereas Saturn's final stages are often the result of things slowly breaking down or calcifying. Pluto's transits to Saturn mark those times when we feel that life demands closure of some sort. We are to take on super-realistic attitudes toward putting to rest issues that have bothered us for a long time. We often feel compelled to totally eliminate certain people and situations from our life. We also may undertake measures to rehabilitate parts of ourselves in ways that elicit greater support from society.

Saturn has no difficulty in materializing form, which is something that Pluto depends on during its rebirth stage. Once our old patterns have been demolished, new manifestations must demonstrate our renewed perception of our inner power and depth. Saturn knows the physical world better than any other planet, except maybe the Moon, and it can handle the reconstruction work required by Pluto for the successful transition we need. When these two planets work together in true harmony, nothing seems impossible. We can show an impressive amount of stamina and persistence while enduring set-backs and eliminating tough obstacles that block our path. Pluto admires Saturn for not being a quitter when life puts on the pressure to persevere. Pluto wants to make sure that we don't think that the material realm and the power to be gained on worldly levels are all there is to life.

Saturn is reluctant to descend too deeply into the inner realms of our unconscious (this time in Pluto's belly), but this is just what is needed during these transits. The underlying motivation behind our outer ambitions needs to be psychologically examined to determine just what drives us to succeed in our professional endeavors, as well as what's behind any secret fears of personal failure. Pluto is intent on showing Saturn the ringed planet's well-guarded shadows so that we do the inner work it takes to clean up our act and stop stonewalling our greater potential. See Chapter Fifteen for more.

URANUS

Here's an instance in which two "transpersonal" planets come together. Transits between Pluto and Uranus dislodge energies that normally remain unconscious and untested in the outer world. Pluto and Uranus both have revolutionary intentions and are not interested in coaxing us to gently reform ourselves and our environment. They both come at us like gang-busters when urging us to take more extreme measures to sweep out frustratingly stale elements of our life. Pluto has a special interest in gutsy, fiery planets, and Uranus is certainly known to willfully trigger fired-up electrical sparks on the mental level, pushing us to take unconventional action without much hesitation.

Pluto knows that it's impossible for Uranus to remain stuck in the tar pits of mundane living for long. It will explode out of any stagnant, limiting condition without warning. Pluto appreciates the boldness of volatile, live-wire Uranian energy, yet Uranus is often too impetuous to satisfy deeper Plutonian needs. Pluto in action is slow but thorough, whereas Uranus in fast but uneven in its influence. Pluto believes in laying low while shrewdly plotting the best time to strike. It waits for an opportune situational vulnerability and then goes in for the kill. Uranus can't stand the waiting game, hates sneaky tactics, and will rapidly plunge headlong into situations without a well-considered plan of action. Sometimes Uranus doesn't even take the expected plunge but suddenly and surprisingly redirects its energy elsewhere—again, with no overall plan in mind. This erratic activity bothers Pluto, who wonders how such a brilliant and intuitive planet as Uranus could also act so stupidly and recklessly when motivated by defiant self-will, rather than by an in-depth, pervasive understanding of the issues in question. Pluto doesn't enjoy surprises, especially unpleasant ones brought on by throwing caution to the wind.

When Pluto transits our Uranus, we must harness—not kill— that rebel within us. We'll need to slow our pace and look before leaping into experimental ventures. ("Gotta have a better sense of strategy," warns Pluto.) Wherever a triggered Uranus wants us to go may be the right direction for us in the near future, but our timing could be off if we rush things and fail to properly research matters. Uranus ignores conventional Saturnian timing and doesn't probe issues. Still, once Uranus' button has been activated, it's hard to apply patience and reason. Pluto is ready for an eruption that will shake up our familiar patterns. However, Pluto also wants this to be a profound experience rather than just a crazy, disruptive phase during which we're baffled by our own behavior. Pluto insists that we realize why we must break out of old shells that have hidden our individualism from the world. We will be coming out of the stuffy closet of social conformity, but we must emerge prepared and empowered to face our future.

However, Uranus has a problem with Pluto's instinctive takeover mentality. Even if we are oblivious to our inner Uranian processes at work, being subject to the dictatorship of another heavy-duty archetype is not high on this planet's wish list! Pluto often acts in ways that inevitably set up power-struggles, probably because of its forceful, uncompromising style of action—and Uranus will certainly fight to remain free and unregulated. Uranus is not too sure that it even likes the murky realms where Pluto hides—shadow-infested and filled with unprocessed psychological pain. This is where the zombies and the vampires roam our psyche's darkened landscape. Uranus wants to come alive in excitable mental states where illumination and self-enlightenment abound and the mind rockets us into limitless "inner" space, and where there are always avenues of escape available when things get too complicated in predictably human ways. Yet Pluto won't let Uranus get too detached. It's time to learn about a few less ideal, gut realities that have kept us from the inner liberation that we must achieve in order to further individualize. See Chapter Sixteen for more.

NEPTUNE

When Pluto transits Neptune, both feel a sense of kinship. Once symbolized as mythological brothers entrapped in the tight confines of dark matter (confined inside Saturn's body), these planetary archetypes believe in unrestricted possibilities in consciousness that time, space, and physicality cannot destroy. In temperament, they share some traits. Both like the quiet, shady retreats of the soul that dwell below the surface of our waking self. Each planet is introspective, contemplative, and cautious about being swallowed up by the dense world of form. Both love mysteries and are good are creating them and, at times, solving them. They are each at home within the unseen realms of life, where invisible energies are active, powerful, and interconnected. Pluto and Neptune are highly sensitized to underground or underwater currents in our psychological atmosphere, and both have an uncanny ability to uncover what's hidden within our depths—probably because they are the ones who hid that stuff there in the first place. Subtlety and the ability to penetrate barriers to superconsciousness are their strengths. Being less obvious about the silent moves they make also allows them to successfully operate behind the scenes.

Yet at some point, Pluto—possessed by a raw, primal fire—periodically erupts in dramatic ways that completely alter the scenery. (Neptune occasionally lets loose its fury when in its hurricane-like "Poseidon" mode—see *Alive and Well with Neptune*.[2]) Pluto is decidedly more critical of human flaws than all-forgiving Neptune. Pluto vigorously picks and picks at the rotting parts of our psyche like a hungry vulture, until nothing is left but the bare bones. This is why we can feel wiped out or nearly annihilated after a stormy Plutonian period, although we do come alive again with even greater vitality once the fallout has cleared and deep wounds have healed. Neptune wants an inner healing to take place as well, but Neptune won't put us through a raging inferno in an attempt to burn off what keeps us feeling unwell. At least, when Neptune does soul-surgery on us, it uses anesthesia. Pluto never believes in numbing us first; it wants us wide awake to see and feel what's being removed!

A big difference between these planets is that Neptune clings to its idealistic but illusionary impressions of life. Its vision of how flawless things "should be" blindly glosses over the real underlying crud of reality. Neptune feels that believing in something or someone strongly enough makes matters magically turn out the way we wish them to be. This may be true when consciousness is operating on purely cosmic levels, where love and beauty—working as active universal forces rather than merely uplifting concepts—have the power to unify existence. We visualize and recreate our ever-changing perfect reality.

However, on the grittier levels of the physical, gravity-bound world, Pluto realizes that beautiful thoughts and images alone are not enough to transform harsh reality. Of course, Pluto is not always right about this assumption, because effortless miracles can sometimes occur. Demolishing illusion and confusion at their root source is what motivates Pluto.

While Pluto transits our Neptune, we may have some life-dreams that are put under the microscope and examined in detail for their strengths and weaknesses, with special attention on those weaknesses that we typically refuse to acknowledge. In some cases, Pluto will put a lot of vital energy into a dormant (collective) Neptunian dream that now needs to surface and become a life-altering reality. Pluto definitely wants to pump up those Neptunian inspirations that can spur us to have a powerful and humane impact on our environment. In general, both of these planets are comfortable working within our inner realms, so we can expect a phase of empowered imagination and soul-yearning. There's more on this in Chapter Seventeen.

Pluto

When Pluto transits Pluto, it's obvious that whatever this planet symbolizes in our chart—in addition to whatever has slowly been brewing in our psyche—will be in high focus now (especially if our natal Pluto already aspects a few "personal" planets). That doesn't mean that this will automatically be a conscious experience for us, considering that inscrutable Pluto is quite comfortable hiding out in the depths of our psyche. Usually, however, a timely eruption is due, during which we get to unload psychological baggage from our past. If we are creative and becoming increasingly self-aware, this transit can turn on our regenerative power and internally revamp our life (usually the parts where we've resisted tampering the most). Our ego has very little opportunity to interfere with the process of internal revolution demanded of us at this point, since it's often our outer environment (both people and situations) that determines how far we can go with this life cycle—fate plays a role. We can, at least, monitor the deep and seemingly unfamiliar feelings within us that are seeking to find suitable surface expression.

Some of our emerging feelings will seem passionately malcontent, even angry at life. Such qualities have been unduly suppressed for a long time and now need to vent their stored-up hurt and rage. Why have these parts of ourselves been so ignored and dishonored? It's usually because cultural programming has steered us in predictable directions of safer social conformity, where our primal energy and authentic selfhood have no place to thrive. The pain of inflicted psychological injury is never properly addressed when we try to meet society's expectations rather than our own. Therefore, this energy stays trapped in our emotional underworld where it can fester. When this transit occurs, we usually are forced to recognize such underworld qualities, especially if we are at a critical juncture in life (the most dynamic

Pluto/Pluto phase is the transiting square, which happens around the "mid-life crisis" years for most people born in the twentieth century).

We're not going to have many Pluto/Pluto transits during our life span, because this planet moves too slowly for that. Perhaps it's also because such intensive phases could prove too hard to endure—evoking Pluto is seldom a picnic, even if it only stays active on our unconscious levels. In fact, we can feel oddly discomforted with ourselves and with our life when Pluto is only operating on the subconscious plane. Consciously confronting this energy can help us to release long-term resentments and hostilities. This can be a transit that stirs up subterranean forces within us. Therefore, some of us may not view the outer manifestations of Pluto/Pluto as having anything whatsoever to do with who we think we are, especially if we've unquestioningly adopted conservative social roles. We fail to undergo the renewal process that can provide extra vitality and inner strength for years to come. For more on this see Chapter Thirteen.

Now that the planets of our life's drama have been introduced, the next part of our birth chart to be reviewed are the twelve houses. In the next chapter, we will take a detailed look at each natal house and how Pluto might feel about transiting it.

NOTES

1. The dates when Pluto switched orbits with Neptune came from the NASA/Jet Propulsion Laboratory web site: http://www.jpl.nasa.gov/ice_fire/990201.htm.

2. Bil Tierney, *Alive and Well with Neptune,* Llewellyn Publications, 1999.

CHAPTER FOUR

A PLUTONIAN TOUR OF OUR NATAL HOUSES

THE USUAL PLACES

The following is a preview of transiting house themes and life issues that will be covered at length starting in Part Two, Chapter Six. Most of transiting Pluto's action will take place in the natal house that it moves through, especially when conjuncting natal planets in that house. Our environment slowly creates just the right stage setting for us to discover how to better actualize constructive Plutonian values, once we deal squarely with our semi-conscious fear of letting go of parts of our past.

OUR FIRST HOUSE

The First House is a life zone were planetary energies work best when they surface and meet present situations head-on. There's nothing subtle about this sector of our chart. What you see is what you get—a planet in its most conspicuous expression, operating visibly when we take direct and personal action in the world. Of course, if that planet is mysterious by nature—as are Neptune and Pluto—those characteristics may be obvious when natally in our First. This is a house of upfront self-presentation, so it's usually difficult to hide any transiting planet's intentions. The First House doesn't condone keeping matters hidden for long. It seems that Pluto feels a little too exposed when passing through a house where everything's out in the open. After all, this is a planet that would rather maneuver in the dark, all alone and undetected. It would prefer to be an unseen but powerful presence. The First House, however, pushes for disclosure.

Thus, it would make sense that Pluto would be more at home in the Fourth, Eighth, and Twelfth Houses, which deal with our less observable interior environment. Yet Pluto knows that— regarding every successful transformative process—there comes a time when its concentrated energy must rise to the surface in full strength so that it can effect a total regeneration of our being and our environment (that old "rising out of the ashes" feeling). The First House can relate to the fiery resurgence of a well-managed Pluto, because it's a place of new starts and fresh beginnings— attributes that resonate with Pluto's theme of rebirth. Neither planet nor house wants to get stuck in a frozen past.

Transiting Pluto likes the First House's ongoing support for our attempts to face up to here-and-now challenges. Moving forward in life, even under adversity, appeals to both Pluto and the First, as does showing the courage to be ourselves and to act autonomously. This is a life zone where the focus is exclusively on us, which makes transiting Pluto's efforts to revitalize our self-image a little easier. There are no other people to directly cater to in this house, unlike in the Fourth or Seventh, for example. Pluto gets to concentrate on just one "research project" whose main focus is the emergence of an empowered identity that will not easily be manipulated by society. Pluto has a lone-wolf streak, and our First encourages self-sufficient, solo activity. Much of what we have to do to bring out Pluto's attributes will involve intense moments of solitude. We are able to draw upon deep, untapped resources, allowing them to surface in highly personal ways that strengthen how we project ourselves into the world.

What Pluto doesn't like about operating in this house is that it often feels like a walking target for those who are fearful of overtly revolutionizing energy. Pluto magnetizes controversy in the collective realm, and that typically stirs up social power-struggles. Pluto's not aggressive in the way that Mars is, although this is a house with Martian undertones; Pluto doesn't need to openly fight the world if it can secretly undermine the status quo. However, the general atmosphere of our First House is such that whatever is transiting must surface and make itself known. Our environment, during this transit, can readily pick up that some of us are a mighty force to reckon with—either a courageous power-house with potent transformative energies, or an anti-social troublemaker who can sabotage much of what society seeks to uphold. Of course, a few of us could also appear to be withdrawn introverts who seeks minimal social contact—just enough to fulfill our power drives. Read more about this transit in Chapter Six.

OUR SECOND HOUSE

The Second House is where the renewed sense of selfhood forged in the First needs to be given a stable environment in which to grow and develop—just as a tender seedling needs the right soil and weather conditions before it can successfully grow long and sturdy roots. Everything about our Second House deals with what we can magnetize to ourselves for our material structure and support—whatever assets enable us to survive in the physical world as the independent, individualized being we began to actualize during our First-House phase. Pluto is interested in any planet or house that has a strong sense of its own resources. Naturally, Pluto wants to eventually take over those resources and do something really dynamic with them. Pluto knows that the Second is a fertile life zone capable of much material manifestation. But how much of such materiality is truly valuable, at this point, to the growth our deeper self?

When we're out-of-touch with this house, we typically collect and stockpile things that distract us from developing any sense of real self-worth. Our hoarding instinct is tied to unaddressed insecurities. We may feel safe only when buffered by physical objects and unchanging circumstances. We sometimes purchase items that are mere status symbols simply to please others and gain social acceptance. Transiting Pluto is ready to throw out goods that have little to do with our authentic self. A thorough revamping of our value system may be called for. However, our Second House guards its possessions well. It doesn't easily let things go, and can function like one big junk closet into which we toss everything we own. Therefore, this planet and this house usually have a conflict of interest.

The Second House also doesn't do well with the thought of physical deprivation or loss. Sacrifice is not something it understands—it must be on solid ground with the material world. However, planets in this house may have different attitudes. Transiting Pluto itself is not necessarily against having powerful resources to wield in society—many successful Plutonians in business are filthy rich. Pluto just wants us to realize that we're not to be owned or defined by what we have—our real wealth comes from an interior source of well-being. If we are stubbornly addicted to mindless materialism—whereby any sense of our power comes from overvalued, external objects—transiting Pluto can enforce a nearly total wipe-out of our possessions. Sometimes, strictly impersonal outer forces are involved—such as a natural disaster victimizing many people at once—that symbolize our inner, unconscious dynamics. In other words, we have unrecognized but conflictive feelings about want and desire—and even darker feelings of greed and envy—that become provoked as a result of a circumstantial calamity that destroys what we own.

Pluto is not an intellectual planet caught up in ungrounded abstractions. Instead, it has powerful instincts that allow it to get right to the heart of any problem that we face in whatever house it transits. It strips away pretenses and lays bare the inner workings that have led to the deep sense of unfulfillment with which we may struggle. We feel slowly uprooted when Pluto is at work. There's also something about our Second that doesn't tolerate illusion. It's a house that demands a reliable dose of reality. It wants us to stick to the no-frills basics in life whenever possible. Pluto will force us to get back to the basics as part of our process of rebirth.

A well-attuned Second House means that we follow our prag-matic know-how and survival awareness when fortifying ourselves materially. Pluto enjoys those houses that encourage using gut instinct as the radar we need to help us better navigate certain realms of experience symbolized by those houses. In our Second, Pluto wants us to start functioning in less artificial, socially-pro-grammed ways; we have a lot here to unearth of much inner value. This transit is covered in more depth in Chapter Seven.

Our Third House

Pluto may not be an intellectual whiz like Mercury, but part of its mission while it transits any house is to make sure that its talent for depth-perception is consciously recognized, understood, and used by us. In the Third House, our conscious mind seeks clear information about our local environment. In this stimulating area, we must develop our mental capabilities in basic, yet essen-tial, ways if we hope to function intelligently in the real world. We learn to observe and translate our hectic surroundings, which helps us to adapt to constant situational change. Communication skills to be found in our Third are those that help us to deal with day-to-day reality. Deep, philosophical understanding or meta-physical revelations have little to do with the needs of a Third-House mentality. There are so many mundane things we have to learn here to even marginally get by—including remembering lots of numbers. We also can be in pursuit of the trivial in life as long as it is momentarily stimulating.

Obviously, too much Third-House focus keeps us humming along on a superficial mind track, unaware of more profound underlying realities. We may be informative and apparently ver-satile, but do we know what we know deeply enough to satisfy Pluto? Transiting Pluto tells us that we can learn much more effectively when we're in a quiet state of solitude, where we can concentrate fully and reflect on our studies. In contrast, the Third House has a social element to it that seeks out bits and pieces of information from a wide range of people met in casual, short-lived situations. Often, these verbal exchanges—while interesting for the moment—are forgettable in the long run, like yesterday's local news. Sometimes the conversation smacks of pure gossip. These methods of gathering incidental information are natural to the Third-House process, probably because they're usually done spontaneously and with relatively little structure. We really don't have to retain much of what we hear for future reference. No wonder Gemini and the airy side of Mercury are at home with the breezy atmosphere of this house!

Pluto, however, wants us to dig deep to uncover hidden realms of relevant data that need our serious analysis. It knows that our Third-House mental equipment is up to the task of such digging, once we are motivated to probe life intensely. Pluto makes sure that our curiosity is so aroused that we feel as nosy as Sherlock Holmes! Assuming that we've made peace with our Second House—so that we value ourselves on our own terms, not by society's standards—we won't feel threatened when transiting Pluto enters our Third and starts to re-educate us regarding our usage of brain power. We've learned, perhaps the hard way, about developing true self-sufficiency in the Second. In our Third, this means that we are ready to be an independent thinker who dares to look below the surface for answers. This house also encourages flexibility regarding change, a trait that Pluto always looks for in a planet or house.

Pluto can take advantage of many options while revitalizing our mental patterns in this house, because the Third supports a variety of self-expression. Of course, Pluto doesn't need to be presented with too many choices—it likes to zero in on one target at a time. We don't get the impression that mythic Pluto was a talkative god—he seemed to be the strong, silent type. Yet the Third House, although appreciating a sharp and penetrating mind, still believes it is important to allow thoughts to travel freely—in other words, our ideas should be directly transmitted to others for their immediate feedback. This is how we develop a little intellectual objectivity. (The first two houses are subjective in orientation and somewhat closed to the influence of others.) If necessary, Pluto can turn us into verbal dynamos for our optimum growth. All of our latent communication talents can come alive and energize those to whom we relate. As long as we don't sabotage our mind with an onslaught of self-destructive thoughts, this planet/house combination can be rejuvenating. Read Chapter Eight for more on this subject.

OUR FOURTH HOUSE

Pluto looks at our Fourth House as an excellent place to lie low while working on our consciousness from the inside out. Our Third-House Pluto transit was educational but, being such a high-visibility zone, the Third was perhaps a little too busy and socially interactive for a planet who would rather learn things by prowling alone in the dark. In addition, Pluto just isn't used to animating itself in the expressive ways encouraged by the Third House. In our Third, thanks to Pluto, we learn when to stop talking, and when to stop knee-jerk reactions toward communication that are based on societal pressure. If anything, Pluto tells us that, by remaining silent, we actually hear more, and can quietly evaluate information in ways that help us to develop a discerning, insightful intellect. Now, in our Fourth House, with its water orientation, Pluto knows that it will be absorbed without saying a word. Pluto penetrates the roots of our being while touring this sensitive life zone. Here, it can reach a place deep within us that we could never expect to contact in our Third House.

We seldom visit our internal psychological roots unless we decide to undergo therapy to explore what's operating unconsciously. We typically hold on to a lot of mixed childhood messages and images in this house—those that unconditionally support us and those that have deeply disturbed us. It's the overall nature of this house to retain elements of our past that become entrenched in our inner foundation, for better or worse. Pluto knows that a lot of depth-awareness work may have to be done in this impressionable area. With Pluto, we have little choice but to drop our defenses and allow certain vulnerabilities to surface—no more shell games. This will take a while, but Pluto needs plenty of time to kill off emotionally crippling factors within us. Our dependency patterns are usually under attack by Plutonian forces intent on teaching us about unearthing our neglected or rejected inner strengths, particularly those that foster self-sufficiency.

Ideally, our Fourth House is not where we resort to phony behavior or social pretenses—that is more likely to come from our Seventh and Tenth Houses, especially when our public image is at stake. Of course, one of the pitfalls of our Fourth is being subjected to family conditioning to behave in ways that do not represent our authentic self. Even then, such conditioned responses seem real and natural to us until we mature enough to reject them. Our subjective Fourth House deals with real feelings and needs that we experience in private, when we are in a safe, secure environment sheltered from a potentially threatening outer world. Pluto senses that an awareness of self-authenticity can be had here if we first peel away the layers of familial influence that otherwise thwart the emergence of our real nature. The Fourth is not a superficial zone where we are content to skim the surface of life—a fact that pleases Pluto.

Here we see an emotional planet entering a feeling-oriented house. Plutonian emotion is not easily evident to others and includes a volatile mixture of passion and anger—such emotionality can get raw at times and turn volcanic. Our Fourth House is a little too guarded by nature to open the flood gates and invite a Plutonian tidal wave of turbulent feelings that could, if not kept in check, possibly wipe out our inner foundation. Therefore, this house is highly cautious about Pluto's attempts to infiltrate our established security system, because Pluto's true intentions are never freely revealed. This house needs guarantees of security before any radical action is to be taken. In our Fourth, we often wonder, "Is this going to hurt?" "Yes," admits Pluto. That is, if everything goes according to evolutionary plan—but it will be the kind of hurt and pain that enlightens and empowers us. Both planet and house also deal with the need to finally resolve or bury matters and put them to rest for good. Chapter Nine will explore this transit further.

OUR FIFTH HOUSE

Assuming that we've survived the overhaul implied by a vigorous Fourth-House Pluto transit—"the mother of all plumbing jobs"— our next soul assignment takes us back up to the bright surface, where once again the eyes of the world are on us, more intensely now than in the Third (where we could at least hide out in libraries doing heavy Plutonian research while avoiding unwanted publicity). There is something still innocent about our state of being while we're exploring Third-House issues (it's the house of the wide-eyed student, not the wise professor). However, that changes once we undergo our "learning to get real from the roots up" Fourth-House Pluto transit. In the Fifth, Pluto can be a little more demanding of us, because we realize that we're not dummies who are still caught up in unexamined, unconscious behavior. We already know too much about who we are and what it took to get here! So, let's stop with the lame excuses and start to really turn on our power drive and see what we can dynamically create for ourselves.

Actually, we may emerge from the Fourth House still in shock, depending on how many symbolic "security blankets," not to mention the rug under our feet, have been forcefully yanked away from us. However, within due time, the Fifth House becomes Pluto's playground, where we realize that reclaiming our own ego-power can be a joy. Something fiery and vital within needs to surge forth and dazzle the world. What Pluto likes about the Fifth is that this house never wants to dim its bright lights—no false modesty or humility gets in the way of our ability to reveal our own greatness (at least to ourselves). Pluto likes to go full blast once it can no longer contain its pent-up creative forces. The Fifth House is always ready for grand displays, the showier the better—but let's not burn the place down with our creative fire.

Pluto may seem to be mostly a cosmic destroyer, ready to level life-depleting structures in order to recycle the energy trapped within those structures. However, even as the lava still flows red-hot, erupting volcanoes create new land masses where fresh forms of lush life will some day thrive. Likewise, Pluto transits are as eager to improve ongoing life as they are ready to annihilate whatever needs to die. Our Fifth House is primed for personalized creative release, whereby we experience our ability to give birth to something wonderful (our precious offspring on all levels). Pluto knows that we can undergo a full-blown renaissance regarding our talents, which this planet will support without question. The suppression of such gifts is not part of Pluto's ultimate plan. Our ego's strengths are now rising to the surface, and Pluto wants to make sure that we do this transit right by shining brightly. In other words, we're not just coming on strong because we're trying to overcompensate for any murky, unresolved psychological issues that still fester in our psyche's hidden closets. We shine in our creative outpouring because it is our divine right to do so, the result of the flowering of our spirit and the resurrection of our child-spirit within.

Meanwhile, Pluto says that we can have fun learning to do this. "Oh, by the way," interrupts Hades, "have you ever heard about my little song-and-dance routine? Ah, probably not, because I never took that act on the road as Hermes suggested when he was trying to talk me into letting him be my agent." Pluto loves a little drama, and the Fifth House is capable of a lot of flair. Both planet and house can handle healthy amounts of intensity and vivid self-expression. The Fifth is also the house of gambles and risks that offer big pay-offs. Pluto will risk all for the right cause. It appreciates that the Fifth is willing to stick its neck out in order to be what it wants to be. Now that's authentic, robust living! Pluto will always reward the sincerely courageous—it abhors cowardly behavior. What's more, our Fifth knows that being chicken-hearted is no way to approach such an adventuresome house. More about this transit is covered in Chapter Ten.

OUR SIXTH HOUSE

Transiting Pluto gets us in high-gear as it transforms our will and ego in our Fifth House. We can feel possessed of supernatural powers—that Midas touch—at least, those of us who aren't wasting Pluto's time trying to convince the world that we have nothing spectacular to offer life, and that we really don't mind continuing to exist in relative obscurity. Maybe we say, "Let others get all the glory," as long as we can fantasize about the radiant lives of Hollywood celebrities—if so, that sounds a bit like we're caught up in Neptune's trance. If that's really how we feel by the time Pluto leaves our Fifth—and be warned, Dark Face is now mighty disappointed in us—then we're in for trouble as Pluto begins to transit our Sixth. Pluto certainly didn't spend all of that time in our Fifth just so that we'd end up underrating ourselves!

The Sixth is a house that takes a no-nonsense approach to ridding us of thoughts and behavior that no longer work, and that includes a self-defeatist or even lazy attitude about coping with mundane reality. The Sixth is also willing to fix anything that's broken but is still salvageable. It's time to do needed rehabilitation work on ourselves as Pluto moves into this zone of our chart—even if we may not be aware that parts of us are chronically malfunctioning.

If, after Pluto's passage through our Fifth, we turned out feeling on top of the world—due to recreating our personality to reflect a powerful sense of high self-regard and utter self-confidence—we may need to tone down our act by the time Pluto contacts our Sixth House cusp. Personality excesses and ego-indulgences are easy to develop in the Fifth when we're feeling a little too sold on ourselves, and when no one has the guts to tell us to our face that we're going overboard with our "Ain't I fabulous?" sales campaign!

A little real humility before the gods is now due, and Pluto in our Sixth will make certain that we learn to be big and noble enough to willingly serve others without misconstruing this as strictly punishment for once being over-impressed with ourselves. Those "glory days," when we could intensely revolve around ourselves and attract captivated admirers and obsessed fans, are over. Pluto hopes that we at least learned a lot about heartfelt values, such as generosity of spirit, because we'll need to apply ourselves less egocentrically when tackling the down-to-earth chores of living. It's time to cope with life's more mundane matters once again—even health matters and the mortality issues they raise. Still, some of us can't help but feel that we're unceremoniously being kicked off our throne.

Pluto scrutinizes the smaller details easily overlooked by the other planets. Its eagle eyes don't miss much. The Sixth House also teaches us to carefully observe those little things in life that are essential to keeping everything running smoothly and steadily. If it's a dirty job that nonetheless has to be done for the welfare of many, both Pluto and the Sixth will not cop out—they are ready to handle the hard work involved. Transiting Pluto will teach us to hang in there, no matter how difficult our job. Pluto doesn't prompt us to quit something until we've almost exhausted our resources. The Sixth is an area where patience and conscientious application are rewarded—the singular focus here is typically on work well done. Both planet and house support industriousness and high levels of productivity. However, Pluto is not into a slave mentality, whereas the Sixth can lapse into a robotic kind of functionality that—while it may make us look busy (if not overworked)—is really not getting us anywhere. In fact, it's burning us out! When we mismanage this transit, we toil away without a compelling vision to sustain our inner fires.

Pluto breaks down toxins that can undermine our physical system. The Sixth House is especially interested in doing the same on various bodily levels so that optimum health is ours to enjoy. Healing channels dedicated to physical or spiritual wellness are obviously a shared interest. Pluto realizes that many people don't take good care of their Sixth-House physical health needs, and so there'll be plenty of opportunities for this planet to turn on its rejuvenating power to help us to reformat our energies and make better use of our life-force. See Chapter Eleven for more.

OUR SEVENTH HOUSE

As Pluto transits each house around the chart, starting with the First, life's challenges get increasingly complex. Other people begin to enter the picture more often as we move away from our First- and Second-House self-preoccupations. Actually, relationships will always be part of our reality, no matter at what cyclic stage transiting Pluto is to be found. But things seems to really pick up steam as Pluto enters our Seventh House (and thus opposes our First House). Here we not only deal with adjusting to another human being, but to someone who reflects, on the outside, a lot about who we are on the inside—only we don't acknowledge such qualities in us at first.

Because a potential intimate partner in our Seventh holds the key to those unconscious, projected parts that need to be better integrated with our conscious, waking self, we are powerfully drawn into such a relationship. Nobody else we know leads us to react the way our Seventh-House partner does—we feel that we must have that partner for ourselves, to be shared by no one else. Pluto appreciates the magnetic power of this life zone and the complex dynamics involved in such partnership exchanges. One of mythic Pluto's big life issues was to secure a mate to co-rule his underground world—meaning a partner to interact with on deeper levels of involvement. Interestingly, unlike other gods, Pluto didn't run around and cheat on his partner—she was his main emotional focus.

Transiting Pluto knows how transformative this particular relationship setup can be for us and, because we have so much of our unrecognized self invested in our significant other, we have much to gain once we reclaim some of those projected qualities for ourselves. The Seventh House is not just where we learn to harmoniously cooperate with others, it's where we also must engage in open, one-on-one conflict from time to time. Pluto is not the best planet for such direct confrontation—Mars is. Still, when the pressure is really on us to fight to keep a healthy balance of power in our union, Pluto will erupt and do battle. Pluto, however, tends to be a dirty fighter when under stress, hitting below the psychological belt a little too much or taking vicious stabs. In contrast, the Seventh House believes that an argument can be elevated to an art form, and that fighting should be based on fair-play, not underhanded manipulation or sneak attack.

Pluto cannot resort to its more primal, lethal ways of dealing with interpersonal conflict and still expect to satisfy Seventh-House sensibilities. This house, like Libra, appreciates a more civilized approach. Perhaps, in business partnerships, Pluto feels it's entitled to be more ruthless in getting its way, because these ties are not as emotional as marital unions, where the level of vulnerability is different. Nonetheless, the Seventh House believes that fairness is to be applied to all one-on-one relationships. Transiting Pluto is now above the horizon as it enters our Seventh. It has to play by new house rules if it is to achieve its goals.

This is a life zone where we learn to observe others very keenly and where we begin to develop an awareness of human psychology that helps us to figure out people. We become intrigued by the motivations of others (although this is even more true in our Eighth House). Pluto is also interested in sniffing out what happens below the surface, especially if it should contradict outward behavior. Transiting Pluto teaches us to follow hidden trails that lead us to another's well-guarded, inner truths. We'll need to respect a partner's psychological territory rather than forcefully intrude into his or her private space. Both planet and house are alert to subtle signals sent by others. Both want to clearly read people's intentions, even the unspoken ones. If anything, the Seventh House teaches Pluto about how difficult it is to achieve true, intimate sharing. It's made even more difficult when we refuse to let go of any tenacious psychological grip we may have on another. Read Chapter Twelve for more.

OUR EIGHTH HOUSE

In the Eighth, transiting Pluto tours a house that feels just like home—Hades! However, it would be incorrect to assume that Hades was just an earlier version of biblical Hell, with flames and demons leaping all over the place as sinners are eternally tortured for their temporal wrong-doings while on Earth. Actually, Hades was a cold and dank place with just one flaming river—the Phlegethon—that flowed outside the gates leading to the Underworld.[1] Even in the worst parts of Hades, such as Tartarus, fire imagery was non-existent, although torment was often designed to be psychologically punishing and physically taxing to those condemned to this dark realm. Astrologically, there are facets of our Eighth-House experience that feel much like doing time in Tartarus. We are often in deep psychological hell when we totally mismanage our Eighth-House energies.

Yet Pluto is on familiar turf here and knows how to navigate its way around this shadowy labyrinth. There's very little about our Eighth House that scares Pluto. Actually, Pluto admits to no fears whatsoever, which is a way to deny having hidden vulnerabilities—after all, mythic Pluto was secretly afraid he couldn't get a partner to commit herself to him by just going on a simple date and seeing what chemistry naturally developed. This is a house where we are to get in touch with an entirely different underground realm, an area that we guard closely and are unwilling to share with others. Yes, we hear about the wonderful self-renewal work that can be had here, which leads to the self-restorative ability to be completely reborn. Yet none of it comes without first being willing to let go of old, powerful defenses that have kept us well-armored and impenetrable. Deep pockets of hidden pain can be found here when we refuse to look within and heal ourselves. For many of us, this can remain an unconscious place that nonetheless has a powerful, insidious influence over our behavior—especially in intimate relationships.

Pluto knows all of the tricky passageways of this house—after all, it helped design them—and realizes what it will take to make them more accessible. At first, we may be tempted to say, "Thanks, but no thanks, Pluto!" However, eventually we'll need to become sensitive to the impact that our deepest, darkest secrets have had on us, and the cumulative, psychological toll they have taken. Of course, not everyone has tremendous heaps of rotting garbage to contend with here. In that case, Pluto is less focused on difficult plumbing work and is more energized to speed up the transformative process—we shake off old hang-ups and allow latent strengths to surface for the first time. We find that we don't struggle with our internal conflicts as much as we used to because we discover appropriate ways to vent our hidden frustrations.

Pluto and the Eighth obviously have a lot in common. However, Pluto is a lone-wolf at heart, while the Eighth needs a willing partner to play out much of its complex dynamics. Jealousy and possessiveness are two features of a mishandled Eighth House that can really damage the foundation of any existing relationship. Plutonians can have these unattractive traits as well, but keep them bottled up inside. In the Eighth, outer situations provoke periodic stormy confrontations, and circumstantial eruptions that we cannot control. Both planet and house will need to know where to best put their passions to use. Pluto loves the fact that it will be guaranteed arousing levels of intensity in this house. Pluto brings out its best during times that are the most tempestuous or crisis-ridden. However, we're only human, so we get anxious at the thought that transiting Pluto is now in a house where it can really let its hair down and turn on the heat! Boy, is it hot here in Hell, or is it just me? More on this can be found in Chapter Thirteen.

OUR NINTH HOUSE

When Pluto rises from the smoldering ashes of our Eighth-House transit, let's hope that all of the deep, inner work was worth the struggles and losses we had to endure. We emerge knowing that our inner world is not the same anymore, and now we're ready to see everything with new eyes. The Ninth House likes it when we're wide-eyed, innocent, and hoping that the Truth shall set us free. In our Eighth, Pluto strips away most of whatever would thwart or retard the next level of growth awaiting us in our Ninth House. We are to approach this next Plutonian transit with a cleaner psychological slate, especially in terms of being free from any long-standing demons in the form of biases, blind spots, hatreds, prejudices, or power trips. This is important, because, for once on Pluto's journey, we are entering a realm of universal scope involving the ability to influence the masses.

Pluto has the potential to offer us a vast awareness of many levels of existence operating simultaneously; this can result in an awesome perspective. The Ninth House is known for its wide-open, mind-expanding spaces, as well as its breadth of spiritual understanding about the human condition when viewed on a large scale. This is no place for Pluto to bring along any toxic residue from an unregenerated Eighth House. In the Ninth, many may undeservingly end up poisoned by what we've failed to heal within ourselves. Adolph Hitler, born with Pluto in his

Eighth, had this planet transit his intercepted Ninth from the age of twenty-one until about fifty-two, which takes us to 1941. History has documented his maniacal and terrifying grab for global power during World War II, as Pluto moved through his Tenth. Pluto can be a master of propaganda, and the Ninth is where political rhetoric is given a wide audience. The seeds of Hitler's ideological venom, planted throughout his Plutonian Ninth-House period, unfortunately sprouted deep, strong roots. His mesmerizing influence on the collective unconscious of Germany was unparalleled. This extreme example emphatically shows how unresolved Eighth-House wounds can serve to injure the collective in some manner when Pluto transits this house of mass awareness.

This may sound a little too dramatic, because many of us are not expecting to do anything globally significant or history-making no matter what transits our Ninth House—our grand, future vision might be to take a few weeks off to enjoy the sun and the surf in Maui! Still, a few of us with different destinies are going to have a far-reaching impact on society. We're the "chosen ones" who have to make sure that we don't introduce unredeemed elements from our Eighth that will pollute our Ninth-House collective aspirations. Assuming that we've made the most of our Eighth-House Pluto transit and are harboring no underground grudges against the world, the Ninth is a marvelous area for Pluto to feel that it's on a healing mission to restore an uplifting sense of constructive power to society.

The one thing here that's different, however, is that now we're less able to solely manage that power. The Ninth House believes in a more democratic, group approach. Our ego is getting the message that it must take the back seat, be philosophical, and learn to enjoy the ride, because now a lot of folks are involved in how this Plutonian energy is to be dispersed. Distributing Plutonian power far and wide to many people for their greatest good becomes an ideal goal that warms the heart of the Ninth House. Here, we can burn with idealism as we fire up our faith in a promising future for all. The collective unconscious is in a better position to call the shots, and we'll have to surrender our reformative Plutonian impulses to a higher, guiding principle. Here's when Pluto starts really feeling its transpersonal juices flow! Read further about this transit in Chapter Fourteen.

OUR TENTH HOUSE

Pluto and the Tenth House have one thing in common: both deal with themes of power and mastery. Control over the environment becomes a tempting ambition. Yet from Pluto's entrance into our Ninth House all the way through its passage in our Twelfth, this planet's orientation is increasingly transpersonal, even transcendental. Our assertive self-will in action seems to have a less direct influence on Plutonian outcomes, because an inscrutable fate causes our life to take a few significant turns that are beyond our control. Of course, such twists of fate can still work in our favor, perhaps because we're not allowed to control every move.

Other people, barely known to us, play a pivotal but impersonal part in our Tenth-House experience. This house symbolizes mass organization of people by assigning them to various life roles based on class structure, economic status, and educational background. It's in the Tenth that we can feel at times like just "another faceless number" who's caught up in a System that forces us to conform to its ironclad rules of conduct. However, Pluto is going to have a hard time bowing down to such rules. It's a revolutionist with subversive intentions, not a conformist willing to toe the line.

Therefore, while Pluto is transiting this house it's hard to feel as if the world really knows and cares who we are deep down inside. We're pressured to live out a broader identity within the collective framework that may have less in common with our private self than people close to us realize. Still, our waking, ego-supporting self likes to assume that it's always in charge of personal matters—fate be damned! We may be intensely driven in our Tenth-House endeavors as we devise Plutonian strategies to help us snare a power role—which we won't easily surrender once attained. After all, we learned a lot about the power of faith when

Pluto was moving through our Ninth, and now our beliefs about life give us the extra stamina and focus needed to survive the life-altering changes instigated by Pluto in our Tenth.

This house deals with how we adjust to authority figures and how we feel about those in charge of us. Is being supervised by a boss a humiliating or a humbling experience? For a passionately anti-boss planet such as Pluto, being under the yoke of authority can be a hostility-producing situation. Mythic Pluto ruled the Underworld with an iron fist. His "show no mercy" policy made him a formidable figure that kept many intimidated, even when at a safe distance. He was unbending with the rules of his game. Today's Plutonians can be just as unapproachable and intractable when functioning in the power seat. Closet dictators seem to come alive when their Tenth-House dreams finally come true and they are granted a position of significant leadership. This is a transit that warns us about abusing social power. The combination of Pluto and the Tenth can imply that a few of us take unfair advantage of society by manipulatively using our position in the world, especially if we already have a commanding role to play.

If so, transiting Pluto has a big cosmic, karmic surprise awaiting some Tenth-House power-trippers. It may seem, at first, as if this planet encourages behavior that leads us to positions where we get away with dominating others and forcefully bending them to our will—but that's because transiting Pluto initially intensifies the path to which we are already committed. All stages of a Pluto transit tend to be vividly expressed. However, at some critical and fateful point, Pluto turns against our power-hungry ego and sets patterns of destruction into motion. At that stage, Pluto treats our ambitious ego like a voracious cancer that needs to be stopped dead in its tracks. What's worse, our downfall—our judgment day—is for all to see and remember. Ultimately, Pluto heavily penalizes people who think that they are above the law (some of the worst punishments in Hades awaited those guilty of hubris, the crime of mortals arrogantly assuming that they were better than the gods themselves). Read more about this transit in Chapter Fifteen.

OUR ELEVENTH HOUSE

Many people survive their Tenth-House Pluto transit by establishing a new outlook on their social contributions to the world—very few suffer public shame of social infamy. The Tenth House is eager to honor excellence in achievement, while it also punishes those who are a disgrace to society. Hitler didn't want to face the judgment of the world for the horrific results of his unbridled hubris, so he committed suicide while transiting Pluto in his Tenth quincunxed his Capricorn Moon (suggesting a maladjusted instinct to self-destruct under critical life conditions). If we have successfully endured our professional ups and downs while channeling our power reserves into relevant, broad-based directions, then Pluto entering our Eleventh can be a time of inner and outer rewards for public services rendered in the name of social advancement.

Such a theme of social progress continues as part of our Eleventh-House journey. Exactly where collective energy is going with its progressive idealism is very important to this house. Ongoing technology is both worshiped and vilified, depending on how insensitively it addresses the ecological needs of the planet and the human rights of the world's citizens. We realize that our future goals are best fulfilled when they include everyone else's welfare—a tall order, for sure. This life zone is even more impersonal in tone than that of the two previous houses. Pluto here is not quite a transcendental force, but it is helping us to reach a transitional shifting-point in our consciousness. Pluto obviously is relieved to hear that the Eleventh House is willing to daringly experiment with the concept of collective freedom and the social exploration of untapped human potential, with no stiff rules and tight-fisted laws to defiantly battle.

Pluto knows that it's on Uranus' wild turf and therefore realizes that unchecked domination by governing authorities will be met with the threat of social revolt. This is a place where disgruntled rebels, cultural outlaws, and other colorful, free souls band together and form coalitions that let the world know that "group power" is a potent force. The suppression of civil liberties will be dealt a deserving deathblow, especially now that outraged Pluto has come on the scene. A spirit of activism may rise within, urging us to deeply think about how unfairly collective power has been distributed throughout history—especially when those at the top put "the big thumb" down on defenseless people at the bottom who are not allowed to rule their personal lives.

Such social inequalities make Pluto's blood boil when it's in this house. This planet is capable of stirring up much turmoil in society, triggering major upheavals in government and even in religion—all in an attempt to balance the books. Plutonians on the warpath can be frighteningly loud, chaos-inducing, and under-mining of all that tradition preciously guards. However, we'd have no individual freedoms without the efforts of dedicated—albeit fanatical—Plutonian (and Uranian) insurrectionists.

Most of us can expect to use this Pluto transit as a time to look at mass instability on the global front in a different light, seeing it less as something scary and threatening and more as a sign that deep universal discontent needs to surface—even if vio-lently—before it can be healed. World peace will come at a heavy price, if it is to come at all. What we need to remember is that our personal enlightenment doesn't have to require that we take extreme measures to reform society to fit our vision. Many people claim to not be political animals, so this transit means letting go of group associations that may have worked for us in the past, but not anymore. Besides evaluating our acquaintances, we need to also examine the organizations of which we have been long-stand-ing members. If the strong energy we felt by belonging to these groups has peaked, it's time to move on—not necessarily to another group. It may be important to be alone for a while. All in all, with Pluto we can step back and gain an in-depth overview of how pervasive and invasive society can be in the lives of each individual. We realize that we're less willing to surrender our individuality to the System without putting up a fierce fight to defend our rights, and yours, too! Check out Chapter Sixteen for more on this.

OUR TWELFTH HOUSE

Pluto entering the Twelfth is ready to shed all of the other skins that it wore during its passage through the previous eleven houses, because now it's time for this planet's transcendental light to burn brightly, even if only internally. Pluto is a planet that impels us to make periodic descents into the lower, shadowy regions of our underground world—our personal unconscious. The society we live in doesn't promote the undertaking of such an inner journey, because it associates the need for that kind of "mystery trip" with unsettling signs of mental illness. For that, we have trained psychiatrists (rather than initiated shamans) who will attempt to light our way in the realms of darkness. The problem is that the more orthodox among them inadequately use a flickering match instead of Hermes' glowing torch to illuminate the path.

Pluto has the temperament to go all the way when descending into the black pits of our netherworld. This is very familiar territory for Pluto to fearlessly investigate. The Twelfth-House abyss serves as a comfort zone for Pluto, who realizes that no matter how bright the sunlight, the surface of life doesn't always reveal much (at least, not much of what intrigues Pluto about human consciousness). This house deals with the closing stages of a cycle that began with our ego-emerging, self-sparking First House. Things now are in varying states of dissolution, and such phases of deconstruction can make us feel strangely unstable inside. We can experience an ineffable feeling of deflation and exhaustion on a deep soul level. Pluto, however, feels quite in its element as it helps to accelerate the process of psychological disintegration that must continue without interruption.

This is, metaphorically speaking, the period when the caterpillar has spun its cocoon and is in the pupa stage, where a lot of metamorphic magic takes place, behind the scenes, in a protective world of darkness and unconscious sleep. Our Twelfth-House experience can seem to be a period of rest, because little about this house encourages the dynamic thrust of worldly conquest more evident in other sectors of our chart. Much can go on deep within us that will fundamentally change the form we take when our recycled self appears once more in the First House. In this phase of soul retreat, Pluto breaks down anything that still can be toxic, while it also supplies our spirit with visionary seeds that will need to germinate as we move into our upcoming phases. Meanwhile, the breakdown period is intense but crucial. It may feel as if we're caught in a strange limbo, merely existing rather than actively doing things. Nonetheless, an internal overhaul of our psyche's ᵗ ture is under way. Actually, a lot of junk is being swept out of our psychological system, and Pluto is obviously having a blast being in charge of the invisible demolition crew at work.

Pluto loves the mysterious, subtle nature of the Twelfth House—a place that's amazingly quiet, which is a trait that this planet finds most rewarding. Pluto is not always happy to be erupting all over the place and devastating the scenery—it also needs down time, where it can deeply ponder what it has previously destroyed, and what it has given birth to in the process. The Twelfth House accommodates Pluto's thorough inspection of the psyche's most guarded hiding spots. It surrenders to this experience knowing that a new cycle of birth can best come about once we have properly broken down our unintegrated psychic debris, to then be released and reabsorbed by the all-loving, all-understanding Universe. Read Chapter Seventeen for more on this transit.

NOTE

1. Brian Clark, *Hades as Place: The Underworld in Myth and Antiquity*, Astro*Synthesis Publications, 1988.

PART TWO

OUR REVITALIZING
PLUTO TRANSITS

CHAPTER FIVE

HIDDEN LIGHT WITHIN OUR DARKNESS

ARIES VERSUS SCORPIO

After an unrelenting period of psychological strain and emotional upheaval, transiting Pluto's energy constructively recycles itself as fresh starts and vital beginnings—sounding at first as if it should rule Aries instead of Scorpio. Dane Rudhyar proposes this Pluto/Aries connection in *The Sun Is Also a Star*, where he states, "Germination is a Plutonian process, and this is why in astrology Pluto should 'rule' Aries."[1]

Pluto may indeed tie into the "forever young" aspect of Aries, emphasizing this sign's fiery sense of periodic self-renewal, the "springtime" of our soul. Yet it's hard for me to link Pluto's darker intricacies with the Ram's simple, basic survival psychology. Aries has an innocent directness about itself. It's not one to avoid the exposure of broad daylight. It unhesitantly takes straightforward action, but with a naive self-interest that doesn't sound much like a collective-oriented planet better known for its calculated, stealthy maneuvers. Secretive, complex, motivation-analyzing Scorpio makes more sense here.

However, the loner quality in Pluto is similar to that of intently self-reliant Aries (a sign that doesn't need committed relationships in order to function—as least Aries *assumes* that it doesn't, until it meets up with irresistible, partnership-ready Libra—its polar opposite). Actually, Scorpio also shares a bit of the isolationist streak that we find in some Plutonians. However, seeking total isolation (not to be confused with privacy) is usually only an emotionally wounded Scorpio's defense, brought into play when it cannot trust anyone enough to permit the psychological exposure that long-term intimacy requires. Normally, this sign desires totally committed companionship, more so than lone-wolf Pluto.

INTO THE UNDERWORLD

Much has been written about astrological Pluto's association with our psyche's underground world, that mysterious realm of the unconscious where our primal desires boil and bubble—the desire to survive anything in order to keep the life-force alive being one of them. A volcano's hidden layers of molten rock (magna)—where enormous pressures slowly build—would be an apt metaphor for this inner Plutonian underworld. Hot but hidden psychological material belongs to Pluto. The more we suppress our Pluto (which is easy to do), the more concentrated becomes our untapped power base. Yet as long as that power base remains inaccessible to us, our greatest potential remains sadly unrealized.

Natal Pluto shows us where pent-up energies result when we attempt to disown stormy feelings or keep tremendous passions and "magnificent" obsessions from surfacing. Our capacity for emotional blockage is great. We may feel compelled to tightly control (or unconsciously let others control) these parts of our being for fear that they would become overwhelming once unleashed. It may be a fantasy that we can indeed control and master our Plutonian parts. Still, no matter how irrational, the threat of annihilation can be felt when our natal Pluto is activated.

Pluto's urge is to kill anything that no longer works for us. However, everyday living doesn't comfortably support the venting of Plutonian energies such as lust and rage. Pluto's power source, although deeply internal, is unrelenting in its slow ascent to the surface of our consciousness. It eventually must emerge if we are to self-actualize its promise of renewal. Many of us tend to thwart the easy release of these deep Plutonian forces, creating more turbulence for ourselves as a result of this power struggle. In addition, what emerges from the depths may scare the heck out of us. Feeling torn in two extreme directions is a typical Plutonian dilemma.

Transiting Pluto seems to show a different dynamic. It doesn't support a further concealment of issues that have already proven to be chronically intense or painful. It's had enough of our cowardice and silence, our hiding in our personal underground, and our tactic of wearing our protective helmet of invisibility when in public. Wherever Pluto is transiting in our chart, certain facets of our life are set up for glaring exposure or full disclosure. By the way, this "let's get everything out in the open" theme sounds like upfront Aries' way of handling crises. The message here is for us to come clean with our interior motives. We may need to recognize any devious methods with which we deal with life. A rousing Pluto transit demands honesty. However, it can take a long while before anything is laid out on the surgeon's table, which doesn't sound like a characteristic of the Aries principle. Again, it appears that Pluto pretty much belongs to Scorpio.

If natal Pluto symbolizes the hidden rumblings deep within the bowels of both a volcano and a human psyche, transiting Pluto represents the fury of a full-scale eruption of whatever has been deeply hidden and compacted under high internal pressure. Natal Pluto can let things fester and further infect us for a long while, but transiting Pluto indicates that it's time to lance our angry, red, psychological boils and enforce a healing stage.

Just like that uncomfortable last image, transiting Pluto in action can be discomforting and offensive to our sensibilities, especially if we've been using those sensibilities to unwisely shield ourselves from in-depth self-confrontation. This is not a planet that honors superficial niceties, especially when it's on a rampage in the name of the unflattering Truth. It's even more fierce than Uranus in this regard.

Facing hard-core reality becomes part of this "what's the bottom line" transit, even if that means we're forced to see parts of ourselves and our lifestyle that are doomed to destruction. Hesitant, uncertain Saturn wants a fair chance to repair faulty structures before it becomes resigned to dumping them. In contrast, decisive Pluto would sooner bring in the bulldozers to demolish the place. Unlike Saturn, it's less apt to seek security in existing structure, and therefore can destroy form with little regret. We can try to fool ourselves into believing our distortions and illusions during a Pluto transit, but that will end up backfiring on us. The real conditions underlying our pretenses and phony facades eventually erupt, sometimes dramatically.

Pluto has been likened to the fabulous Phoenix of Egyptian myth, the fabled firebird able to consume itself, only to reemerge from the flame and ashes to regenerate. It is a perfectly apt symbol of Plutonian rebirth. Transiting Pluto provides such renewal as an option for some of us, as long as we realize that we may have to writhe about in a little ash and flame before we ascend to headier heights. It's not going to be easy. In fact, it's bound to be a scary proposition to face off with our darker parts and be willing to engage in a deadly battle in order to exorcise the power those parts have had over us for so long. Perhaps that sounds a bit overstated, but not to those who have been struggling with self-destructive addictions and compulsions. Any of us who has been in the iron grip of soul-deadening predicaments should welcome every Pluto transit we can handle. To others, these transits may seem horrific, like sky-diving into the pit of Hell.

There can be an almost reckless, *kamikaze* quality to transiting Pluto (and to natal Pluto as well, under certain aspects). Kamikaze pilots in World War II certainly did not see themselves as involved in senseless suicide missions; they most likely felt profoundly honored to play out a meaningful, reverential role in deciding the ultimate fate of their beloved country. That kind of unrelenting intensity leading up to some fateful ending or showdown is a condition that belongs only to Pluto. We may find, during our Pluto transits, that we can be equally dogged and single-minded about pursuing our goals and ideals *to the very end,* regardless of consequences.

Under Pluto's influence, we may be willing to be put through the acid test in the name of what seems utterly right and true. Sometimes, we put ourselves in great peril as well. We can defiantly polarize ourselves against the societal status quo in the pursuit of Plutonian goals. For example, after many years of legal threat, assisted-suicide advocate Jack Kevorkian—a.k.a. "Dr. Death"—was finally charged with first-degree murder when transiting Pluto opposed his natal Sun.[2] He was eventually convicted and given a prison sentence.

So, what can we do during a major Pluto transit to help us feel alive and well? Pluto can either bury the rotting corpse for good, or resurrect the dead, or revive that which is near death but still salvageable. The drastic measures that Pluto urges us to take when intent on action is driven by evolutionary necessity (keeping that fundamental spark of life going strong). Ironically, this planet, typically associated with "death," is really on a mission to ensure eternal life. Compromise is not part of Pluto's vocabulary, so its demands have an "all-or-nothing" quality about them. Here's a dead-serious planet that brings ultimatums into our life, major crossroads where we're expected to burn our bridges behind us and realize that there's no going back. Sometimes there's nothing left to go back to.

To deal with all of this, we'll need to draw on inner resources of strength and courage that we've always had but never before needed to test—at least, not like we're having to test them now. Our total commitment and unflinching involvement is required, and that implies an uncommon level of concentration. This can be a vibrant time of soul validation, arousing tremendous, risk-taking urges within us. Certain things that seem psychologically dangerous to us can now hold a key to self-affirmation once we learn to conquer our fears. That's not easy, because Plutonian-triggered fears are buried deeply within us and firmly entrenched.

The once-popular fad of fire-walking seemed like a Plutonian exercise in overcoming fear. Everyone who was successful in walking barefoot over burning coals certainly felt an amazing sense of instant empowerment. It would be interesting to know how some of these people later translated that empowerment into other areas of their lives. Or was it only a one-time experience brought on by the collective power of *participation mystique,* which is actually more of a Neptunian phenomenon?[3]

RESURRECTION CITY

A well-handled Pluto transit can help us to feel in charge of our lives, because we learn how amazingly strong and indomitable we are at the core of our being. However, we may have to fight for this self-knowledge. It doesn't magically come about. Eventually, we find that we can take a lot of "crap"—a good Plutonian word—from life without being blown away. We learn that we have a sacred "fire down below" that is never totally extinguished, even under the harshest of outer conditions. This eternal flame will always be there to light our way, even during the darkest and bleakest of internal nights. However, Pluto's fire is not gentle and cannot be applied in a casual or superficial manner.

Pluto has been associated with the *kundalini,* a serpentine life-force of undulating "spiritual fire" that—as Hindu yoga masters and saints have long claimed—makes its passage up the spine, eventually fully awakening our seven *chakras* (the specialized energy vortexes in our "etheric" body). This must precede true enlightenment, it is said, and it must be done correctly to avoid psychological and physical harm. Likewise, astrologers link Pluto to psychological trials by fire in which we sometimes get badly burned when we become dangerously out-of-kilter. Such trials also help us to undergo awarenesses leading to a profound process of self-healing. Pluto may sear and scorch all that it touches, as does a rushing stream of lava, but it also burns away any negativity from our past, which extends far back into our soul's history. One reward of surviving this is a capacity for full-bodied living, because this planet is associated with an enormous appetite for life experience.

Transiting Pluto allows for the awesome release of forces that natal Pluto has concentrated within us for years, even if the two are not currently making an aspect to one another. A little bit of our natal Pluto potential gets to surface every time something in our birthchart is triggered by Pluto in transit. It's as if transiting Pluto resonates at a special frequency that natal Pluto has no trouble receiving. Uranus and Neptune act like this, too.

During this planet's transitional periods, we will have a hard time internalizing anything for long. Life forces us to "throw up" on some level. Pluto also compels us to "throw out" whatever is no longer needed. Excess psychological baggage becomes too weighty to carry during a major Pluto transit. It has to go. During Pluto phases, we get to play the role of a detective looking for clues at the crime scene. If we are still attaching ourselves to oppressive people or energy-sucking lifestyles, a little self-honesty is needed to determine why we continue this behavior, even when it does us nothing but harm. Meanwhile, Pluto is scrutinizing the situation and making plans to give certain elements of our life the old heave ho!

Pluto is associated with the body's elimination system for a good reason—it deals with the neutralizing, drainage, and total removal of toxic, corrosive by-products. Keeping such injurious material inside us, physically or emotionally, during our Pluto transits only renders them lethal at some later date. Therefore, it's best to flush them out now in preparation for a healthier future. But do we need to always unload in a drastic manner? Must we destroy everything in sight? Perhaps such extreme measures are the outcome of our total resistance to letting things go a little bit at a time, long before we reach the boiling point. An unyielding attitude on our part only creates Plutonian complications that press for uncompromising resolutions. Maybe we've remained aloof and remote in the past, but now, during our Pluto transit, we find ourselves in the thick of situations that demand that we act decisively and allow for closure. Why secretly desire to return to a past that no longer has any fire to offer us?

PLUTO TRANSITING A NATAL HOUSE

Pluto's transit through any natal house marks a lengthy period when certain circumstances of that house are ripe for a clean sweep. Not every house affair will call for a Plutonian death and rebirth. Regarding currently non-problematic circumstances of this house, Pluto urges us to seek gradual but significant empowerment. Situations slowly evolve to help us feel stronger and more capable of dealing with the issues. No dramatic turning-points are required. However, it's the darker areas of this house—areas where we routinely avoid self-examination and thus keep our shadow material intact—that are subject to the most serious Plutonian make-overs.

If something must be stamped out for good because it has chronically impeded our development by holding us back from deeper self-understanding, Pluto will ensure that problems associated with that troublesome "something" become apparent—and Pluto will use *anything* it takes to force us to confront ourselves or others in this area. Being a basically amoral planet, it can play dirty if it has to. Certain issues may slowly build up in intensity and eventually erupt, demanding our full attention, as stark reality repeatedly hits us in the face. The more we have resisted analyzing and acting on such matters in the past, the more pressing they become now. We mustn't be too rigid or obstinate during a major Pluto transit, because that will only provoke this planet to come down harder on us, emphatically driving its message home.

However, Pluto is exceedingly slow in its operations. Time is on its side. Pluto seemingly can wait an eternity to fulfill its desires. We only get to see Pluto's raging fireball during the later, incendiary stages of this transit, when the critical issues in question are ready to explode, forcing a non-negotiable ending to a major life-chapter. Usually, by then, Pluto's aspecting a natal planet or two, triggering our inner self to actively engage in—and often do battle with—critical outer conditions.

I think that things also take so darn long because Pluto, more than any other planet, demands that a vast composite of situational factors be present before it will rev its engine and speed up the process of transformation or devastation. Complexity is its middle name. All pertinent details must be in place before major Plutonian action can occur, and that includes those special people who are to become triggers for our Plutonian growth. What ushers in these people and situations seems to be an impersonal fate that defies logic and justice—a fact that we find very disturbing.

Meanwhile, how does the theme of being alive and well fit into this? So far, Pluto sounds like a can of vipers waiting to be opened. The real truth is that Pluto can seemingly be dormant for a long stretch of time (like a sleeping volcano) as it inches—about 3° to 4° per year—across the house it transits. We might wrongly assume that our inner Pluto, operating so far below the surface of life, is not really paying much attention to the daily, mundane activities of each house. Therefore, if we are messing with things that we honestly know we should avoid, we may convince ourselves that nobody's going to really know about it. Boy, is that a big mistake!

Some of us may even feel that we have a right to slowly destroy ourselves in the pursuit of our pleasures—or, more accurately, the right to please ourselves in the pursuit of our destruction. The bottom line is that whenever we detour too far from the sane path of psycho-spiritual wholeness—a path destined to lead us to the creative integration of our many parts—distress signals are sent to our psyche's underworld to alert our Pluto, an archetype with an uncanny knack for sniffing out trouble. Tempting an agitated Pluto to surface under these conditions is not a smart idea. He may not even bother to wear his helmet this time, in which case his presence may be frighteningly conspicuous!

However, there are many occasions when the right dose of Plutonian energy proves restorative. The affairs of the house involved may sorely need an overall resurgence of vitality. Pluto can turn on its invigorating power to bring a new direction or vibrant ambition into the picture. When it trines or sextiles a natal planet during its stay in this house, Pluto can coincide with small bursts of rejuvenating energy that make us feel as if we have another chance at bat after hitting too many foul balls or even after striking out. These mini "bursts," though, should not be confused with Jupiter's hope-filled surges of pep and positivism regarding our future's promise.

Pluto doesn't share Jupiter's boundless optimism. Jupiter offers its goods freely. Pluto typically takes away something that we've held tightly on to for a long time before it is willing to bestow anything of long-lasting value in return. After all, something or someone needs to be eliminated during our Pluto transit if we are to function better than before. What's usually needed is the courage to act. Even with a Pluto conjunction, square, or opposition, we can clear away stagnant patterns that have only served to clog our passageways of consciousness. Such aspects can be equally rejuvenating once we work through our resistance to change. If we don't cooperate, however, drastic alterations are forced on us.

Often we do not recognize or appreciate the reconstructive surgery that has been done in Pluto's transited house until long after it has moved out of that sector and we've had a chance to reflect and recuperate from any opened wounds. It's at such a time that our perspective on this pivotal era of our life becomes clear. We see the results of the internal and external struggles that existence forced us to undertake; we also see what we made out of strained situations that were sometimes grueling and sometimes soul-fortifying.

Although Pluto eventually pulls out of this house for good, it leaves its indelible mark on us. If all turns out for the better, we find ourselves less fearful to be our real selves. In that case, we refuse to accept the false masks that others try to make us wear. Such people may permanently remove themselves from our life as a result. Our response should be, "Good riddance!" Even if everyone walks away from us, we're now less afraid of being alone, if that's the situation handed to us. Now we know, deep inside, that we can muster up whatever it takes to make it through life all by ourselves. Our survival skills have probably been upgraded the hard way. One reward that comes as a result of this is a tremendous coping ability. After a point, less and less in our world can shake us up. We develop a ruggedness that helps us to handle life's ups and downs with aplomb.

Pluto Transiting a Natal Planet

Natal planets aspected by transiting Pluto are invited to journey below the surface of day-to-day living in order to take a hard look at their own inner motives and less-examined needs. Pluto becomes a private investigator, knocking on doors and asking each planet a few pointed questions aimed at identifying probable suspects and witnesses. Sure, Pluto is nosy and a bit intrusive, but if a planet has an airtight alibi (and no criminal record) or if it swears it saw or heard nothing fishy, there's little to worry about. Pluto gets back into his unmarked black stealthmobile and, before driving away, reminds each planet to keep both its front and back doors locked at all times. You just never know who could break in in the middle of the night and burglarize the place—or worse!

The truth is that very few of our birth planets have a squeaky clean record by the time we're past our first Saturn Return. There'll always be some dirt to dig up on us. Pluto will use its special investigatory power to force those little secrets about us and our relationships to surface. It's time to "fess up" when Pluto's making the rounds. However, there's no need to become petrified with terror—this is not the Inquisition of bygone days. Remember that Pluto works on us very slowly; the wheels of fate take a long time to turn. With its eagle eyes, Pluto misses nothing. It's likely that we are the ones who aren't paying attention to telling clues along the trail, left here and there by the subtle Universe. If we find ourselves in a sticky predicament, loaded with circumstantial complication, Pluto's detailed notes show that our troubles built up long before things reached their critical level.

Actually, these transits can make us face ourselves like never before, and that can be unsettling or cathartic. Pluto transits suggest that we could also hit the motherload of a gold mine, because this planet rules underground riches of Earth. Pluto carries a theme of attaining massive wealth and super-powerful resources. It's the planet of mega-mergers in business and industry. However, the primary enrichment to be sought during a major Pluto transit involves, first and foremost, something of inner value. Chasing obsessively after the external temptations of worldliness can sidetrack us from the personal psychological work that now needs our attention.

The drives and urges associated with any natal planet are typically forced to rethink their strategies for getting what they want during a Pluto transit. If something in our lives is not working, it's time for us to adopt a radically new perspective. How we go about doing this can be dramatic. If we've repeatedly used strong-arm tactics to have our way in life, Pluto is ready to strip us of our power tools and our intimidating manner. The buck stops here with Pluto. If, instead, we've been too meek, non-confrontational, or willing to bow down to our oppressors, Pluto announces that it's time to feel a surge of our own inherent power as symbolized by the natal planet being transited.

Pluto abhors naiveté (Kore was plenty naive before she "met" Pluto and was made over into his vision of her hidden potential). Pluto demands that any transited planet let go of its innocence and instead take a crash course in hardening its survival muscles—a dose of stark reality is needed. As this is happening, we can feel waves of defiance as we probably become stormy with our current life conditions and with the people involved in them.

Any talk about "spiritual transformation" during this time is premature, because we won't be feeling very spiritual while we are caught up in a raging Plutonian transitional phase—some of us are so ticked off that we could even self-destruct if we don't wipe out our past frustrations. A few of us are human A-bombs at this time. Yet this may be just a temporary stage we go through in order to finally release trapped inner qualities that have been repressed for too long. If we are feeling "spittin' angry" during a Pluto transit (but hopefully not murderous), it's a good sign that we are ready to turn our energies around and kill off our old and tired behavior. Even if anger is not our issue, we are still not very accommodating regarding the demands of others.

Something about the natal planet involved usually feels as if it's dying during our Pluto transit—and we can feel like we're the executioner, sharpening the ax. For stubborn, stagnating types who hate any sort of personal changes in their lives, the environment—with Pluto's blessings—will conspire to make things come to an ungraceful, possibly shocking end. Think of the sudden devastation caused by hellish wildfires swooping down hills or racing through canyons to engulf home after home. That kind of tragedy has Pluto written all over it. An extreme and soul-wrenching manifestation such as this will rarely occur, even during the worst Pluto transits. Yet for some, it has already happened, and astrologers don't know exactly why. We can only speculate: maybe it's karmic retribution or maybe the "victim's" unconscious elements are in a severe state of outrage, demanding the complete annihilation of some deeply held idea or behavior as the only solution for soul relief.

Usually, death doesn't happen in a concrete manner, such as the death of a loved one or the total loss of a possession. Seldom is Pluto symbolizing a threat to our own life. However, planets represent our psychological urges, and Pluto is eager to terminate internal attitudes that have continued to poison our consciousness. What we have spent many years hating or resenting may now become an issue that vividly captures our undivided attention. Pluto says, "Enough already!" Such hatred is starting to destroy us. We'll need to release our darker emotions once and for all. Otherwise, concentrated levels of venom will begin to damage our psyche in major ways that spill over into our situational life and even jeopardize our health.

We don't have to turn our energies around and start sending spiritual love to any loathsome, horrible so-and-so who's betrayed or abused us. After all, Pluto can't pretend it's Saint Neptune. However, we also don't have to obsess over that person or any disturbing past event. Why sadly relive the memory of old woundings again and again? Pluto helps us to kill whatever has been negatively symbolized by the transited planet, at least inside ourselves. We no longer allow past traumas to control our lives and keep us from the psychological freedom we deserve. Getting to that level of detachment is not easy, considering how long we have dwelled on such troubling factors. If peace of mind is our ultimate goal, Pluto leaves us little choice. We can't continue seething forever without injuring ourselves badly at some future point.

In the following chapters I'll point out transiting Pluto's redeeming features whenever possible. Realize, though, that this planet doesn't like us to fake things just so we can temporarily feel better. It doesn't believe in quick fixes to problems whose histories go way back. Trying to remain calm and "in control" (like a good little sleeping volcano) won't help the Plutonian process become any smoother. Note that it's the sleeping volcanoes that, when they finally erupt, really blow their stack sky high. We'll need to be real with our emerging feelings during our Pluto transits. Pluto has a lot to offer us, once we are willing to lose everything in the process. The surprise is that only truly unneeded things leave us, while whatever is essential to the support of the real person within us remains and becomes further fortified.

NOTES

1. Dane Rudhyar, *The Sun Is Also a Star,* E.P. Dutton & Co., Inc., New York, 1975, pp. 66–67.

2. According to various reports, Dr. Jack Kevorkian was born May 26, 1928, in Pontiac, Michigan. Some astrologers speculate that he has Scorpio Rising, but no confirmed birth time has been made available as of this book's publication date.

3. See Chapter Four of Liz Greene's *The Astrological Neptune and the Quest for Redemption,* Samuel Weiser, ME, 1996.

PLUTO TRANSITING THE FIRST HOUSE

STORMY WEATHER

Pluto moves so slowly around the chart that many of us are guaranteed not to have this transit during our lifetime, although we probably will deal with transiting Pluto squaring or opposing our Ascendant at some timely point. If any planets smack of destiny or fate, Pluto and Neptune fit the bill. The moment a person is born, an astrologer could scan that individual's birthchart and quickly see that Pluto and Neptune will only be able to pass through a limited number of predetermined houses in a typical life span—usually no more than seven, and fewer if any of these houses have an intercepted sign.

Pluto's fate-touched houses have been chosen for extra scrutiny. With that comes an earned ability to recognize and draw power from experiences of essential worth and enrichment, according to the particular themes of each transited house—*if* we dig thoroughly and allow any long-buried parts of ourselves to be exhumed and revivified.

Mundane house situations that have encouraged our shallow involvement will, in time, become stripped of their appeal and eventually forsaken. Pluto wants us to let go of dead-end patterns that have long had a stranglehold on us. If we cooperate with Pluto, we will voluntarily take out our psycho-trash and clean up our act. If we resist, more forceful removals take place in our outer world—life-dramas beyond our control that are immune to the objections of our will and the protests of our emotions. Things need not escalate to such an extreme state unless we're doggedly determined to resist available, growth-inducing options. Being so unyielding to change—especially now that Pluto is passing through our First House—will probably produce more pain than we can bear. Why put ourselves through that kind of prolonged and not-so-cathartic suffering?

Pluto crossing over our Ascendant is one of those milestone transits—a period when brutally honest self-confrontation is almost unavoidable, although this crisis point can be suspended for years as psychological pressure continues to build within. Eventually we erupt, releasing a lot of stored up intensity, and that can be a "good" thing for a while. Our Ascendant represents personal traits wrapped around our need to create a functional self-image. It describes an identity that we semi-consciously package as our initial way to project ourselves into our immediate environment and interact with other people.

The sign on our Ascendant—our Rising Sign—also serves as a ready defense against the imposition of other people's influence. This is what we thrust at them when they attempt to oppose us. However, some Ascendant behavior is conditioned by our earliest surroundings, giving us the impression in later years that certain Ascendant characteristics are actually innate. We assume that they've always belonged to us. However, we probably adopted such traits at a tender age as our way of coping with our dependent existence. Pluto realizes that there's more going on below the surface of this ongoing daily presentation of ours than we dare reveal or even acknowledge.

Pluto wants us to have a profound awareness of whatever it transits—in this case, our Ascendant sign's potential. Identity issues involving this sign are targeted for Plutonian inspection and harsh analysis. Nothing is sugar-coated. This is not a time to apply superficial "let's think positive" keywords to our Rising

Sign's profile. Pluto intends that we deepen our Ascendant sign's approach to self-expression. We'll need to figure out just how complex and multi-leveled this sign can be, and then we're to determine how we can best facilitate the surfacing of less-obvious qualities. Something more profound about this sign needs to be unearthed and strengthened by the personal action we take.

Some of us begin this transit feeling that inner, psychological parts that have long troubled us need to die, because they're killing us on some level, draining us of a vital sense of being. Pluto intensifies this conflictive, vulnerable experience. Some of our internal elements are in a state of revolt. Perhaps our most offending characteristics are those that repeatedly misrepresent who we are, deep down inside. We've displayed these outer traits to the world—again and again—until we've learned to perfect our superficial facades.

What if we have Sagittarius or Leo rising and we're sick of coming off as so darn optimistic and upbeat all the time? What if, instead, we feel inwardly hostile because nobody seems to come to our rescue or show strength on our behalf? Of course, this is probably because we never let on that we're vulnerable and that we could actually use some emotional support. It would not be surprising to find ourselves feeling stormy and malcontent during the start of this transit, and wondering why people can't figure out who we really are and what we really need.

THE UPPER HAND

When Pluto conjuncts our Ascendant, it also opposes our Descendant—our Seventh House cusp. It's no wonder, then, that existing relationships may start going through a rough patch during this transit, especially if we have a natal planet or two near our Seventh House cusp. Our inner discontent may not be so obvious at first. One result is that we can become overtly touchy about people trying to control us, change us, resist us, or openly thwart our needs. Pluto triggers us to be boldly assertive when it comes to protecting our autonomy (a basic Ascendant theme). If in the past we typically would silently brood when feeling intimidated or dominated by others, now we may have frequent outbursts in an attempt to get the upper hand in our relationships, simply to force the restoration of a balanced exchange of power. We cannot stand to be manipulated or guilt-tripped for even one more day. We're ready to reclaim our ground by establishing a more self-empowered pattern of interrelating.

However, things are dicier when it's a long-term marriage at stake and resentment on both sides is a key issue. We are then more apt to put our grievances on the table and fight for our rights. We can show a surface toughness and marked lack of cooperation that may frighten our partner and upset our marital status quo. The unaccustomed intensity of our overt self-will may even disturb *us*. We could be feeling ferocious about claiming our independence.

Actually, we may not be quite ready for an all-out confrontation. We're just warming up and starting to get our lava flowing. If anything, passive-aggressive behavior may be the way we initially work out some of our Plutonian issues. If so, it's our partner, in frustration, who will transform into the juicier role of the one who erupts—a role that's more appropriately our challenge to play. We'll explore this issue again later, when we get to Pluto stalking the Seventh. For now, realize that our perceptions of our partner can radically change as we initially adjust to Plutonian ways of reshaping our identity. The people who threaten to leave us at this time are those who only know how to relate to our old identity, the corpse that's now being discarded. To effectively be ourselves, unapologetically, we'll have to let some folks go who otherwise would hold back our growth. Still, that doesn't mean we have to scare them to death in the process by becoming a walking A-bomb!

Boiling over

The First is not a house known for its developmental skills in handling people, but that's not its prime function. Sharing is not a theme to be emphasized here. That's to be found in our Seventh House, where learning to give-and-take can become a

big challenge. Our ability to thrive independently without external intrusion is a First-House objective. We are to be left to our
own devices here, for better or worse, to see what we can self-
reliantly initiate for ourselves. In fact, basic survival skills are to
be developed in both our First and Second Houses. Here, first
and foremost, we look out for ourselves. Our First-House self-
expression is to be immediately actualized, even if unpolished
and limited in scope. Qualities of temperament described here
are less under the full control of our conscious self. We can't
totally manipulate these instinct-driven traits. They act according to a subjective agenda of their own.

Transiting Pluto is now in a position to stir up primal
instincts from our underground world that will fight to keep our
selfhood intact, rather than allow it to be overwhelmed by others.
One way some of us might keep people from having power over us
is to display a nasty temper. A Plutonian temper is much more
scary and can do more damage than anything Mars can muster.
Mars will go directly for the face and throw a few fast punches;
Pluto hits below the belt or strikes when one's back is turned.
Pluto is a dirty fighter and probably is the one who invented the
sucker-punch!

People might feel psychologically ambushed and undermined
by our anger. Hostility can build up to such a degree that we
viciously lash out at others, catching them off guard. With Pluto,
we can sting people in their most vulnerable areas and reopen old
wounds. We self-assert in ways that are much too psychologically
aggressive. Such one-on-ones with others can reach a boiling
point and someone could end up scalded.

However, it's probably not a good idea to suppress our
Plutonian rage too quickly just because of the fear that things
could get ugly—that is, unless we've always been rage-aholics who
consistently refuse to exert self-restraint once provoked. If this is
the case, Pluto transiting our First sets up an unsympathetic
environment ready to stop us cold; our aggression can result in
severe restrictions and penalties. If we're a destructive firestorm
that's out-of-control, something or someone has to put out our
dangerous blaze. Should this be the situation—that we are

uncompromisingly forced to stop being so enraged with life—this could be the first step toward the rebirthing process for which Pluto is famous. We probably will rant for a while longer, until we settle into the deep stillness of core-being that Pluto guards and protects—that part of us that is indestructible. Tapping into that hidden reality of ourselves can help to reroute our power drives toward less self-damaging outlets. However, it can't happen overnight. We struggle to renew ourselves, and we often struggle alone. Hey, anyone got something breakable we can throw against the wall?

BORN AGAIN

Speaking of self-renewal, this transit is a marvelous time to shed old skins and push for heightened psycho-spiritual growth. We can unload heavy baggage from our emotional past that has weighed us down and kept us entombed for too long. It's usually only when we're totally by ourselves that we peek at our darker self-portrait and privately brood over inner sorrows and past dis-illusionments. With Pluto, an inner strength from our depths can arise, giving us the will to examine our unfulfilled desires more honestly. This requires the intense self-focus that best comes from voluntary solitude. We'll need to clear out the life distractions that, by their very nature, would otherwise eat up the quality time needed for Plutonian soul-work. Some of us may feel that it's wise to go underground and become less accessible. The fewer people around us right now, the less complications we endure. The fewer outer obligations, the more we can concentrate on prob-lems that must be reevaluated.

Some of us may be ready to emerge from our shell to show the world a new self-concept soon after Pluto crosses the Ascendant. Maybe we did a lot of fruitful soul-searching when Pluto was passing through our Twelfth. We are now ready to eliminate all traces of old social programming. The First House supports spon-taneity in behavior and action, so transiting Pluto now offers us moments of surging energy when we courageously refuse to hide what we are or conceal what's cooking within us. We can take on a determined "in your face" stance if need be, because we're no longer willing to let others dictate our actions.

Pluto can transit our First House for at least a decade, usually longer. Significant sociological changes can occur in a decade to signal that it's the right time to emerge with a confident display of identity in sync with our essential self. We can come busting out of our closet ready to defy and condemn those happy to put us there. Others may be disturbed with how we reveal ourselves in this new light, with our unsettling, militant undertones. Well, that's just too bad, since stuffing our feelings and closeting our truer nature just to placate someone else simply doesn't cut the mustard anymore!

If "loved ones" can't cope with our sweeping changes, it's their hang-up and their ultimate loss. Should we emerge renewed but a bit edgy with life at this time, well then, so be it! Eliminating old ties is sometimes the price we pay for authentically living out our life according to our vision of ourselves—so is temporary social isolation. Still, it might prove desirable to make this a less-drastic transition by first attempting deeper dialogues with those who claim to be uncomfortable with "what we've become" compared to the predictable way we used to be.

GOODBYE, OLD COCOON!

I bet that's what every liberated butterfly thinks when it first takes wing and looks back at the dark, empty shell that used to be its total reality. The same goes for us when a fulfilled Pluto transit allows for a successful metamorphosis and the chance to show the world our greater light. For some of us, our rejuvenated self-insight illuminates a path where we can have a powerful impact on the collective.

The Ascendant doesn't symbolize the core of our being—that's the Sun. However, the Ascendant does describe what people see "rising" out of us moment-to-moment during our life—which influences their immediate perception of us. It's important that we periodically rework our self-image, fine-tuning it so that it seldom misfires, but remains true to the intention of our spirit. After all, the Ascendant serves as a gateway to our concrete experience of conscious living in the world. It's our initial contact point with earthly reality. We do not benefit by putting forth false or unworthy images of who and what we are.

Let's say that we have struggled and succeeded in coming out of the darkness created by our self-ignorance, and now we proudly feel ourselves to be a survivor, with all of the self-empowerment that implies. What are the ongoing rewards? How do we sustain our profound feeling of being alive and well? We probably have a lot more vitality now that we have released trapped energy from our psyche and unraveled psycho-complexes that had vampirized us for a long time, robbing us blind of our zest for living.

Our First House supports action and movement, so we'll need to do whatever it takes to keep our physical system energized. Any bad health habits will have to go, because overall fitness becomes a burning goal. The life-force that Pluto protects can freely run through our veins to enable optimum functioning of our body systems, if we help co-create this potential. We fought hard to attain this precious resource under trying psychological conditions; let's not lose it. Our days of self-loathing—leading to self-abuse—are over. With a well-managed transiting Pluto, we can be brimming with life and passionately active in our personal pursuits.

We'll remain on friendly terms with Pluto as long as we never again betray our integrity by caving in and surrendering to the will of others who refuse to acknowledge our right to be ourselves. People not interested in our greatest good need to be removed from our lives—within legal means, of course! Redemption-obsessed Neptunians may be appalled to hear that, because they have hope that others in our life will eventually see our light and become compassionately understanding. Pluto knows that life is too short to wait around for such an unlikely miracle. Thus, Pluto terminates rather than wastes time negotiating such matters. It has a reputation for taking unsentimental, unsympathetic approaches to obstacles, including human ones.

From here on, we'll need to take charge of our direction and observe our ups and downs with greater detachment. Life's slings and arrows become less wounding or soul-damaging. That surely doesn't mean that we have to take further abuse from anyone, as perhaps we did in the old days. We can still fight off any frontal attacks coming from those who are threatened by our newly forti-fied autonomy. Yet we may find that raging fury is no longer something that erupts and takes over our sensibilities. Our power base is now healthier than it ever has been; we no longer overre-act to the attempted underhanded tactics of forceful egos. With Pluto, we show a steely determination to follow our impulses with masterful self-assurance.

PLUTO/MARS TRANSITS

SMOKIN'

When transiting Pluto aspects natal Mars, the results can be provocative. Mars doesn't easily allow itself to be influenced (unlike the Moon or Mercury). However, Pluto isn't one to merely "influence" a planet by offering a few casual suggestions. It astutely sizes up a situation, invades, and then takes over opera-tions—all in the name of needed rehabilitation. Both of these planets represent a combination of energies found in Scorpio—although with this complex sign, we're dealing with a darker and moodier expression of Mars. This transit is a period when life pushes our psychological limits and tests our strength under strained conditions. Luckily, Mars is not a planet to fall apart eas-ily under stress. It sees Pluto's challenge as another chance to build up its muscles and sharpen its survival skills—which is good, because we'll probably need these assets. However, Mars innocently expects Pluto to show what it's got to offer up front, because Mars is not sneaky and likes things out in the open. Yet tricky Pluto has something else in mind for Mars, besides activat-ing the displays of aggression and self-interest in which this fiery war god excels.

Although pumped up for some kind of action, Mars doesn't have a clue about what's to come because Pluto refuses to disclose its ultimate plans ahead of time—and that's enough to drive any impatient planet loaded with testosterone crazy! When joining forces in a frictional manner—such as in a square or opposition aspect—Pluto intensifies our Martian instinct to put something dynamic in motion, to move forward with an indomitable "outta my way" attitude and powerful "can do" spirit. This is assuming that we have already learned how to focus energy and take effective action. If we haven't, then disciplining ourselves to concentrate on very specific goals becomes our first big challenge.

We get nowhere fast by scattering our forces or procrastinating. Plutonian energy doesn't do as well when it's diluted or needlessly diverted. It wants us smokin' with industrial-strength power. We just need to be careful not to obsess about any personal activities that we pursue during this period, because fixated self-will can be psychologically and physically taxing. Mars is not used to operating under that kind of prolonged stress.

UNLOADING RAGE

During a frictional Pluto/Mars transit, some of us may fear that we'll blow our top and physically hurt someone else, or ourselves, although most often any harm done is psychological. Mars doesn't willingly turn its forces inward, especially when more stimulating, external targets are available. Our temper can surface more vividly than usual, with an extra dose of Plutonian fury that erupts quickly and inexplicably. What triggers us may seem minor, but nonetheless is symbolic of unfinished business regarding frustrated attempts at self-assertion. We may overreact to threats, offenses, interruptions, or delays of personal gratification. What gets us so worked up can seem highly irrational to those upon whom we unload our anger. We're running on primal, emotional energy at this point—and we're ready to knock Godzilla's block off!

A few of us may realize, perhaps for the first time ever, that we have a temper and that we harbor suppressed urges to strike out at anyone who tries to control us. (Geez, and after all those blissful years of meditating twice a day and giving our unselfish, humane support to elevated social causes!) Pluto loves to snoop around the basement of another planet's home to see what's lurking in its musty, unlit corners. Thanks to this planet's keen vision and sense of smell, whatever's rotting away will be found out. Dark, aggressive urges that we have avoided confronting in our past might now rear their ugly head and generate enough heat and noise to finally get our attention, as well as the unfavorable notice of others who may now start to back away from us socially. Few wish to become intimate with our newfound rage.

It's too bad that some of us first lash out at folks—usually those near and dear—before we understand why we now want to crush those who dare to foil our Martian desires. Any other personal planet would claim, perhaps falsely, that it would never want to actually "kill" anyone no matter how outraged or violated (although Mercury has been known to talk people to death). Mars, however, knows that its true, unvarnished nature includes less civilized expressions of self-preservation—which can involve "doing in" the opposition first before being done in by them! Pluto feels right at home with the courageous temperament of this feisty, gut-driven planet.

Layers of social cultivation have made sure that we rarely tap into this selfishly anti-social, "animalistic" side of Mars, at least not without penalty. However, during a Pluto transit, we take off the white gloves of civility and allow ourselves to feel raw passions—over which etiquette experts would (politely) have a fit. It may not be raw or passion-filled if Pluto sextiles or trines Mars. Yet with the conjunction, square, quincunx, and opposition, the intensity level rises. We are alive, that's for sure. The blood is racing through our veins. But are we well? In time, perhaps—but first we need to acknowledge that we're steamed up about certain unsatisfying elements of our lives. What can we do with this realization besides attempt to attack and destroy anything close at hand that we deem to be an aggravating interference specifically designed to torment us?

For starters, we could benefit by analyzing all personal actions that have led up to our current, pent-up state of affairs. Did we play a passive role in situations and allow others to take charge and manipulate our will? Mars hates when that happens. Have we acted in ways that go against our inner grain in order to appease others and gain their superficial approval? That's not a good idea if we're trying to fortify our Mars awareness. Are we still grappling with long-time feelings of cowardice and a lack of fighting spirit in the house ruled by Mars? That's bad news again. Answering "yes" to any or all of these questions could suggest that we're getting ready to shoot Plutonian fire from our nostrils and roar with righteous anger, given the right situational trigger. We're mad as a hornet and we're not going to fake it anymore. However, if all we actually do is brood and smolder while unconsciously discharging heated sparks into the environment, we can provoke lots of unwanted turbulence.

Pluto knows that we very much need to get a few things off our chest, which means facing up to certain fears about being straightforwardly real with others in both word *and* action. We can better develop our inner Mars by taking direct and unambiguous approaches to removing obstacles, as if using a machete to clear thick tangles of jungle vines. Attempting to suppress our Martian impulses goes against Pluto's desire for the powerful release of hidden tensions. The longer we bury such energies, the more powerful the force of our eruptive revolt later—and the more violent.

DETERMINED TO WIN

Mars represents that part of our ego-system that needs to claim victory in its battles with adversarial forces. Mars is a poor loser, so the only outcome it finds acceptable is winning every fight. It's a planet that can create conflict scenarios even when none exist, which underscores its "me" versus "them" mentality. Mars gives us clues about how we demonstrate both our competitive streak and our determination to act alone without supervision. Without Mars active and strong within our psyche, we could easily be overtaken by domineering types who bully us into ego submission.

Pluto, being an Outer Planet, doesn't care much for catering to our own ego's petty demands and our emotional insecurities (it has it *in* for the "whiner"). Pluto simply wants Mars to survive all circumstantial challenges without losing its appetite for living vibrantly. This transit can be a shot in the arm, injecting us with a willful vitality that spurs us to self-reliantly take on personal projects single-handedly. It shares the gutsiness of a typical Uranus/Mars transit, without all that cerebral idealism getting in the way. There is little about this transit that is detached in action. We can become fully engrossed in what we are trying to accomplish, bolstered by our refusal to be easily defeated by doubt or uncertainty.

Obviously, with a sextile or a trine, Pluto is not as driven to probe and to expose Mars' vulnerabilities, while Mars itself is less on the defense and more ready to adopt a Plutonian strategy when initiating action. These "softer" aspects are not as psychologically intrusive—though they're not necessarily mild-mannered, either— so transiting Pluto doesn't seem to be coercively bearing down on us. Still, we may have an itch to bring a new sense of vigor into various facets of our life experience (first check natal Mars' house placement). Situations can now become enlivened by a healthy dose of Plutonian power. Whatever needs to be permanently removed from our lives by our own actions can be done without the anguish and power struggles of a Pluto square or opposition. Efforts will require persistence. To succeed, we'll need to resist any situational distractions that could throw us off-track.

A Pluto/Mars conjunction, square, or opposition drives us to desire to come out on top in life, even though we may not feel thoroughly confident about how things will turn out. Transiting Pluto can seem to undermine our plans of action while also com- pelling us to continue to take risks. It's a weird mix of feeling strong and yet not in full control of situations, at the same time. Remember, our ego and will alone can't call the shots.

We can exhibit a laser-sharp focus regarding our desires. Our strength of conviction at times allows us to make remarkable progress. In fact, this transit is known for tremendous productiv- ity, making us appear unstoppable in the conquest of achieve- ment. But "unstoppable" can also transform into "ruthless" pur- suit, whereby we allow no one to steer us toward advantageous alternative paths. We might become too adamant about going after what we want, intimidating and alienating people who oth- erwise could offer us creative support. Such overdrive can be our way of compensating for a gnawing feeling that fate might rudely intervene at any minute and dramatically stop us cold. It's almost as if we unconsciously know about Pluto's reputation as a "terminator." With Mars involved, we'll try to fight that possibility all the way.

Transiting Pluto sometimes forces life to come to a screeching halt for those on decidedly self-destructive paths. However, part of this transit's purpose is to help us face up to life with courage so that we become less wavering in our solo ventures. It's important that we don't go to extremes and allow seductive feelings of invincibility to make us assume that physical limits won't deter us. Should we defiantly ignore them once too often, such limits will permanently stop us. Still, we may try to do the impossible during a Pluto/Mars transit, even if that means flirting with evident danger.

SEXUAL DYNAMO

What about sex? That's a topic that interests both of these planets. For Mars, sex is a simple biological release. Its procreative function doesn't seem particularly important, probably because having offspring creates dependency relationships—which Mars finds confining. However, Pluto views sexuality from a broader perspective. Survival of the species is important to Pluto, but so is deeply personal, erotic fulfillment. Sex becomes a rejuvenating force that can help us to tap into our power base. In some instances, sex can also be a Plutonian way of transcending ordinary consciousness. Sex also can trigger disturbing unconscious components when Pluto is involved, whereas, for Mars, sex is typically only a disturbance when the subject of its desire is unavailable or has a headache!

This transit could spark a renewed interest in sexual activity for those who've been low on fuel for a while. The transiting square, quincunx, and opposition can arouse Mars in potent ways, giving our libido a needed tune-up (including new spark plugs). Still, such transits can result in a level of sexual tension that is not easily satisfied. Pluto can have insatiable appetites that defy quick fulfillment. We can be sexually hungry and greedy at this time, or at least obsessed with gratification. A problem with Pluto is this planet's inclination to be forceful in its pursuits. Sexually speaking, this means that we can be more aggressive with our Mars energy than normally would be the case. Or, we could project this tendency onto others, who then come on to us much too strongly, putting pressure on us to submit to their surges of animal magnetism. Sex could become a game of strategy, a battle of wills, or an arena in which to play out power drives. True romance is not part of this picture.

For some of us, a retreat from sexual involvement may be important now, especially if we've shown ourselves to be addictive in this area in the past (maybe we were born with conflictive Mars/Neptune or Mars/Pluto aspects). We could also start thinking about celibacy if our sex life has already been much too complicated and turbulent due to our unwise partnership choices. In this case, Pluto wants us to cool it for a while and sublimate our sexual energy into areas requiring enormous physical or creative output. It's good to have a big project to tackle. A natural Plutonian activity would be renovating a house or restoring old furnishings. Getting out the old sledge hammer and knocking down walls may make us feel pretty satisfied. Finishing a basement (the "underground" sector of the house) would be an especially appropriate Plutonian endeavor requiring of us a lot of Martian sweat and physical endurance.

TOTAL EFFORT

Whatever we attempt, it will appease both planets if undertaken with an element of passion, with nothing done half-heartedly. The worst we could do during this period is to bottle up our desires by providing ourselves little dynamic activity, or by remaining fearful of taking action. We'll need to direct our energies toward some meaningful area where they can have a dramatic impact in our lives and, perhaps, out in the world. If we need to recharge ourselves on the level of will, this aspect can provide us with the right motivation. If we have ineffectually asserted ourselves over and over again in the past, we now can make our mark in ways that make people take note. Therefore, we'd better keep our actions legal and above board! All in all, we'll find it's so much better running on a recharged battery and a full tank of gas. This is what transiting Pluto can provide our Mars.

CHAPTER SEVEN

PLUTO TRANSITING THE SECOND HOUSE

TREASURE HUNT

Mythic Pluto—just like his brothers Jupiter and Neptune—was to govern a specific territory within the vast empire of his paranoid, cold-hearted daddy, Saturn, after the old man's downfall. We know that Pluto's domain was the mysterious underground realm, Hades. There he ruled unseen over the spirits of the dead. All who died and descended into Hades, including honorable heroes and other virtuous souls, were allowed to have their eternal rest as ghostlike "shades." All were essentially the property of Pluto.

In addition to managing this dark place and its inhabitants, Pluto was also given dominion over the buried riches of Earth. In some myths, he was also associated with fertility. His guardianship included a wealth of Earth's hidden resources: gems, minerals, and precious metals. The ancient myths made no mention of oil, but in today's world, petroleum ("black gold") is a highly valued commodity that first shoots up from someplace "way down under," giving oil-wells a Plutonian association. Everything that was a source of power, wealth, or beauty from deep below the surface belonged to Pluto—and still does. By the way, a lot of the goods of deep Earth fetch a pretty steep price on the market. Pluto's resources don't come cheap! There's a lesson here in that for us.

Although Pluto is a "water planet" in astrology (with fiery undertones), it also has its roots in primal earthiness. Geologists tell us that the small, solid inner core of Earth is a tremendous source of energy and heat—with temperatures as high as 12,000° F—which sounds very much in sync with astrological Pluto's symbolism. When transiting Pluto enters our Second House, we will need to probe for latent but valuable resources that are waiting to be tapped from the deep, hidden recesses of our psyche. These inner resources also don't come cheap! Before we own them, we must first examine those personal values that are less reflective of our inner core and more the byproduct of our social conditioning. We who live in materialistic cultures are subjected to a bombardment of societal messages that we absorb and process as if they were inborn attitudes—even when, blatantly, they are not. Pluto's Second-House transit provokes a necessary crisis, targeting our value structure. This doesn't come about all at once. Pluto will slowly shed its hidden light on such issues after many soul-searching years have passed, perhaps after a period of prolonged financial frustration.

OWNING UP

The Second House deals with ownership themes. Here, Pluto may coincide with a major turning point, forced on us, and that involves our means of material support—imagine if transiting Pluto squares our Uranus or opposes our Saturn. Any possession to which we blindly cling for everlasting security may be the target of Pluto's no-nonsense elimination program. A very easy-to-understand consequence, which may apply to a few of us, is bankruptcy. We may have lived beyond our means or made a mess of money management, to the point that we are now spiraling downward into the dark world of debt and hopelessness. Authorities are likely to be breathing down our neck and demand that we pay up or suffer severe legal consequences. Transiting Pluto sets up these complex situations so that our big financial crash occurs, and our freedom to overspend is effectively terminated. From then on, our job is to repair the damage we've done in our material world, and then allow ourselves a brand new start.

Usually, with Pluto, drastic measures are used as a last resort, rather than as inevitable karmic penalty. We may have become too reckless with money, and with consumerism in general, to the degree that we've become addicted to having things that give us a power boost, even if we don't actually enjoy them for their own sake. In other words, what we covet and eventually hoard has nothing to do with who we really are. In addition, we're not very discriminating in our purchases. How could we be, when deep down inside we don't really value them? Yet we know that the outer world values material possessions, and therefore feel that we must have such items in order to keep up the appearance of being a social power player. That alone can trigger the urge to compulsively spend. People who use their goods to manipulate others get Pluto's attention real fast. Those who abuse what they have or who deliberately and defiantly waste resources can expect old Dark Face to pay an unexpected visit in the heat of the night! If we have been guilty of wrongdoings of a Second-House nature, it's time to own up and pay the price for our willful, maybe criminal, actions.

Normally, we don't wake up one day and comprehend that the damaging things that we've done along these lines have jeopardized our long-term security. Life usually has to "get in our face" and strong-arm us to surrender what we own by using what seems to be impersonal forces. Sometimes we haven't done anything wrong—certainly nothing illegal—to deserve this, or so it seems. Yet a few of us may discover that an "act of God" named Hurricane Fernando has roared through our sleepy little coastal town and destroyed all that we've accumulated in a relatively short moment of chaos—everything that once gave us emotional comfort is now in ruins! Or perhaps we've invested most of our savings for our retirement years, only to find that we've been swindled by unscrupulous individuals whose demonic greed becomes our stunning loss. (These are two extreme examples, but they do happen in people's lives, and they smack of Pluto playing hardball in the Second.)

In situations like these, where we feel totally blameless and supremely victimized, we'll have a hard time understanding why Pluto makes us travel down this misery-producing path. There might be too much destruction in our lives at the moment to see how anything at this stage could happen in the name of inner growth and spiritual evolution. However, in the aftermath, we realize that we cannot depend on the material world for our inner security. Life has shown us the hard way that nothing is permanent, and that when things leave us, we must allow ourselves to let them go without suffering devastating withdrawal symptoms. On some level, we need to be free of the bondage and nagging insecurities that physical attachments can create.

LESSONS IN SURVIVAL

Transiting Pluto, as it patrols our Second House, doesn't sound like much fun, but that's not necessarily always the case. This planet is an excellent rejuvenator. If we have struggled with personal issues of self-worth for decades, with not letting ourselves receive first-class comforts from our environment, Pluto can help us to radically alter this picture. We now have a chance to become reborn in the area of gaining self-appreciation, although it will take time and lots of inner work. Pluto doesn't give us anything unconditionally, with no strings attached, the way big-hearted but indiscriminate Jupiter might. We may have to fight long and hard for our right to be treated well by those in our personal world.

Those of us who have taken a lot of abuse from others will finally be pressured to tap into Pluto's power to "resurrect the dead" (for example, those very essential parts of ourselves that we've buried in order to perpetuate relationships that we've been too scared to end). Not all of us can relate to having such a potentially destructive pattern, so we might expect issues of self-value to be less problematic during this transit. Yet for some, it's a matter of physical and psychological survival.

A few of us may have to walk away from a lifestyle full of material temptations, because to live in such an atmosphere could further diminish our self-value. Maybe we feel owned by another, who has the financial power to make the rules and control our moves. Pluto will stimulate us to feel at odds with ourselves, in a state of inner turmoil, until we realize we must treasure our independence and value our ability to pay our own way in life. The First and Second Houses need us to operate autonomously, with as little interference from others as possible. Pluto transiting our Second has much to teach us regarding the forging of inner strength through the capitalization of our talents. We can't afford to waste such assets as a result of neglect or indifference. Qualities that have been dormant are now ready to come alive and get us highly motivated or, in this case, at least motivated enough to make sure we get paid what we now are starting to realize we're worth—which may be a lot more than anyone has ever admitted to us before.

FINANCIAL REBIRTH

Pluto usually insists on first getting rid of whatever impedes our life-force before offering a needed transfusion of vital energy. One goal of this transit to make sure that we know how to take care of ours material needs. That doesn't mean being disgustingly rich. We'll need to adopt a healthy, empowering psychology about moneymaking and resource-building. We need to establish respect for the law of physical attraction and for how we are to secure what we want, particularly now that we are, more than ever, strongly magnetic on this level. This requires that we learn to become well grounded in the art of self-preservation. Taking charge of our existing material responsibilities is not anti-spiritual, but parasitically living off of others rather than fending for ourselves *is!*

Transiting Pluto doesn't permit us to have a "loser" mentality. Any self-defeatist attitudes regarding our earning power will eventually be lined up against the wall, blindfolded, and shot at dawn! Often, when we have Second-House troubles, an unrecognized

source is our capacity to be stingy with ourselves. We're too insecure to enjoy what we own; therefore, we're never content. Pluto
will force some of us to explore why we punishingly short-change
ourselves. Where is the origin of this tendency to allow for material insufficiency? An inner journey to uncover the source of our
pattern of self-denial is a must if we are to break this cycle of
impoverishment and Spartan living. The god of hidden sources of
wealth is waiting for us to enrich ourselves in many ways. It probably requires a major crisis or two to force us to realize how important money is to living a more effective, responsible, and empowered life.

If we've over-accumulated possessions for all of the wrong reasons (conspicuous greed), Pluto is ready to rid us of our excesses,
often in a fate-drenched, dramatic fashion. While not many of us
need to be brought to our gold-plated knees, a few of us cannot
learn Pluto's lesson any other way but through an extreme rever-
sal of fortune—a stunning "riches-to-rags" turnabout. We've seen
this happen to a few celebrities in the entertainment business, or
to everyday folks who won the lottery—they had it all, then self-
destructively lost it all. Pluto hates mindless waste, so reckless
squanderers beware!

We might start making money during this transit in fields
that are distinctly Plutonian, perhaps explaining that strange
and compelling urge to become a taxidermist or an undertaker's
assistant! Most often, however, it's our approach to whatever we
do to earn a living that has the stamp of Pluto on it. We can
make our money doing something that we feel quite strongly
about—a magnificent obsession that impressively pays off. While
it can be a very self-focused path to take, some of us may find
that we're eager to contribute on a larger social scale. Perhaps
we want to tear down old, worn-out ways of conducting business.
Pluto is a revolutionary at heart and, like Uranus, symbolizes
being on the cutting edge and pushing for radical change. Down
with the safe status quo. Let's give those time-honored social
institutions a complete overhaul! That could be our outlook. It's
no wonder that some Saturnians in power view Plutonians as
subversive and dangerous.

BODY BEAUTIFUL

There is another side to the Second House that doesn't get as much coverage as its more popular, financial element, yet it has long been dear to the Taurean/earth Venus level of Principle Two: the sensuality of the physical senses. Part of being an earthling means opening ourselves to a wide range of bodily sensations. The human body is built for the enjoyment of its surroundings via sight, smell, touch, taste, and sound. Our Second House includes simple experiences that put us in touch with being alive and well and very much in our bodies. We seek gratification through physical form and through our embrace of Nature. Playing with mud when we are young can be an elementary Second-House activity. Pampering ourselves via a deep full-body massage or a "mud" bath at the spa is an activity that may appeal to adults.

Assembling uncomplicated forms of beauty—like arranging fresh-cut flowers and picking the right vase in which to display them—can also be a very soothing Second-House activity. We use raw or natural materials, such as plant life, to create atmospheric effects that please us and make us feel connected to planet Earth. It's a sensual way to love and respect our state of physicality. In a purely Second-House sense, our human body is never bad, "dirty," or evil. The wise old pagans knew this to be true and ensured that this part of our life experience was celebrated as another valid expression of manifest divinity. It was to be honored.

If we can look at the sign on our Second House cusp and interpret how its dynamics play into the way we enjoy being of this Earth and owning a sensitized mammalian body for a lifetime, it becomes easier to see how Pluto can deepen our soul-body connection. Pluto sees no need to pit body against spirit, which is something that has led to the destructive shaming of the body for centuries throughout many "civilized" cultures, typically on the basis of religious teachings. A few of us may grow up wanting to have nothing to do with satisfying our earthy, physical or sexual needs.

Therefore, those who find physicality fundamentally repulsive or even sinful will certainly trigger Pluto into action during this transit. It could be that our physical system revolts in life-threatening ways or stops working for us (such as having an obstructed colon). This is an unlikely consequence, but it bears observing. Still, is our body currently suffering a self-attacking disease (lupus, cancer) that eats away at us or compromises our ability to cope with our natural environment?

More often, we'll have experiences that finally allow us to feel full physical pleasure without the dampening restrictions produced by nagging guilt. After years of feeding a warped belief in the unholiness of "the flesh," some of us may have a catharsis in which we come alive and reclaim our previously despised "animal" nature. Usually we meet some wise Plutonian who shows us the light about true body-love. Of course, we can also experience this through the awakening of sexual energy—a Plutonian theme to be repeated in our Fifth and Eighth houses. Pluto demands the surrender and release of trapped energy in whatever manner it is found. Sex is as good a channel as any for such release.

Most of us are not hung-up about ordinary physical pleasures (if we were, we would never need to diet). Yet many of us fail to find quality time to love our bodies. This transit is great for discovering what sources of needed pampering are available to us: aromatherapy, reflexology, relaxing in a sauna, mud treatments (although not the cost-free ones of our childhood), facial massage, or even wearing something sexy and silky to bed. Perhaps, for the first time ever, we start sleeping in the nude. All forms of gentle, therapeutic indulgence can keep us on good Second-House terms with Pluto, as well as help to restore our vigor and the spark of youth. Addiction to tobacco, alcohol, drugs, and compulsive sex only keep us alienated from this loving dimension of physicality. Transiting Pluto says, "Turn up the heat and feel the warmth that a well-loved and well-treated body can radiate." Others to whom we are close to can happily feel it, too, and the results can be transformative.

PLUTO/EARTH VENUS TRANSITS
MIRROR, MIRROR...

Much of what was just said involving sensuality, including the hang-ups, also applies to the earthy side of Venus. While we are having our Pluto/Venus transit, how we relate to our physical appearance is often an issue. Our reaction may not be one of self-acceptance. Should the aspect in question be a conjunction or a square (or sometimes an opposition), we could find ourselves attacking our looks (earth Venus) and blaming them for a host of relationship problems (the airy side of Venus), or even for why we are currently not so nice to ourselves. However, if this is so, Pluto is only bringing to the surface a hidden uneasiness that we've had for long time regarding our physical features and people's response to them. Raging against how we look in a full-length mirror may now lead us to do something more than just wallow in self-loathing.

Earth Venus seeks beauty that reflects the harmony of the natural world. Due to years of bad habits—especially those involving eating things that go against Nature—we throw that harmony out-of-balance. What results is a body image that makes us feel ashamed and unlovable. Pluto motivates us to rehabilitate ourselves physically, but not so that we try to conform to coercive cultural standards of bodily perfection. Transiting Pluto simply wants to achieve optimum body equilibrium, as well as restore the vital flow of the life force. Exercise is usually part of our self-renewal (physical inertia is one of earth Venus' life-long problems).

Some of us may obsess about plastic surgery, which is a drastic "quick-fix" Plutonian solution (the possibility of post-operative complications is stronger with Pluto's stress aspects). Still, getting a total facelift creates a radical outer transformation that would satisfy Pluto to some extent. Critics love to point out that one's outer beauty is of less value than one's inner beauty, but I think it's a two-way street connecting our outer and inner self. When we look good, we feel good about ourselves. And when we feel good about ourselves, we are more ready to let our attributes rise and shine. Our outer self also gives us clues about what's going on with our internal self. This explains why chronically mean-spirited or pessimistic people often have that sour, crabby look. They never appear serene. Usually their tense, down-turned mouths are a dead giveaway regarding their inner disposition.

Shaping up

Transiting Pluto wants earth Venus to become more body-aware in a power-enhancing manner. Perhaps we can make practical changes to ourselves, like shedding a few unwanted pounds or adding a little shapely muscle to our mass. We do that by exerting Plutonian self-control over what we eat—but let's not turn this into a compulsive's sense of over-control. Actually, with Pluto, what we eat is often less important than why we are eating it. Certain foods that we crave have deep, symbolic meaning. Sweets are particularly Venusian (throw in a little Neptune as well, depending on how much mind-altering chocolate and sugary stickiness is involved). Earthy Venus, being a bit lunar in its needs, gravitates toward all kinds of comfort foods, such as mashed potatoes, stews, meatloaf, and macaroni and cheese. However, while our caloric intake can be amazingly high, we may remain mysteriously hungry. That's when it's clear that we're using food to serve a psychological purpose that has little to do with true physical appetite.

A well-managed tensional Pluto transit can help us to dig into what's eating us whenever we compulsively grab for something to fill our stomachs. It's also important to not go to extremes: starvation diets, prolonged cleansing fasts, or even ravenous forms of pigging out. Pluto sextiling or trining Venus, in theory, should be less apt to misuse food simply because psychological hunger is less of a problem. In fact, the smoother influx of Plutonian energy made available in that situation can give us the incentive to first burn off excess weight and then tone up what's left. These issues will be explored again when I analyze Pluto transiting our Sixth House. I also suspect that there's a lot of natal and transiting Pluto energy involved with folks who are passionate about weightlifting (especially the elite class of "power-lifters"); this easily can become an all-consuming interest for some—and that's how we know it's a Plutonian thing!

ANIMAL MAGNETISM

Pluto/Mars gives off strong sexual sparks that suggest that the animal within us is alive and ready to howl at the Full Moon. Hormonal activity heats up and an itch for sweaty physical release builds. Earth Venus also understands sexual heat, valuing it as a good and very pleasurable thing. It symbolizes Aphrodite's appetite for bodily gratification. Sexual contact becomes an opportunity to get close to and bond with someone we find very appealing and desirable—someone who adds to our own framework of emotional security. However, poor air Venus, with its Libran connection, doesn't fully understand why such earthy physicality is so necessary for love's chemistry. The element of air is far too cerebral to appreciate basic animal magnetism and the wisdom of visceral response. So when you hear those old tales about frisky Mars chasing flirty Venus, and vice versa, they're talking about a robust, earthy Venus. Airy Venus doesn't send out the pheromones that arouse Mars—and doesn't get physical on the first date, anyway!

During this transit, our sexual response can become heightened. Sexual desires intensify, which could pose a problem for those who have no easy outlets for release. We'd really like to try our emerging Plutonian passions on a willing and suitable partner. If no one is available, we'll have to find private ways to give ourselves pleasure. Pluto tells us that it's okay to explore and discover whatever turns us on. It could be something we've tried to keep a tight lid on for years for fear of being judged "abnormal"— or a sex maniac. With the sextile and the trine, we normally have desires that have a better chance of being fulfilled. Our intensity is better matched by a partner who has a healthy attitude toward sex. This could be a juicy transit to write about in our secret journal—think of it, the time we awakened sexually to our greater erotic potential!

With less flowing aspects (especially with the opposition), our appetites are probably stronger, but so is a compulsive, predatory element. Some of us hunger a bit too much for intimacy and thus find ourselves uncommonly possessive of our love attachments. We're also capable of being bitter and destructive when things turn sour. Holding on too tightly is an earth Venus trait to begin with, and Pluto's intensity simply aggravates the problem.

Perhaps this potent energy is expressed through rewarding our body—such as having a luxurious bath using fragrant oils, with glowing candles around us and soothing music in the background (a Venusian atmosphere, perhaps borrowing a few seductive Neptunian touches). In short, we learn rejuvenating ways to relax by slowing down our emotional pace. Attractive surroundings are always important to both earth *and* air Venus. When we add a steady lover to the picture, Pluto aspecting our Venus means that we can give and expect to receive serious satisfaction. This is not a light-hearted combination, but one driven to attain the depths of gratification.

Pluto has a reputation for being insatiable and therefore not easily fulfilled. Having a bottomless pit of burning desire sounds like torment, especially when a part of us demands total ecstasy, while another part feels starved all the time. The conjunction, square, quincunx, and opposition can introduce an element of distrust if we haven't already gotten our Venusian self-worth issues ironed out. Earth Venus may enjoy being artfully seduced, but it won't tolerate being demeaned. We find ourselves undergoing internal conflict when engaged in sexual activity that goes against our need to be valued and appreciated. This practical Venus seeks a quality experience. While a mishandled air Venus might find ways to rationalize remaining in a coercive relationship, a well-managed earth Venus will shut down and go on strike rather than suffer prolonged emotional or physical maltreatment.

HOLDING ON TIGHT

Both planets can relate to the realities of money and possessions. Earth Venus knows the value of a buck and wants to keep its purchasing power alive and well. It's very much into securing worldly attachments and will instinctually safeguard what it owns (especially when in signs like Taurus, Cancer, and Scorpio). Just as mythic Pluto kept a lot of his wealth safely hidden below the ground, astrological Pluto is also good at preserving wealth and protecting financial assets. When combined, these planets focus on the obtaining and managing of valuable resources.

Pluto's transiting trine or sextile might be great for motivating us to add breadth and power to our material structure, except that earth Venus here sometimes is less willing to work hard to acquire things. Perhaps a fat inheritance comes along, or our "Lotto" fever finally pays off. Still, this is the side of Venus that doesn't easily part with what it has, and typically wants to accumulate more—and more—of whatever it values, which is not always money. We've got to watch our hoarding instincts when the earthy facet of the Venus archetype is triggered. This Venus symbolizes a drive within us that often hangs on too tightly to tangible goods—even relationships, if we unconsciously feel that we own our partner.

Transiting Pluto, always believing in trimming the fat, has plans to downsize our material load so that we only keep what's essential. It's even more serious about reducing our stockpile than is Saturn. We can still end up with a lot left, but whatever we keep either is what we deeply value, or what has great resale value. We could facilitate this Plutonian process by organizing what we have and then deciding what really needs to be discarded or recycled. Others in the community may desperately need certain things that we own but never really get to use. (These folks in need are having their own tough, Plutonian survival challenges on the material plane.) It's a good time to part with items we no longer need, through closet cleaning and yard sales.

If we resist cooperating with Pluto's urge to purge, another type of desperate "other" may want what we have and may try to take it by force: the thief who burglarizes our home or steals our car. Don't spend too much time worrying about this, because it's not a common manifestation of this transit. However, Pluto will go to extremes in certain cases to vividly make its point: let go of compulsive attachments based on unresolved greed or an unexamined hunger for security, and realize that nothing of a material nature can be owned forever. Having our goods stolen, vandalized, or legally confiscated (hmmm, we should have paid those back taxes!) makes us realize our degree of attachment to worldly items. Nobody relishes being robbed, but if we become devastated and almost incapacitated due to our losses, then things we own and continue to own have too great a power to own *us*. Pluto would like to break that wicked spell once and for all.

FINANCIAL REVIVAL

While we could be forced to file for bankruptcy, clear our debts, and start rebuilding financial security all over again during this transit (more so with the square, quincunx, or opposition), most of us will want to seek ways to fortify our financial future before we find ourselves in the thick of a major crisis. Usually, we have no choice. Maybe we haven't made the best use of our moneymaking talents, or we've stayed in a job where we haven't been paid what we are truly worth. This can be an introspective time, during which we're forced to confront issues of self-value that, in the long run, will help us determine our worth in any career. Pluto can always be counted on to vitalize our desire. What we may desperately want is better pay—in fact, we want any major financial boost that allows us to feel less shortchanged by life. Resentment and fear may have the upper hand if we continue to feel devalued and exploited. If economic complications enter the scene, we can feel pressured to make unwanted lifestyle adjustments just to make ends meet.

By the way, predicting how our transits will turn out is extremely difficult, because our possible life-scenarios are endless. This is especially so with the Outer Planets, due to their direct link to our boundless unconscious self. The aspects they form can operate in a subjective manner as easily as they do circumstantially. It may be best when they arouse both our inner and outer worlds simultaneously, or maybe, as is more often the case, inner work is needed before effective outer change can occur. For particularly stubborn types, dramatic situational shocks are needed to precipitate internal processes of outer change and internal revolution. We need to discover the best way to introduce any transiting Outer Planet to our consciousness long before a situation that shakes our very foundation is unfairly forced upon us (a typical feeling when Uranus, Neptune, or Pluto invades our life).

So, with earth Venus involved, what can we do to appease Pluto? What can be done to circumvent drastic outcomes (like being financially wiped out)? We can start investing, perhaps in small amounts at first. We can also put money into a financial plan geared toward retirement security. We need to meaningfully empower ourselves. In the short term, we can unclutter ourselves of rarely used possessions—for example, what can we sell to flea market buyers or consignment stores? Not only do we need to hang on to less during this time, but, if possible, we should try to get paid for these unnecessary items (after all, earth Venus has to be satisfied with how things turn out as well). Mysteriously leaving town while abandoning everything we physically own is not the answer to our Plutonian dilemma. Earth Venus demands responsible use of possessions—besides, Pluto despises escapism. We'll just have to tough it out, if need be, until we can arrive at a sensible solution.

In simple terms, we can undergo a financial rebirth. If money used to be our big enemy (because of poisoned attitudes adopted from our childhood, or due to unrelenting economic frustrations as an adult), we can finally comes to grips with material reality and our need for self-sufficiency. Money in itself is not a corrupting influence. It could be that a few of us will have to readjust our metaphysical assumptions about earthly attachments by making room for healthier approaches to material success—heck, think of all the spiritual workshops and retreats we could attend if we just had enough cash flow. Pluto provides the right incentive to make sure that we don't end up struggling to pay bills or to have a few nice things in life we can call our own. We need a meaningful financial make-over based on a new philosophy about the necessity of balanced materialism.

CHAPTER EIGHT

PLUTO TRANSITING THE THIRD HOUSE

DEEP THINKING

Pluto is a planet of potent instinctual knowing. It can be frighteningly street-smart when survival is at stake. When cornered, it can plot and deviously scheme out of a tight squeeze. It uses a primal form of gut-intelligence that manifests as the cunning we see in some animals. Watch the panther stealthily stalk its prey before striking—this is a complex form of instinct at work. In contrast, the Third House is interested in using conscious intellect to objectively observe things while also remaining emotionally detached; a little breathing space is required here. There's nothing underhanded about this house's way of getting its hands on information. Ask a direct question and hopefully get a clear answer—that's how the Third likes it. However, Pluto does little in life that we'd call direct and up front.

When it transits our Third house, the one thing Pluto is determined to kill off within us is our potential to be superficial. The shallow use of our brain power keeps us skimming the surface while caught up in life's inconsequential matters. Pluto wants us to dig deep, and maybe get ourselves a little dirty as we uncover buried material that could put us in contact with the raw realities hidden within us and others. This is especially true if we have natal planets in our Third. A transit like this could be an intense eye-opener, revealing emotions and feelings that we've learn to rationalize away in the past, or that we've simply never recognized or validated. Usually, a Third House dynamic is to talk out our stress, rather than just feel it. In contrast, Pluto demands that we shut up and start to internalize our dialogues, even if that becomes painful and unsettling. We shouldn't be so quick to intellectualize the inner truths to which Pluto wants us to expose ourselves.

Transiting Pluto always sniffs out the less obvious problems that we've willfully neglected for years. Often, we simply don't realize that we have such repressed, heavy-hearted issues to deal with until a Plutonian crisis occurs. This period can demand our total re-education regarding life and how it works. We've been fed a lot of socially sanctioned ideas about how to cope with the real world and how to obtain knowledge, but now Pluto is ready to reveal a whole new level of understanding that may seem alien to everything we've been taught. This powerful new information can and will uproot our intellectual foundation.

We may find ourselves starting to distrust the authority of experts. Some of us could begin to suspect cover-ups and conspiracies by people in power who aim to keep us, or the public in general, in the dark about sensitive material or controversial subjects. Let's not get too paranoid. Our new mental explorations will require a depth of study that we may not have been ready to pursue until now. This is a good transit for research projects, as well as for the unraveling and decoding of complex data. But first we'll probably go through an initial period of mental agitation, feeling that the pat answers we've depended on to solve problems no longer work as well as they once did, if they work at all. We sense that there's more to whatever interests us than meets the eye. However, enlightenment doesn't come easy. We're forced to investigate our world like never before, with a passionate persistence uncommon to the Third-House process of development. We'll also have confrontational dialogues with ourselves.

Moodiness can be a sign that Pluto is starting to infiltrate this house. Pluto doesn't encourage bubbly cheerfulness. Maybe some of us find that we are no longer as glib or chatty as we once were. A few of us may look at things darkly, with shades of cynicism and streaks of pessimism. This is most common if we were born with a tensional Mercury or Moon aspect to our natal Pluto or Saturn (aspects that already condition us to take a dim view of rosy outlooks or smiley yellow faces telling us to have a nice day). We might brood more than usual. All of this is preparing us to observe and analyze the world in-depth from now on. When our mental perspective deepens like this, we cannot tolerate the narrow-minded life interpretations of others, or safe, simplistic solutions aimed to ensure a "happy" but shallow existence.

JOURNEY DOWN BELOW

This book is about what we can do in practical ways to make our Pluto transits smashing successes or, at least, productive moments in our lives. My overall tone is upbeat and hopeful, although Pluto probably never gets to have a good laugh about the frustrating side of the human condition—unlike crazy-loving, absurdity-appreciating Uranus. Pluto is so deadly serious about everything. However, it will be necessary to squarely look at the problematic side of any Pluto transit before real progress can be made.

Some of us could already be in a vulnerable mental state by the time Pluto, covering the outside peephole, knocks on our door. Seductive and persuasive Pluto has plans to take us deep within ourselves to visit the underground chambers of our mind, where we can view the decay and demons that haunt us. We can even feed a few hungry bats while we're at it! Pluto leads us to a dark and swampish place. We'll need to be careful where we walk and especially what we step on. Let sleeping serpents lie. Just pay silent attention to the dramatic scenery and take plenty of mental notes for personal research later.

If some of us are a little too imaginative in our everyday dealings with reality—if we already inappropriately intensify our day-to-day emotional experiences—then this transit can seem hellish. If we're touchy, our thin-skinned nature now becomes magnified. We may find ourselves erupting at others and lashing out verbally. Or, instead, we turn within and implode, doing battle via fiery arguments with ourselves, perhaps related to unresolved conflicts from our past. It can be scalding either way, yet this is probably a good sign that Pluto is arousing our thinking patterns in a major life-reforming manner. If things remain too calm, then nothing's really clicking as it should. Serious self-interrogation is a common experience during this transit.

Thank goodness, the lava doesn't flow from our mouth throughout this long Pluto transit. Who could stand being around us if it did? It's probably best to stay down below and probe our interior self for a while before we set off verbal firestorms in our outer world. If we externalize Pluto too soon, and without any real depth, then we'll likely project all of our rage onto others, who then appear to be the sole source of our and the world's misery and deep discontent. They become the villains in our drama, the dragons that we'd love to slay. Keeping Pluto contained for a while also helps us temper its energies somewhat (not actually control them, but reorient their flow). We can learn about the power granted to us by focus and concentration. In the Third House, we can typically go off in many directions at once, but Pluto insists on a mentally disciplined, single-minded approach. We will need to learn how to quiet our minds and become less distractible. In this regard, it probable helps to already have a steady natal Saturn in our Third or our Mercury in a fixed sign such as—you guessed it—Scorpio! Taurus can concentrate long and hard as well.

TOUGH TALK

It's unlikely that we'll be able to stay quiet for long. Remember, transiting Pluto is less secretive than is natal Pluto. Its goal is to expose whatever's been kept under wraps for the wrong reasons. At some point during this transit, some of us will realize that we've been cowards for too long, afraid to say what we think. Pluto encourages our candor and our frankness. We can be brutally honest. This unwavering honesty counts more than the force of our verbal blows. Still, until we learn to do a full make-over of our communication skills, we'll probably blurt out feelings with great emotion and an eye for someone's jugular vein. But, guess what? They'll probably come back at us with both barrels loaded. The Third House supports the free exchange of thought; therefore, communication becomes a well-traveled, two-way street. We'll have to be able to take what we dish out. Others, too, have pent-up Plutonian anger in need of verbal release.

If this is not understood, that others have strong "opinions," then our Third House Pluto transit can be a great source of frustration and alienation for us. When Pluto in our Third squares or opposes the fire planets (Sun, Mars, or Jupiter), we can go through an uptight phase of acting like dictators by domineering people with words. Even Pluto aspecting our Saturn can be severe in speech and inflexible in thought. It may feel great to get some hostility off our chest, but it can also damage relationships for good.

The tempering of Pluto mentioned before means that we need to always think and reflect before we blitz others—our words can act like torpedoes rushing toward a target. The results can be devastating to those unprepared for our wrath. Later, we may regret such forcefulness on our part, especially if we're the ones dishing out the ultimatums. Yet it may be too late to patch things up by then. Pluto/Mercury aspects have to watch out about this tendency, as well.

On the other hand, being too subtle and diplomatic with people may not always work, either. Pluto doesn't go in for wimpy approaches—we'll need to lay our cards on the table and get right to the point during our most confrontational moments. We also can't afford to have others miss our point: that, from now on, we are going to think for ourselves and forthrightly say what's on our mind. It could get steamy at times, but so be it.

Most of us will need to learn how to use psychology on others constructively, so that we can emotionally reach them. This doesn't have to be a manipulation game or some sly act of cunning. It's strictly a matter of assessing another's capacity to absorb what we're trying to say. Maybe a little tactfulness here and there will do the trick (which is our natural inclination if we have a lot of planets in Libra). However, others will appreciate us telling it like it is, without including such niceties. I guess we'll have to learn through trial-and-error. The bottom line is that we'll need to always clear the air and get down to basic grievances in our relationships, long before they build up in force and power, then come tumbling down on us in an avalanche of hurt and fury.

Seething Siblings?

It would be wonderful to think that every Pluto transit through the Third resulted in a renewed appreciation of being someone's sibling, with bonds stronger than ever. It does turn out this way for some, usually due to a mutual burying of hatchets or outgrowing of childhood rivalries as both personalities blossom and mature. In this case, Pluto can help to fortify our relationship by materializing situations that turn out to be advantageous to all parties involved—even financially profitable, perhaps by going into a lucrative business with a brother or sister. We can get close to a sibling who historically may have been tight-lipped, secretive, or emotionally distant. A rebirth occurs in our union, and we're finally each other's confidante; we see and appreciate the depth in one another. Obviously, we may have to first air out a few resolvable feelings before we can reach this level of trust and openness, but it is reachable.

It could also be that we've never directly had a problem with our siblings (which is unlikely), yet one of them has power and control issues to work out in his or her life. That brother or sister could be struggling to emerge into a different lifestyle than was offered by family tradition. Perhaps our parents or that sibling's spouse is having a tough time deciphering this person, whose defiant and willful eruptions can cause a family split. Maybe he or she is showing intense single-mindedness and is impossible to influence. We may have an opportunity to become that sibling's behind-the-scenes counselor or therapist, allowing him or her to vent feelings without censorship or harsh judgment. However, at a certain point, this may prove too difficult, draining, and thankless of a role for us to play.

There's one more scenario to be found here that's not very constructive. We may find a brother or sister who considers *us* to be a prime target for attack. Unfinished business from the past degrades into a dramatic showdown of sorts, except that our sibling has both guns drawn and we've been caught off guard and weaponless. It's not a fair fight. The whys behind this apparent rage or bitterness can be numerous and are not particularly rational. Remember, this transit takes a long time to unfold. This alone can add a seething quality to the picture for both parties. In the worst case, we sever ties permanently—or so it seems at the time. Actually, in the *really* worst case, someone kills someone—but that's not what this book wants to promote, at least not without a drastic change of title!

It's sad when a Pluto transit coincides with irrevocable breaks in close relationships. However, survivalist Pluto says that we can and will learn to live without *anyone,* if doing so will prevent our psychological or physical destruction. And frankly, who needs this kind of abuse? We don't necessarily have to waste brain cells hating this sibling forever, but we may be determined to keep him or her out of our lives without suffering needless remorse or guilt. That being said, there is still a chance that a reconciliation, maybe brought on by a crisis, can occur later in life—but only on terms we can live with. Otherwise, forget it!

THERE GOES THE NEIGHBORHOOD

I like to refer to happenings in our neighborhood when talking about our Third House because it's a great way to witness transit influences at work on the circumstantial level. We just have to learn how to associate such outer, seemingly impersonal conditions with our inner states of consciousness. With this Pluto transit, it is doubtful whether we'll even be living in the same neighborhood by the time Pluto enters our Fourth. Major life transitions can occur that cause us to move to a radically different environment. However, perhaps we are determined to stay put, no matter what, and refuse to be uprooted for any reason. It's then that the neighborhood has no choice but to appear to transform before our eyes. Depending on the transiting aspects, we may not like the results at all, mostly because we cannot control them.

Sometimes Pluto will work itself out through our actual neighbors. Foreclosure signs go up because some folks are going bankrupt. Others leave because a major source of income has dried up and they can longer pay the mortgage. If we are apartment dwellers, evictions could become likely for troublesome neighbors down the hall. The theme shared by these scenarios is one of change being forced on people due to either financial hardships, a lack of proper income-management, or severe economic setbacks. Of course, other manifestations could be the deaths of long-established neighbors, news of ugly divorces, or turf disputes that have people at odds with one another. What we ourselves start to feel during this commotion is the demise of a peace-filled era in which we once felt comfortable with our neighborly surroundings, when everything seemed to have a familiar sense of order and security. Now, signs of dissension and deterioration are evident. We can feel invaded by unwelcome elements manifesting a little too close to home.

In other instances, the entire neighborhood is forced to undergo upheavals. Maybe the rezoning of unused land has invited businesses to encroach on our subdivision more than we can comfortably tolerate. Neighbors could be up in arms about it, but we are powerless to stop the onslaught of "progress." It could be that the neighborhood infrastructure of underground water pipes, electrical lines, and its sewage system are in need of repair or a major upgrade (not all at once, hopefully). This reconstructive work, while necessary, can get messy and disruptive. Of course, not every neighbor is also going to have Pluto passing through his or her Third at this time, but if *we* are, our reactions to such disruptions can be intense and filled with resentment. We are likely to overreact to anything being torn down or demolished. It would be better to give this an interpretation that reveals something about our inner world and the pressures on us to grow in new ways. We'll need to stay flexible and become philosophical about the apparent destruction we see up and down the block. Sometimes these major changes, while drastic, are needed—so let's not take things too personally!

PLUTO/AIR MERCURY TRANSITS
COMPLEXITY

Pluto is not known for the intellectual detachment we find in Mercury or Uranus. However, when combined with either of these airy planets, Pluto drives us to deepen our mind's understanding of how something works. Pluto urges us to take things apart and carefully investigate them from as many subtle angles as possible. It is as stimulated by what is unseen as by what is clearly visible. Pluto has the skills of an ace detective who doesn't miss one bit of evidence at the crime scene; all clues are spotted quickly. Obviously, the problem-solving facet of our mind is involved here, yet such superior sleuthing ability suggests the addition of a gut-level awareness and uncanny sixth sense. Pluto has X-ray vision and can also see quite well in the dark.

When Pluto transits our Mercury, evoking its airy side, we may find that we are less distractible and more apt to focus energy on a few topics that become increasingly fascinating to us. We may be drawn to studying something that enthralls us. We're eager to learn as much as we can about our new interest. This can be time-consuming, so some of us may try to put such demanding studies aside, only to find that we are more obsessed than we realize about further exploring the information made available by Pluto. The more complex our subject matter, the better. Actually, the earthy side of Mercury is more at home with Pluto because it's the part of our mental experience that likes to research and analyze things at length. It also will take its sweet time doing so, because it likes to be thorough in its knowledge. Air Mercury doesn't enjoy being that tediously single-minded about anything. It requires periodic stretch breaks to keep from becoming exhausted or overloaded. Perhaps a walk around the block will refresh us before returning to Pluto's secret underground library. Think of how Gemini would tackle the learning experience in comparison to Virgo, and it will become easier to understand why air Mercury doesn't want to be doggedly focused on anything for too long.

NOSY QUESTIONS

What air Mercury does better than earth Mercury is to ask a lot of direct questions in a casual, chatty, off-the-cuff manner—even when what we want to know is considered private and "hands-off" by another. The air Mercury part of us wants quick, clear, uncomplicated responses. It also wants to impart or exchange information (swap stories) in hopes of learning something new. However, with transiting Pluto, we'll have to be careful not to become intrusive with our inquisitiveness. Both Pluto and air Mercury share endless curiosity as a common denominator.

It would be better to silently observe things for a while, at a distance, and see what we can dig up that way rather than corner and grill somebody for the facts. People caught off-guard may resent being "interrogated"—which is how they'd probably interpret our approach. They also may not care for our intensity. Not everyone feels comfortable being around an amateur investigator who's always trying to ferret out information. Even when we keep our mouth shut for a while, we still may stare at folks in ways that let them know that we're trying to read them like a book, that we're on to their every move, and that nothing gets past us. This alone can give some people "the willies."

A good way to fulfill our need to nose in on secrets is to start reading murder mysteries or books that investigate "the unknown." Air Mercury needs to be entertained while it's learning something. Horror and dark fantasy novels might prove to be thrilling escapes that captivate our mind and imagination. In fact, "whodunits" give us an opportunity to figure out the case at hand long before it's solved at the end. We get to vicariously play the role of private eye or forensic detective. Pluto is teaching air Mercury to pay attention to details (something earth Mercury has little trouble doing), look for the less obvious, and slow down and focus attention where it counts the most. Without the ability to sufficiently concentrate, a restless, hyperactive mind can be a serious handicap.

Of course, if crime-oriented reading material holds no interest for us, other suitable Plutonian learning material involves depth-psychology, cosmology, physics and metaphysics, exploring outer space, and delving into "inner" space in terms of the evolution of soul and spirit—and let's not forget reincarnation. While air Mercury would love to hear about exciting past lives (who? what? where? when?), transiting Pluto would prefer that we learn about the fundamental reasons for karma (the "why?" factor). Pluto never supports the superficial; it likes to get right to the heart of any matter.

FROM THE BLACK LAGOON

Many members of the mid-century "baby boom" generation will recall that famous B-movie involving a reptilian humanoid creature who was pretty non-verbal, but quietly swam about the murky waters of an Amazon lagoon. Research scientists—in true 1950s-style—wanted very much to capture this live evolutionary oddity for observation and experimentation. The amphibious creature didn't care for that idea and reacted with primitive fury when finally caught and chained up in an observational water chamber. When he broke loose, he went on a soggy rampage that made everyone scream and run for their lives! Actually, I don't remember all of the finer details of this flick. They killed him off in the end, and I think that the movie's beautiful, raven-haired heroine shed a tear for him. It could be said that Pluto is very much like that primal creature, and the Black Lagoon is very much like our shadowy unconscious. Of course, the nerdy scientists—low on empathy but high on intellectual curiosity—would symbolize a combination of both air and earth Mercury.

Pluto emerges from the dark, muddy waters of our underworld during this transit to be studied and subjected to experimentation by detached air Mercury. However, we must not try to repress Pluto or kill him off with our weapons of rationality and reason. It won't work. Pluto's fiery fury can turn destructive enough to overwhelm a panicky and emotionally ill-prepared Mercury. It has been suggested that mental breakdowns can occasionally accompany this transit (particularly with the so-called "hard" aspects). We could act as if we were possessed by demons—paranoid-sounding demons. However, it's more common to find us thinking long and hard about our early childhood traumas, wounds, rejections, hurts, or whatever else we've managed to avoid resolving until now—or maybe the adult-size, secret pain that we've never before articulated.

In this respect, Pluto enables air Mercury to feel the power of emotions and then find ways to verbalize them—either to ourselves or to others who are not afraid to hear our angry statements. A few of us could go through a spell of using four-letter words when upset, to underscore how intense we're feeling about our life at the moment. Or, we become surprisingly sarcastic about everything that displeases us. With air Mercury, Pluto tends to vent through the mouth. It would be helpful if, instead, we started keeping a journal in order to release our agitated thoughts onto the page. A journal with a lock and key would probably make some of us feel safer when expressing such raw commentary, because we're going to want to point fingers and name names! Many years later, when we are not feeling as stormy and eruptive, we can look at those honest pages of pain and objectively make better sense of what we were going through. Our journal may become a gold mine of material leading to self-insight. However, to extract the most out of this effort, we must keep our often misunderstood creature-self unchained and free to move about our psyche's deep but familiar dark waters.

Instant Shrink

The sextile and the trine from Pluto to airy Mercury can suggest times of our profound awareness regarding anything that motivates others to behave as they do. With these less-tensional aspects, we patiently wait to gather the information about others that we want and need. Aggressiveness is less our problem. We don't often give in to the temptation to play "I Spy." As a result—and also due to a magnetic quality about us—people may come to us to confess their sins or spill the beans about their private lives and loves.

This can actually happen with any Pluto/Mercury contact. However, when the sextile or trine is involved, we are probably more receptive to and less judgmental about what folks in sticky situations are going to tell us. Hearing other people's secrets requires that we remain honorable individuals who live by a code of ethics. This is important, because an undisciplined expression of air Mercury can turn us loose-tongued and gossipy, hating to keep any juicy tidbit all to ourselves. Meanwhile, others are trusting us to keep what they privately reveal under wraps. Whether we can or cannot do this becomes a real test of our character. Letting certain Plutonian information carelessly slip out can have disastrous results for all parties involved.

Not only do people want us to play a role similar to a priest in the confessional booth, but they sense that we have the depth to be their therapist. Maybe we do have more mature insights into life during this transit than is normally the case. We seem to love to solve puzzles during this period, and people in need become challenging human puzzles. As long as we don't succumb to power-tripping with our advice, it seems to be okay to analyze their situation and give out our opinions on the matter. Airy Mercury always has a point of view to offer—with Pluto, it can be a very insightful viewpoint indeed. However, we'll have to be careful not to trigger thoughts in others that unintentionally open up a can of worms. We may not be professionally trained to deal with the repercussions. This might especially be the case if we are astrologers having this transit. What we say can be more powerful to our clients than we realize. It sticks with them for a long time. We'll need to choose our words wisely and in a timely manner. We also have the power to heal others with the words we say, so it pays to think before blurting out sensitive information.

OLD BLACK MAGIC

There are some astrology texts that suggest that Pluto/Mercury combinations are good for being a magician. Most successful stage magicians are excellent at deft sleight-of-hand maneuvers and can hypnotically convince enraptured audiences that things are dematerializing and re-materializing right before their eyes. Such magic-makers seem to have, in their bag of tricks, ultimate power over the known laws of nature. Yet also suggested with this planetary combo has been a potential for dark sorcery and other shadowy ways to manipulate people—body, mind, and soul.

In a less devilish context, Pluto aspecting Mercury can give us an interest in mind-control, whether we are fully conscious of this or not. It would be great if it's only our mind that we're trying to harness, but often we seem driven to direct the thoughts of others. Our mind can forcefully attempt to influence people to do what we desire, and such magnetic mental energy can be seductive (more than just persuasive). If some folks give us permission to work on their minds for transformative reasons (as in hypnotherapy or psychological counseling), then perhaps we can do wonders for others by helping them see their own Plutonian hang-ups. Air Mercury can be our clear-headed translator while we're descending into someone else's cryptic inner Hades.

If our intentions are less than honorable, we may try to dominate another's thinking in ways that are neither redemptive nor ethical. We can be a coercive verbal bully, intimidating others to surrender exclusively to our ideas. This is what black magic is all about—psychologically trying to break down another's will and their independent thinking just so that they will do things our way. Pluto can transform us into a skilled propagandist, but what is our ulterior motive? In the long run, people will want to vigorously resist our demands by not revealing anything to us, especially with the opposition in play.

SILENT SPACE

Perhaps the hardest lesson for the airy side of Mercury to learn is knowing when to stop communicating, especially in the verbal sense. Pluto's influence can turn us into a dynamic speaker or powerful writer, whose passionate thoughts and words make lasting impressions on the minds of many. If we have something of vital social importance to convey, then by all means we need to put our insights and observations out there into the world in order to shake things up a bit. Usually, what we advocate has an element of controversy to it that unsettles some listeners, but charges up the intellectual batteries of others. A definite impact is made and people's thought processes are deeply stirred.

Still, at some point it's good to practice the mental discipline of silence. Meditating *per se* is not much of a Pluto/Mercury exercise because intensely-focused thought is not encouraged by mediation. There is something about surrendering to the eternal flow of "unthinking" that doesn't work for either Pluto or Mercury. Yet consciously and deliberately clearing our minds of unnecessary thoughts does appeal in part to Pluto, a planet that seeks to annihilate what it deems useless. A first step toward this goal is to talk less (only speak when we really have something important to say). We'll need to pay attention to when we're just idly chattering to siphon off any excess of air Mercury's nervous energy.

With the transiting trine, we may sense when we've said enough and can therefore mentally withdraw from our surroundings in search of peace and quiet. This becomes an effortless way to shut off excess stimulation. The sextile has an "off again-on again" attitude when it comes to conversations (we can be just as happy reading a book on a deep subject as we are having an intense talk with somebody). The conjunction, square, quincunx, and opposition struggle with more compulsive and often frustrated urges to communicate. They become overly-stimulated by what's happening in the environment. With these aspects, everything seems to trigger a strong response. The need for finding silent space becomes even more important to our nervous system's health and to our sanity.

This transit could be a good time to seek out less-demanding activities that won't mentally tax us by over-analyzing life. Maybe we need something that has a more primal connection to the life-force itself, something evoking sensory stimulation—like gardening. The mere act of reconditioning soil with restorative enhancements to ensure robust plant growth fulfills Pluto's urge, while planting orderly rows of seeds and giving them clearly-written labels for identification purposes would satisfy air Mercury. We may have to mull this over and see what kind of non-verbal activities we can engage in to really capture our full attention.

CHAPTER NINE

PLUTO TRANSITING THE FOURTH HOUSE

UPROOTED IDENTITY

Finally, Pluto gets to transit its first water house. The Fourth is a life sector where depth-awareness is familiar. At this angle—the astrological Nadir[1]—a subjective identity takes shape as soon as we are born and find that there are certain people hovering around us during this vulnerable time in our life—infancy. Shortly after birth, we pick up on the general atmosphere of our home life and sense whether our survival needs are met promptly, or whether we'll have to struggle to attract the attention we require. For some of us, our basic needs are seldom satisfied, so we feel rejected or abandoned (in the non-analytical way that babies intuit their immediate surroundings).

The emotional impression that we receive from our earliest environment may be a pattern of solid support, inconsistent care, or near-total neglect. Perhaps it's an alternating mix of all three. What we were expecting was more quality time to slumber in paradise—the womb! Therefore, at this sensitive point when our budding impression of our family is formed, a whole lifetime of security expectations develops, for better or worse.

We could speculate that our Nadir identity doesn't begin at birth; it may have stronger roots that predate our current incarnation. Maybe a series of interconnected past lives created the existing need for the life themes of our Nadir sign to nurture us and provide a foundational anchor. What is symbolized at this angle must be satisfied before we can feel safe enough to venture forth into the impersonal world that awaits us, which is why the Nadir's orientation takes hold very early in life. In any case, what we have going for us at the Nadir/Fourth House level is something we've inherited in one way or another, a carryover from some pre-existing situation (even our genetic legacy is associated with our Nadir/Fourth House). What's represented in our Fourth operates like a built-in part of us that exists even before our ego develops its organizing structure. We have a personal history here that is not found with our Ascendant.

Transiting Pluto is now at a point where many factors of this highly subjective Nadir self-image are ready for an overhaul. Momentous alterations of a complex composite of past factors are about to take place, especially on psychological levels. Karmically, we have played out the dependency patterns of our Nadir sign, for better or worse, during many lives before this one. Soon, we'll close a chapter that was once key to our soul's emotional growth while we assimilate the essence of that extended experience. No longer must we blindly reinforce this pattern again and again through current family dynamics. Breaking away from the pull of our parental vortex will be a challenge, because it seems too easy to continue to get sucked back into these relationships, even though we're painfully aware that we need to outgrow them. They're becoming a suffocatingly powerful influence, and Pluto wants us to acknowledge that at this time.

FAMILY SECRETS

Transiting Pluto is a bloodhound on the trail when it comes to tracking down family secrets. While growing up, we may have sensed that there were a few things wrong with our parents' marriage, behind the scenes, but nobody was willing to talk about it—especially our mom. Everything was shoved under the rug. Those unspoken issues had an impact that we couldn't necessarily see—but we could feel it. If one parent was a closet drinker or was having an extra-marital affair, while our other parent did his or her best to shield us by creating the illusion of family normalcy, our inner radar probably picked up on the "secret" anyway. This resulted in subconscious disturbances to our security-development, especially in the area of trust.

We're rarely conscious of this, especially if we have natal planets in our Fourth House. In that case, what goes on in our family, and later on in families throughout our culture, becomes an ongoing life focus for us. If we have natal Pluto in our Fourth, near the Nadir, this transit marked most or all of our early childhood years. That's strong stuff for any young kid to undergo. A hard-to-understand heaviness and maybe a deep sadness was in the air regarding our family's soul, even if outer appearances suggested otherwise. One parent, usually our mother, was undergoing internal complications, perhaps undetected by the family at large at the time.

Even if we came from a model home where the family virtues outweighed the few minor flaws we spotted (and where everyone claimed to be happily and lovingly bonded), Pluto is now preparing us to acknowledge that most other people haven't been raised in such an "ideal" matrix. We'll probably be meeting more of these people in the next several years. We also may realize that we've been fooling ourselves all this time about how glorious it was to grow up in our household. We'll discover that we've unconsciously overlooked emotional trouble spots that might have been overwhelming if we had recognized them at a tender age. Our parents also may have tried to prevent us from learning certain truths.

Whatever the case, what was once hidden may now begin to surface in uncomfortable ways that definitely get our attention. Transiting Pluto wants us to look at what was really going on in the past, without the distorting lens of sentimentality and nostalgia. Pluto strips bare any warm glow of childhood based on false memory or repression. That can prove initially disheartening during the early stages of this transit. It can be a hidden cause of many black moods and even some soulful crying jags. Yet we won't get stuck in that phase for long with Pluto controlling our current Fourth-House unfolding process.

DEEP NOURISHMENT

If we are full-fledged adults during this transit and are raising a family of our own, we may find ourselves investigating, with a critical eye, our role as nurturer and comforter. Women seem to have different dynamics here than men: they feel that they must look after and safeguard the children they bear. They see their offspring's welfare as more their responsibility than that of the child's father. Regardless of who seems to do most of this active mothering, we could also be supporting other family members while resenting the fact that our own emotional needs have gone unfed or have been sidetracked for much too long. We may build up hidden levels of bitterness or rage that eventually demands a Plutonian eruption—all based on our feelings of being neglected, unappreciated, or overtaxed by those we love the most, who can nonetheless drain the heck out of us with their non-stop neediness and selfish personal interests.

The culprits here can be problematic kids or unsympathetic spouses. Some of us can reach a breaking point where we shut down emotionally and go on strike, refusing to cater to any more family demands. We refuse to give another drop of ourselves to anyone who forcefully gobbles up our time and energy or who becomes abusive. Perhaps we go through the motions of giving in to others, but inwardly we've lost our warmth and any real sense of devotion.

Before we sink into such a hard-freeze stage, one that unsettles and alienates the people around us, it would be good to pay attention to warning signs that say we're under too much pressure to expend our maternal energy in a nonstop fashion—which can result in total burnout. By then, our emotions and physical health can suffer from exhaustion. Pluto allows us to feel as "down" as necessary—it'll even let us double-up in psychological pain inflicted from childhood insecurities revisited—if that's what it takes for us to realize our unconscious tendency to poorly nurture ourselves.

We may feel justified in blaming others for our near collapse, but ultimately we'll have to point the finger at ourselves and ask why we compulsively give too much of ourselves to them. Pluto wouldn't be putting us through such a state if we weren't greatly imbalanced in this area of care-taking and care-giving. Must we wait until we char the Thanksgiving turkey in the oven—and almost burn the house down as well—before we realize that we're steaming mad about this whole situation? Pluto thinks not!

SOOTHING TIMES

What we need—as we'll discover as years go by—is quiet time to nourish ourselves in the deep, healing ways that we'd typically discover if we were just left alone for a while, without people trying to divert our energy toward their personal crises. We'll need to discipline our emotions for this to happen, because we automatically seek to attend to others, almost as if we have a reflex muscle for nurturing. Pluto is trying to help us control this compulsion. We need our own form of tender, loving care, and need to mother ourselves in quality ways.

Being good to our body is one way to get the ball rolling. Sleeping extra hours instead of convincing ourselves that we can get by with less can restore vitality. Taking time to eat without being in a rush is also to be encouraged. Eating wholesome foods assures steadier energy rhythms. (Some of this advice will be covered again when Pluto transits the Sixth.) Taking baths with a little magnesium-loaded, nerve-relaxing Epsom salt added might help to soothe our overstressed body. Let's do whatever it takes to slow the pace and come home to our quiet, inner center.

Let's also stop habitually pushing ourselves beyond our limits. Every so often, we'll realize that routine household chores are less important than attempts to renew our spirit with self-focused activities. We'll have to do some fancy talking here, however, to convince those we live with of this concept. Of course, some of us will probably need to immerse ourselves more fully in house-keeping tasks if we've been habitually out of touch with our living space (again, a sign of poor nurturing abilities). What can we do to bring new life into our home?

NEW NEST

There are lots of things we can do to our home to show that our Plutonian surge of inner rebirth is alive and well. If we live in a place that we have always loved, and if we feel that moving is totally out of the question, this becomes a great time to renovate. However, before we put tremendous energy into painting walls, redoing the floors, and screening the porch, it might be good to first inspect the Plutonian parts of our home which are typically not the prettiest parts of any residence: the water system's net-work of pipes, the plumbing, the septic tank, the furnace, the water heater, and anything hidden behind the walls that involves power transference (such as the electrical system, although Uranus is the key planet for that).

With Pluto in our Fourth, we need to look for previously unde-tected damage that can pose safety hazards. Once we are satis-fied that everything is in full functioning order (maybe because we had to replace a few things with more updated models), then we can have fun beautifying our home with dramatic flair. We need to ensure that we can afford our fun, however, by only encouraging realistic, timely expenses.

If we own a home, as opposed to renting, we have more free-dom to tear down and rebuild. Typically, an expansion of a room is desired (maybe the master bedroom or a bathroom—two pri-vate, Plutonian areas). We also might want to do a lot of remodel-ing with future resale value in mind, which may also include impressive landscaping (with shrewd Pluto in charge, we're always thinking ahead in terms of ultimate gain). The changes we make become a big investment, a gamble on our part to reap satisfying rewards later. We could also have an inner conflict about leaving our home altogether. Sometimes we must move because of pressures beyond our control. If we can't pay our bills due to some economic crisis, we may be forced to sell, or perhaps the bank forecloses on us.

A few of us—inscrutably so—could be vulnerable to a cruel fate entering the picture through major home damage beyond our power to prevent, like a huge sinkhole that nearly demolishes our house and others after a period of freak, torrential rains. Perhaps a disabled plane plunges from the sky, creating a huge fireball when it crashes into our roof (while we barely manage to escape), or a sudden rock slide buries the private mountain-hideaway that we've held on to for decades. These drastic occurrences are rare, but possible, during Pluto's transit. We may be able to prevent such catastrophic scenarios in the first place by not being so irrevocably attached to our home that any threat of loss becomes utterly devastating and unthinkable. That's when our attachment starts to become pathological, giving another meaning to the term "homesick." Pluto will make sure that we let go, one way or another, of whatever has unduly possessed our soul.

NATURE POWER

Some of us will do a lot of metamorphic inner work during this phase rather than become embroiled in ongoing family dramas that result in no-win power struggles. Realizing that true security comes from within and not from emotional attachments, we have an option to use this Pluto transit in different ways. With Pluto hanging around here for years, it's unlikely that any of us will be able to escape from examining our hidden insecurities and probing unresolved dependency issues. Such issues may loom large in order to demand our full, internal attention. However, if some of us have unearthed our own maternal power to self-nurture, we might find that we have developed an empowered union with Mother Earth as well.

This may sound "cosmic" and abstract, but what it implies is that we feel more rooted in the life of the planet (not just with human life *on* the planet). Some of us may discover that we've developed a super-green thumb, giving us an extraordinary ability to grow anything. It makes me think of those magazine ads showing smiling gardeners standing next to colossal cauliflowers, zucchini that resemble baseball bats, and pumpkins almost the size of 1960s Volkswagen Beetles!

This is an example of Nature's awesome power. The energy that allows for this kind of amazing growth may not be coming straight from our fingertips or from space alien visitations (as our imagination would have us believe). It could simply be that Pluto wants us to witness a potential that normally goes untapped because we earthlings are not ready to collectively use that potential wisely. Things grow—and grow—to impress upon us how fantastic the surge of the life-force can be. Our gardening talent becomes a metaphor for our inner self and its potential to bloom beyond our dreams. If we have never tried to grow flowers before—or gigantic tomatoes—this is a good time to tackle a small garden, even if it's only on our patio.

Healing power and the ability to restore vitality may also be associated with this transit. Maybe something special *is* emanating from our fingertips after all. Perhaps our aura is energized more than usual. However, it's best not to become too enthralled with these abilities. We should just let our healing energy flow innocently while we steadily follow the path of our heart—a path that allows us to develop this special relationship with planet Earth. If we try to make this a mind-control thing, we run the risk of becoming power-trippers who think we can manipulate natural forces at will. We can't. Our Plutonian healing energy is best applied to others who have felt psychologically crippled by parental rejection or social isolation in childhood. In other words, those people who have had a history of feeling unwanted and not fitting in—unhappy loners. Obviously, deep studies in psychology and other related fields would fascinate us at this time. We can also have a strong desire to help folks break away from obsessive dependencies of all sorts.

PUBLIC DISCLOSURE

Finally, let's not forget that in the beginning of this transit, Pluto opposes our Midheaven for a while. This suggests a time when our inner security needs start to transform us in ways that might make us feel at odds with our outer professional image (a Midheaven issue). This is especially so if that image is already phony and contrived. Maybe we realize that we're in a career that no longer makes us feel deeply supported for who we really are, rather than what we allow society to think we are, Tenth-House style. Our unconscious may be sabotaging the public persona we've carefully crafted throughout our ambitious years. Personal upheavals in our private life may jeopardize our social reputation. It's a tough phase to undergo if we are already famous and can't seem to keep out of the tabloids. Any messy situations at home, as well as the shadowy parts of our personality's private side, can become well-known to the outer world, resulting in bad press. Sometimes a troubling parental upbringing becomes relived through tensional interactions with our boss or public authorities, with potentially damaging results. All of these areas require our intense inner review and maybe some trusted, expert, outside help. Pluto is teaching us to empower ourselves by reaching out to others who care.

PLUTO/MOON TRANSITS

BLAST FROM THE PAST

Pluto and the Moon are both water planets, so we can expect this transit to revolve around subjective issues that cannot easily be put into words. Sometimes it's even hard to dredge up internal images, such as memories. We can't seem to detach from what's going on inside us, especially with Pluto intensifying our feelings. This transit can describe an internalizing period of brooding reflection, during which we look back on our lives and pick at certain unresolved issues, sometimes mercilessly—at least in the beginning. Our Moon symbolizes a personalized past that we continuously carry inside ourselves, no matter what our age. In fact, the older we get, the more we find ourselves scrutinizing that past in hopes that it will explain the origin of any current unfulfillment. Our built-in lunar function provides us with security urges and an instinctive need to retreat to safer psychological harbors when the outer world threatens to uproot us. Therefore, when our Moon is involved, our urge to protect ourselves from harm is strong as we instinctively seek to hide inside a psychological womb.

One main problem with our natal Moon, from transiting Pluto's vast perspective, is that we are too used to supporting protective coping mechanisms via our accustomed defenses—blind reactions that keep us from making any progressive change in our temperament. It's hard to grow further when we automatically reject the unknown elements that such needed growth may bring our way. Don't think that conservative Moon signs like Cancer, Virgo, and Taurus have the most difficulty with change. Moons in Sagittarius and Aquarius don't do well, either, with letting go of their dependence on finding security through personal freedom, even when a really excellent relationship requiring full commitment is at stake. However, Pluto will not tolerate any part of us remaining stagnant due to our unchallenged anxieties. Therefore, this transit tries to bring to our consciousness, for closer inspection, those old safety issues that have troubled us before—issues we've avoided digging in for years, for fear that they'd upset our psyche's apple cart and alter our security patterns forever—gee, that's exactly what transiting Pluto has in mind!

One way Pluto does this is by bringing up, usually under stressful situations, troubled memories from long ago that disturb us as we relive them. This warns us that what we buried many years before wasn't really dead, and now this zombie is awakening and roaming the isolated streets of our unconscious! With arms outstretched, it's ready to grab our attention, an understandably frightening experience. No voodoo charm comes to our rescue. We need this Plutonian experience if we are to exorcise the ghosts from our past that continue to spook us.

In less picturesque terms, this means that life will help us to shake free from our attachments to powerful fixations and blockages that have kept us from maturing emotionally—especially with the forceful square or opposition aspect in action. If we've been stuck in defensive but immature modes of operation that now hurt our ability to intimately relate to others, Pluto works to make this known to us in vivid terms. Once we see what we're dealing with—recognizing that our unhappiness has been due to unresolved security issues—we can terminate this self-defeating pattern for once and for all. It will require that we look at ourselves honestly and be willing to peel away our defenses. This is not easy, so patience and courage will be needed.

BLAME GAME

When we're not doing well with our adult lunar development, it's always an easy but cheap shot to blame one parent (typically our mother) or both for how weird we turned out and how miserable we are. We can also point a finger at our generally "rotten" childhood and recall that nobody loved us or had time to tend to our needs. When we review those early, formative years during Pluto's transit to our Moon, we do so through the specialized lens of this darkly intense planet, which makes us a harsh critic of all those who denied us our happy childhood.

Our urge to tear down and destroy old structures is strong, so we may feel driven to get down to what was *really* going on with our folks. We want a confirmation of our suspicions, as we hunger for psychological details and hidden facts that actually may be impossible to unearth. Certainly our parents are less than willing or able to rehash the low points of raising us. Yet some of us may persist in trying to uncover painful material that we strongly feel has a great deal to do with what troubles us now. We figure that Mom knows all of this "top secret" stuff but just won't confess. It's heavy denial on her part, or so we assume.

In today's social climate, we are well aware that bad things of a sexual nature can go on in some toxic households. Taboo behaviors, such as incest or molestation, seem more common than previously suspected. The topic has received more air play in the media ever since Pluto made its passage through Scorpio. Pluto in hard aspect to our Moon might pull such combustible memories from deep within us to a level of waking awareness, where we recognize them in all of their horror and disgust.

However, astrologers need to be very careful when venturing into this shadow territory, even when natal patterns seem to be incriminating. Luckily, more clients are coming to astrologers and bravely discussing the subject, giving us permission to explore the astro-symbolism involved. Still, I'm not sure how forthcoming a client would be about this topic with transiting Pluto contacting his or her Moon. Intense issues that already are not easy to articulate may reluctantly surface, if at all. It's a delicate situation that could be approached in too intellectualized a manner by an inadequately trained astrologer.

Sometimes there are specific people to blame in our childhood for the atrocious things that might have been done to us, including many forms of psychological violation. In most cases, however, we'll need to resist angrily finding fault with everyone from our past, blaming them for why we compulsively act out destructive patterns again and again in our existing relationships or toward society at large. It's common to lash out at others with storm-tossed feelings when Pluto and the Moon clash. We can obsess about finding the reason for our emotional unfulfillment, but we'll miss the mark if we fault something or someone outside of ourselves for our continued distress. The same goes for blaming past-life karma. Maybe a former incarnation was the reason that we came into this life with a certain bias against emotional contentment and trusting those close to us. Still, nothing will change until we own up to our internal power to create better emotional realities. Pluto is now offering us the key to no longer feeling trapped by an oppressive past.

IMPASSIONED

Any Pluto/Moon mix can arouse an emotional response that shows how strongly we feel about specific life issues, usually betrayal issues. This can be a volatile combination that can prove to be too much for the people who deal with us—a case of overfeel on our part, fed by a little paranoia. However, transiting Pluto can also be especially rejuvenating if we've been too shy to show the world all that we've been internalizing for so long. Our Moon needs us to make caring human connections rather than remain in a state of isolation. The right signals from our environment help us to open up and respond to our surroundings. We only retreat within ourselves to restore our emotional energy while we digest our outer experiences.

With a stressed-out natal Pluto/Moon, some of us might withdraw too often and become inaccessible regarding our feelings. We may not trust simple human interplay, suspecting that it will lead to exploitation and abandonment. Transiting Pluto energizes us to pour out the tensed-up feelings that desperately need ventilation. We can be ultra-sensitive to our surroundings and feel an urge to make a lasting impact in our relationships.

The transiting conjunction, square, quincunx, or opposition suggests that our emotions may be released too strongly, although they can have a passionate quality that some may find captivating. This could prove effective for motivational speakers trying to persuade an audience, or politicians trying to get re-elected. However, we probably lean more toward a hard-sell approach due to deeply held convictions powerfully expressed. Not everyone goes for that kind of gut-wrenching performance, no matter how sincere we are.

Some of us may feel possessed by a greater force that gives us courage and a determination that we haven't demonstrated before. This is particularly so with the transiting conjunction. Our security needs become tied in with a revolutionary drive to change ourselves and society. We can feel, with extreme conviction, that we know what needs to be overthrown. We can have periodic outbursts that clear the air. Logic and reason can't get their foot in the door. Our passions feed our instinct to eliminate any obstacles blocking our path. Obviously, our mood can be a tad militant.

If we've been "fraidy cats" for most of our adult years, and have resented the fact that others always get to have things their way, now's a time when we can rise up and seize the moment by fiercely fighting to protect our needs without caring how selfish that may appear. However, if we do this too stridently, we may rupture close relationships. That may be just what needs to happen if we are to learn to stop subtly sabotaging our partnerships through compulsive behavior.

CONSTANT CRAVINGS

Insatiable hungers and unquenchable thirsts fall under the domain of Pluto. During a Pluto/Moon transit, we may have enormous desires that are not easily fulfilled. Food and drink (alcohol), sex, or the security of collecting lots of possessions may unduly preoccupy us. This could be a period of hard-to-explain binges, where cravings and impulse buying can go into overdrive. Perhaps our lunar self doesn't realize that we're supposed to be shedding security crutches at this time. Instead we might attempt to over-consume something or someone. The Moon can act like an empty stomach feeling hunger pangs, while Pluto now triggers our urge to devour. A few of us struggle with appetites that seemingly control us. If the point of eating was to appease our hunger, we'd soon be satisfied. Yet pigging out doesn't seem to relieve what's gnawing at us. We still feel underfed.

Until we realize that we are thirsting for something deeper—like a reconnection with our central source of inner power—our cravings and addictions continue to obsess us. Until we work out our emotional security dilemmas, we probably won't respond to life in ways that are self-nurturing. We become our own "Terrible Mother" (an image of the darker, destructive side of the maternal archetype). How we attempt to reward ourselves can, in the end, become an undermining act of unconscious punishment. Our body comes under attack, as well as our emotional framework. Pluto will help us to get down to the bottom of this pattern of self-infliction.

THAT HEALING FEELING

The up side to this transit is that we get to do some needed psychological plumbing, repairing our emotional system so that we can flush out poisonous images and memories. We'll have to process this with eyes wide open so that we know exactly what harmful elements we are eliminating. A clear awareness of what has specifically injured us prevents any future "reinfection." Some of us had to go to Hell and back to realize how much better it is to be made whole again. We don't simply wake up miraculously healed. One positive result of a well-handled Pluto/Moon transit is that we feel much less emotionally fragmented and fragile. We now have a secure sense of being reborn in personal ways that mean a lot to us, even if the outer world sees little radical change. Maybe being free of a few soul-destroying addictions can give us that "new lease on life" glow.

So, what do we do to continue feeling this alive and well for the rest of our lives? That depends on the extent of our emotional transformation. Transiting Pluto sextile our Moon may not be enough to create a sustaining impact, but let's not be too quick to minimize its influence. Pluto is already good at in-depth restoration and a sextile or a trine facilitates this process without needless complication. With a transiting Pluto conjunction, the results are more emphatic. In that case, our Moon has been thoroughly saturated by Pluto's essence.

One way to keep our Plutonian changes positive is to be good to our bodies, mothering ourselves in highly energy-protective ways. Remember, Pluto is the guardian of the life-force, the eternal flame within. We'll need to eat to nourish our body, not to medicate our emotional wounds. Getting proper rest is important; don't ignore physical signs of exhaustion. We'll also need to refrain from constantly intruding into the emotional space of others and thereby becoming entangled and trapped in potential difficult unions.

The Outer Planets require states of detachment to do their most effective work. Such detachment allows us to develop an overview of life that provides plenty of room for our passionate truth-seeking. These planets eventually teach us not to take earthbound realities so personally. Don't expect mundane society to teach us how to do that. All of these revelations have to come from within, so we may feel alone in our awesome journey to discover vaster dimensions of non-physical existence. Our Moon doesn't want to detach totally, nor should it. But with Pluto, we learn that it's best to depersonalize our feelings so that we stop wasting energy trying to defend ourselves against the conflict-creating attitudes of others. Otherwise, we get caught up once again in the power plays and revenge patterns that we worked so hard to escape. Pluto's healing energy allows us to feel less vulnerable to other people's neuroses and their emotionally disturbed evaluations of us. Let others rant and rave, while we remain serene and true to our calm and newly fortified center.

NOTE

1. A technical note: Steven Forrest uses the term "astrological nadir" in his books (see *The Changing Sky* in the Bibliography), probably to differentiate it from that point on the celestial sphere directly beneath the observer—also called the Nadir—used in the horizonal coordinate system; it is this Nadir that is always found opposite the Zenith. The astrological Nadir, instead, belongs to the ecliptic coordinate system and is exactly the same northernmost point also known as the Imum Coeli, which astrologers more simply refer to as the IC. The astrological Nadir, then, is always opposite Midheaven and is not to be confused with the other Nadir. Whenever I use the term Nadir, I'm solely referring to the "astrological" one.

CHAPTER TEN

PLUTO TRANSITING THE FIFTH HOUSE

SURGE OF JOY

It's been suggested that Pluto going through the Fifth House (even natally) will cut an overblown ego down to size, because there is something meglomaniacal about unchecked Fifth-House self-expression. We think we're hot stuff—God's gift—while others merely see us as shameless attention-seekers or pitiful over-compensators trying to cover up our mediocrity. Some truly obnoxious, brassy behavior can come out of the ego's desperate attempts to shine most brightly in this house. It's true that in our Fifth, some of us can go crazy when we don't get the thunderous applause we've anticipated—and we don't take well to bad reviews the next day.

Nonetheless, it's been my observation that, if anything, not enough of us glory in our ego-strengths or bask in self-wonder in this house. It's surprising how many people feel patently non-creative and downright unwilling to stand out and be seen as someone special. Not many are comfortable with taking center stage. Our culture, fueled by ego-stifling Judeo-Christian traditions, puts a social damper on how and where we are to show off our glitzy colors. Unless we are actively involved in the entertainment industry, the understood message we receive is that we must tone it down when in public and not grab for attention. Apparently nobody likes a person who is too full of him or herself.

Transiting Pluto will nevertheless stir something deep in our soul that wants to be heard and seen, defying our culture's bias against too much self-adoration. Both the Fifth and Pluto can provoke passionate displays. The Fifth House is specifically where we are given free reign to be playful with life, to have fun *being* alive and well while also getting a kick out of having others watch us release our energy. We can loudly blow our horn and let people know that we exist. The Fifth doesn't want us to grow too old too soon and sadly become another victim of society's tired, lackluster model of adulthood. Maybe this is one reason why many of us need to have kids, puppies, and kittens around us—to remind us that we can still be young at heart and full of spirit.

However, at the start of this transit, there is nothing lighthearted or childlike about Pluto's process. Think about our two previous Plutonian transits: we've learned to deeply think for ourselves in the Third and to let go of "insecurity" attachments in our Fourth. Together, these transits give us a new power base from which to operate. In the Fifth, Pluto forces us to confront our potential greatness in personal terms. Being humble is fine, but false humility has to take a hike. In the Fifth, we can't hide behind an "ah shucks, folks" attitude for too long. Pluto wants us to make our grand entrance from behind the dark velvet curtains and head bravely toward the spotlight.

This is no easy task, because little that is associated with the enrichment provided by Pluto comes effortlessly or painlessly. Still, we can help this process along by realizing the power of being joyous, which can now surge within us as never before, after enough time has passed for Pluto to transform us. Perhaps we have enjoyed a new appreciation of life ever since we survived the potentially devastating and nagging uncertainties at our Nadir and throughout Pluto's Fourth-House transit. Now, something tells us that we're really ready to rise from the ashes of our old, insecure, uptight self. Pluto is determined to kill the remains of the sour-puss, the grump, the Scrooge, the party-pooper, even the hurt inner child filled with sadness and bitterness. Claiming our state of joy will require facing the coward within who has often stopped us cold from daring to fully enjoy ourselves, for fear of what "others" would think.

During this transit, we learn the source, in part, of our dread of social disapproval: we probe the past and remember the many times that some wet-blanket authority figure tried to quash our talents or muffle our individuality, keeping us from feeling big and important. With this transit, we can make a clean sweep of any lowly feelings of self-worthlessness and inferiority. The environment is ripe for our "coming-out" party. Lights, camera, action!

STAR POWER

Pluto can really turn on the heat of ambition in some of us. We begin to realize that life is too short to waste precious years working hard *not* to get noticed. Hidden talents may emerge from our depths. Our early strivings can strictly be in the realm of personal hobbies; for instance, taking art classes at night or having an urge to brush up on musical skills abandoned many years ago. We sense that something vital is missing from our drab and predictable lifestyle, and feel a hankering to jazz things up by adding flair and color to our lives.

Once we let Pluto take over, we find that we are aroused by our unfolding talents. Our objective is more than just doing something to temporarily entertain ourselves. We feel driven to see how deep and how far our self-expression will take us. If we are still relatively young, we will probably go with Pluto's flow without letting self-doubt set up roadblocks. This could be a fabulous pattern to embrace during young adulthood, when we may already feel invincible and have faith that a promising life lies ahead of us. Pluto smells like power—the power to be ourselves all the way.

No matter what our age, Pluto transiting our Fifth can keep us from getting psychologically stiff-jointed or as dry as bleached bones. In this adventurous, risk-taking house, Pluto gambles for high stakes when it's on a roll. If we only live once (at least with the personality package we now have), let's go for what we'd love to more fully experience in life. Parachuting out of a plane at age seventy? Why not? Swimming with dolphins while on our dream vacation? This sounds rejuvenating. What we will be learning to do during the next several years of this transit is to treat ourselves well, engage our ego in true recreation more than we've ever allowed before, and radiate our star power to the world without any apologies. If we do everything right, others will love our robust, confident performance.

That Special Fire

We look to our Fifth House for clues about our romantic adventures as well as our love affair with our own creative output. Pluto has almost too much to give. It wants to make sure that the genuine sense of self we ardently show the world will be felt by others in no uncertain terms. If we were born with natal Pluto in our Fifth, learning to back off and not force our will in "matters of the heart" may become a character-shaping lifetime goal. We can easily overwhelm others with our intensity and drama. Of course, a few of us with this natal position could also be emotionally shut down, the type of person who hides our lovelight under a bushel. However, when Pluto transits this house, we learn how to become more Plutonian in our appetites, through trial and error, within the limits of circumstances in which we find ourselves. Sometimes Pluto helps us to evolve best when we take a long break from romance—or at least from that idiot version of romanticism in which we may have lost ourselves too much already—especially during Neptune's previous Fifth-House transit.

If falling in love has ever felt more like falling apart at the seams, due to our self-destructive attractions, then Pluto is here to show us how to heal our wounds through a survival technique: a willing period of celibacy. The key word here is "willing." Pluto will put out our flames of passion if we've managed to burn ourselves or others too much in the past. That's when we feel compelled to turn our attention to other things beloved by our Fifth House—

such as the many ways we can enhance our personality and develop a non-sexual charismatic appeal. Transforming our passions for the better sounds nice, yet there's bound to be festering, underground issues for some of us that center around why our love life has been such a wreck, with its dismal track-record of failure and heartbreak. There remains an underlying sorrow beneath the festive outer presentation we offer to the world.

If celibacy is not a realistic option because we're learning about romance and courtship for the first time, transiting Pluto could usher in a love affair that makes us realize just how strong and insistent our emotions can be. The more naive we have been about such things (just as sweet Kore was), the more Pluto wants to heat up our blood and get us in a feverish state of desire. Plutonian desires can be exquisite, but also discomforting, because there's always a chance that our passion could be rejected by a person we nonetheless *must* have. Why has tortuous fate even introduced this individual into our life, if he or she was not meant to be ours and ours alone?

The trine and the sextile, especially to our Moon or Venus, seem like gentler and more moderate versions of the conjunction, square, quincunx, or opposition. However, all Pluto/Venus aspects push us to take bold chances in love that make us face ourselves and our fears of being exposed on deeper levels. We may feel that we have a lot to gain by opening up, but also a lot to lose in any love affair that triggers our passion. Our underlying urge is to control everything about this encounter, leaving little room for being surprised or caught off-guard in any way. We'd better watch our step, says Pluto! Too much control goes against the natural display of spontaneity fully supported by this house.

DARKER AFFAIRS

Pluto is a planet of powerful temptation (so is Neptune, but Neptune is less the ready participant, at least in the beginning—it innocently gets itself sucked in and seduced while blindfolded). Pluto stirs up our not-so-obvious ability to be the tempter as well as the tempted—a situation in which we subtly devise methods to allure, entice, and even entrap another to surrender to our charms. We can be more provocative and devious under Pluto's transits than we'd care to admit. If we are under any illusion that we're morally pure-minded and above animal lust, our unconscious side can surge forth and ignite hungers of a more primal nature. (For example, consider that baffling, hard-to-cure disorder ATS—Acquired Televangelist Syndrome!) If we are married or are otherwise technically not available, we can detonate mine fields of emotional upheaval in many people by embarking on a steamy underground affair. Maybe a few of us are inappropriately fixated on someone who is underage or related by blood; we probably struggle with giving in to such taboos. More often, the object of our secret lust is another married person as emotionally pent-up as we are, perhaps also an in-law. Transiting Pluto in this house can suggest some dangerous, risky attractions.

Variations on this theme all point in the same direction: we are trespassing on territory that society not only frowns on but forbids. To willfully continue to do so invites severe penalty and shame. (This sounds like the confessions of many guests who pour out their sordid tales to shocked but titillated audiences on those tabloid talk shows.) So, is transiting Pluto making a hard aspect to our Mars, Saturn, or Uranus? That could imply that we're susceptible to breaking social codes in our determination to get what we want—in this case, someone we want, and want badly. Being involved in an extramarital tryst is probably the most common of these dark affairs, even when we're not the one who's married.

What makes taking this route so odious is not just the typical moral violations that come to mind, but also our capacity to corrupt ourselves on deep soul levels. We can take actions that tarnish our integrity, based on obsessions that we barely understand but are unwilling to resist. Some of us want to surrender to such compulsivity, even when we end up as damaged as those we hurt. Not all extramarital affairs turn out like this, just the ones inspired by Pluto! Everyone involved takes little dose of poison into their personal emotional system.

Some of us know well in advance that we're playing with fire, but still ignore the potentially drastic consequences. Others anticipate that nothing will block their path, so they find out the hard way that this is not true. Sexuality is a potent ingredient in most Plutonian affairs, but so are control tactics and power games. Transiting Pluto will only permit things to go so far astray before it demands retribution, considering that the health of our soul and another's is at stake. The last act of this psychodrama-passing-for-love often is rich in subplots of betrayal, vengeance, seething hostility, cruelty, and whatever else Glenn Close did in *Fatal Attraction!*

It's best not to clutter our love affairs with such complications. The Fifth House enjoys none of the gut-wrenching storminess or ominous black clouds brought to the party by Pluto. However, we can keep things simple and sane by only getting "hot" for people who are unattached and don't have a hidden criminal record a mile long! We need to make sure that lovers are giving themselves to us without manipulative strings attached, and that neither of us feels hopelessly addicted to the other. Nobody is to own anybody in this Pluto-sanctioned relationship. If we follow these guidelines, we'll find that we can become thoroughly engaged in a love union where a mutual exchange of depth and sensitivity make us both feel special and important for all of the right reasons.

THE POWER OF KIDS

Pluto is a planet that, ideally, can provide conditions suitable for fertility. After all, it's associated with compost heaps in gardening as well as with the regenerative power of sexual biochemistry, which ensures the survival of any species. The miracle of conception is related to Pluto. A female's transformation during pregnancy qualifies as a bona fide Pluto experience. During this transit, some of us not only may bring children into the world, but become parents at a time when we are to deeply focus on what it means to raise a child. We're probably unconscious of this until the blessed event has occurred and we take charge of this person who depends on us exclusively—a situation alien to some of us with strong natal Uranus patterns. But then it hits us, the profound responsibility that's been placed on our inexperienced shoulders!

Sometimes this sense of profundity is felt early, because transiting Pluto makes us painfully aware that conception is not always a given. A few of us may patiently have to try harder to reach that critical first step (a visit to a fertility clinic for evaluation may be required). We may discover that carrying a fetus to full term can be fraught with perils if we have hidden biological or health problems that are just now being brought to light. If we are the mom-to-be, it is imperative that we have a clean diet and a calm emotional life for nine months or so (although achieving serenity is easier said than done with Pluto going through our Fifth; and the baby inside us feels every intense emotion). We'll need the full cooperation of our body during this often taxing experience, and therefore we can't afford to carry on like an edgy soap opera character who thrives on high drama. We need restful conditions and plenty of quiet, still moments.

Let's say that all turns out well and our new baby shows, from the start, that he or she is a tough little survivor, a hearty soul with a penetrating stare. That's what we might project onto our precious one—lots of Plutonian traits. This "old soul" could indeed have Principle Eight emphasis (Scorpio, Pluto, the Eighth House) all over his or her chart. Several years later during this transit we may discover that child-raising is more than we bargained for, especially if we're mild-mannered. We could be dealing with a five-year-old tyrant who has mastered adult psychology at a tender age—and we discover that we don't enjoy having certain buttons pushed by such a shrewd little squirt!

Of course, some of us may discover that our little one has the wisdom and inner strength of a Zen master, and can teach us plenty about depth-awareness. But that's rarely the case. We'll need to be careful, during this first decade of our child's life, to not set a fixed pattern of parent-child power struggling that only brings out the worst in us. That could keep our child in a continuous state of inner rage or outer defiance, which school teachers will eventually have to deal with when "Pluto Junior" gives them a taste of his or her wrath. If we're in heavy parental denial, we'll be shocked to hear that our little "angel" has a mean streak. School bullies from our early childhood were often Plutonians testing their intimidating power on easy victims: gentle Neptunian kids who probably had their own host of inhibiting Saturn problems with authority.

The toughest scenario by far occurs during the turbulent teenage years. Plutonian rebellion is as strong as that found when Uranus goes through our Fifth, except that with Uranus, our teenager is up front about defying us and fearlessly breaking our "dumb" rules regarding appearance and conduct—even brilliantly debating with us about them. In contrast, Pluto is sneaky in its underground maneuvers. Our kid—and if we have several, usually one stands out as our special Plutonian challenge—may seem to be going along with things on the surface, but then transforms into someone unrecognizable by nightfall when he or she hangs out past his or her curfew with mysterious pals wearing black leather. We don't even know what's really up, because we're getting the famous Pluto silent treatment and that impenetrable blank stare.

However, we'll need to do some investigating if we sense that things are not right and that our child has eerily withdrawn from us. The same advice goes for our adult children who seem more remote than usual. This doesn't mean that we have to become flaming paranoids ready to invade our child's privacy at any moment. Still, we can't afford to skirt serious teen pressures like booze, sex, and drugs. Heck, the problem could be shoplifting or vandalism. Whatever the case, we'll need to bravely discuss those touchier matters that we've dreaded talking about ever since our kid was born. Rats!—we knew this moment would eventually come.

PLUTO/SUN TRANSITS
AUTHENTIC SELF

The Sun symbolizes key characteristics that unfold as we mature and further individualize. Pluto deals with a reorganization at the core of our entire being—not just within the ego's structure—

that leads to total renewal. During this transit, emphasis is put on our ability to undergo fundamental inner changes whereby we become more conscious of what we essentially are. It's what we essentially are *not* that has to die. Yet the Sun feels that it must defend itself and hold its ground against any process as ego-threatening and finalizing as Pluto's.

We could be at a critical point in life where self-definition is most important, especially with the conjunction, square, quin-cunx, or opposition. Have we used our ego's power to create false images of ourselves that have nonetheless impressed the outer world? After all, misguided solar urges would have us strut around like big shots or proud peacocks, further feeding our illusion of inherent superiority. However, if transiting Pluto catches us in the act with our crown on, it will surely try to thwart our ongoing attempts to make ourselves more valuable and important than everyone else. The Outer Planets have transpersonal goals in mind for all of us and they cannot abide any individual's arrogance and conceit—especially if it is based on willful ignorance of one's true nature.

Expect part of this transit to focus on the tearing down of whatever blocks our self-integrated identity from shining. When we strive to make ourselves whole, our spirit radiates strongly and our hidden light surfaces easily. Pluto's job is to clear the way for such inner radiance to emerge without letting our short-sighted ego try to control the whole show. This process may not be all that magnificent to behold, at first. It can turn into an internal battle as life forces us to reorient our seat of consciousness. It's also scary to expose the real parts of our being to the world, because many of us have been more comfortable grooming ourselves according to what society expects and rewards. However, this is a time to present an authentic expression of self that is more in alignment with our prime purpose for existing in this incarnation. We are to unearth our essence and openly appreciate it as the hidden treasure it is.

BATTLE OF WILLS

Our ego may think that some of Pluto's power-enhancing perks are desirable—that is, as long as our ego can take over the entire operation. Pluto knows that's impossible if any true progress is to be made on the soul level. Evolutionary growth has always used the ego to do its bidding, not the other way around (although during the "involutionary" arc, developing a full-blown ego becomes the prize to be won after many, many lives). If we think we can push circumstances around to make everything turn out our way, this Pluto transit warns us that we have another thing coming— especially with the square or the opposition ready to play hardball with our personal reality.

As the transiting planet, Pluto will provoke powerful authorities and uncompromising situations to put us in our place if need be, which usually means that, first, we get bounced off our throne. Life may boss *us* around for a change if we've had a sad history of being a dictator who controls others by keeping them scared of our threatened retaliation if they disobey our commands. Bullies do get older and often better at their game, and must be stopped.

Therefore, if a few of us have not developed healthy solar values (maybe our natal Sun's already in a mishandled hard aspect with Pluto, Mars, or Saturn, and we've opted to take the low road), our self-centeredness seemingly knows no bounds. Our heart certainly is not in the right place when it comes to handling people. External power-clashes are one method used by the Universe to let us know that we've met our match in the outer world. Depending on our age, opposing forces can manifest as parents (usually our father) who totally refuse to go along with our plans, our chosen lifestyle, or our real self. We can feel attacked and emotionally deserted, instead of being the recipient of full parental support and praise.

At this point, we had better reassess ourselves and analyze why we are meeting such resistance—no sense getting disowned because of our extremism or our absolute contrariness (even though Pluto itself is associated with banishment and exile). However, due to wounded pride and an inability to take "no" for an answer, we could get so pushy when exercising our will power that we force even minor issues to become major crises—and we deeply wound and alienate others in the process. Things can get even more complicated when we ignore the signs that tell us to stop being an island unto ourselves while making everyone else "out there" our mortal enemy. That's when paranoia can set in, and before we know it, we don't trust any authority to do right by us. At that point, it's showdown time. We may either give or receive ultimatums that lead us to burning our bridges behind us.

Obviously, a Pluto sextile or a trine can help us to negotiate better terms, so that we're not fixated on seeing things in an all-or-nothing manner. Other transiting Pluto/Sun aspects suggest that we're probably much too intense and obsessed at times to make smart moves. Our gut's on fire and our raw, uncontrolled reactions are directed at anyone who appears to usurp our power, with fateful consequences in some cases—there is something irrevocable about certain Plutonian decisions. We may have to live with the results for a long time. That's why it's good to think things through before dramatically setting certain scenarios into motion.

NEW LEAF

If we know that we won't be enduring the above power struggles because we've already done a lot of honest self-exploration, then we can look forward to whatever major changes Pluto may bring our way. It still is a time to show courage and inner strength, because a few personal conditions will seem completely beyond our control. The external environment has the ball in its court, and we must be poised in a dynamic state of readiness for whatever happens next. We can assist this process by consciously engaging in simple Plutonian activities, such as getting rid of anything that doesn't represent the "real" us. Usually, things from our past that remind us of innocent, bygone days—when we knew little about ourselves—become prime targets for permanent disposal. We may keep a few cherished items, but gladly let the rest go. That can include people from our past. From now on, we need around us only that which best defines us and underscores our true identity. Of course, we're still in the process of learning what that real identity is all about.

When things go well during this transit, we are eager to turn over a new leaf and take on a vital approach to living the life *we* want to live without fear of failure. We're using our solar power in a manner that we never dreamed possible. It may take a while before we see the results we desire, perhaps not until this transit is finished and an additional year or so has gone by. Long-term changes at the level of our core self are being made, and that's never a quick, superficial process. In some cases, our life alterations can be drastic due to situational pressures that demand an overnight death and rebirth—as when a tornado wipes out the structures of our entire town. Our urge thereafter may be either to rebuild or relocate. Either way, things are never the same.

Even when we're having a relatively smooth Pluto/Sun transition (beating the odds and surprising ourselves), this is still Pluto we're talking about, not Jupiter or Venus. Every so often, small eruptions can occur as hidden pockets of anger and resentment are stirred up within us. We could find ourselves incensed about someone else's disrespect (the Sun wants to be honored) or about some other form of humiliating mistreatment (our ego is touchy). Simply being ignored or overlooked can set off little tantrums and crazy fantasies of crushing those who have dared to offend us.

If our anger is not provoked, there can, instead, be deep fear of being overwhelmed by impersonal elements of life that don't care two hoots whether we survive or not. It must be awful to have such a Pluto transit *and* be homeless and unemployed at the same time, without sufficient means of receiving multi-level support. Pluto can hit us really hard when we're already down and out and barely making it. However, even in such a desperate situation, a fighting spirit within us is determined that our life will turn around and restore our human dignity and sense of purpose—both of which we *must* have if we are to go on living.

LUST FOR LIFE

The upside of this transit, when well managed, is that we physically feel recharged and ready to do a lot of big, important things. Our inner Pluto is all fired up for constructive action-taking. We need large projects to pour our hearts into, and that means societal or collective enterprises—even those that are not necessarily humanitarian in nature (although astrologers usually try to push us in that direction). Sometimes our destiny involves obtaining business power in a commercial sense that ends up affecting the mundane lives of many. Social progress on a technological level can fulfill the spiritual evolution of the "collective," as does work that promotes inner healing for the masses. The main thing needed with a Pluto/Sun transit is that we feel in command of ourselves, doing what we do best, and getting results on which others can build later, if necessary. We'll want our share of glory. Some of us may even feel gung-ho about leaving a worthy legacy for future generations.

The Sun deals with our sense of having a central mission in life. Therefore, this could be a destiny-unfolding time when our greatest power resources are at hand and are ready to be put to the test. Not all of us will have some great masterwork to produce that will garner tremendous recognition and acclaim; in fact, few are so privileged. Yet in our private world, where we have less of an impact on collective destiny, we still may reach heights within our inner universe that can remove self-doubt regarding our ability to overcome limits, self-imposed and otherwise. Rising self-esteem can become a source of healing, making up for the many years during which we were unsure of our intrinsic worth. Our lust for life is based on our passion for being the best we can be in our own eyes. We're just now realizing that this goal is within reach.

LIVING IN PLUTO TIME

Peak Pluto periods involving our natal Sun are moments when everything can seem new again. Life becomes a vivid experience.

We certainly have less reason to feel blasé about anything; apathy is not a Plutonian or solar trait. However, such vivid awareness of life on our planet can sometimes be too heavy to bear. More than ever, we'll feel outraged by the horrible injustices and atrocities done to innocent people around the world by tyrants, war lords, brutal dictators, gang leaders, torture squads, and other Plutonian light-destroyers. We'll wonder about the incomprehensible miseries caused by Nature's out-of-control fury, resulting in human destruction from hurricanes, volcanic eruptions, avalanches, mud slides, earthquakes, famines, and killer viruses. When we're caught up in "Pluto Time," these realities hit us harder than ever. We also bristle at the human greed, psychological meanness, and sheer senseless violence we see perpetrated by societies that look less sane, and less civilized, as each year goes by. It may deeply distress our soul that this deterioration is happening around us, yet we are powerless to stop it—one of the agonies of living in Pluto Time.

Actually, we *can* do something to help alleviate the human suffering we are now seeing with our eyes wide open. For one thing, we can start by cleaning up the garbage in our ego's backyard. That means not taking offense as readily when others, especially strangers, give their rude opinions about us, our country, our religion, our politics, our sexual orientation, our ethnic heritage, or whatever else we consider a direct insult. This only helps to pollute the collective atmosphere further. We also shouldn't be too ready to hit, slap, kick, punch, push, shove, or scream at people who displease us—not if we're also praying for world peace. People toss their little A-bombs at each other every day and fail to see the accumulated fallout that this creates in our society.

When operating in Pluto Time, we have a special ability to defuse tensions before they escalate into ugly scenes. We can get to the heart of any matter by realizing that blind frustration is largely responsible for people behave badly—frustration, plus painful feelings of being devalued by someone else. This may be a cause of our current epidemic of human rage on highways as well as battle fields. Everyone wants to feel honored, but some go nuts when they aren't validated by the people around them.

During our Pluto/Sun transit, we can offer strength and hope to those who strike out when feeling disenfranchised, impotent, or very much like unwanted outsiders living on the fringe of mainstream culture. We may be willing and able to descend into society's underworld (Pluto's realm) in order to cleanse and heal gaping wounds that otherwise continue to putrefy and infect others. Maybe that becomes our new life mission. Even though we can only make waves on a small-scale basis—such as trying to stop World War III from breaking out down the block—all of our earnest efforts impact on the psychological health of the rest of humanity. And that makes us feel regenerated, as well.

CHAPTER ELEVEN

PLUTO TRANSITING THE SIXTH HOUSE

UNDER THE MICROSCOPE

There are several features about the Sixth House that allow Pluto to feel right at home. For one thing, this is where all sorts of annoying problems crop up in need of real solutions. That's great, because Pluto loves to investigate and repair whatever's malfunctioning; the Sixth should keep transiting Pluto quite busy. Both Pluto and the Sixth feel compelled to tinker with objects and people—taking them apart, studying their innards, and putting everything back together again in, hopefully, better shape than before. This sounds therapeutic for all involved. Our Sixth requires that we take time to study the details of our life and the environment around us. Pluto naturally likes to scrutinize situations, size things up, and have thorough knowledge of how something works. Actually, both planet and house are even more fascinated with why something *doesn't* work. Each is eager to carefully study complex conditions and painstakingly research and compile essential data to better understand any matter.

When Pluto transits this house, we find ourselves slowly undergoing important attitude adjustments regarding our ability to use working talents and skills effectively and efficiently. Both

Pluto and the Sixth hate to waste time and energy; they demand high productivity. We may now find that we obsess about the work we are doing or will be doing in this lifetime. Have we allowed ourselves to be put to good use, or is our current job a dead end where our abilities are being underused, or not used at all?

It's common to find ourselves increasingly self-analytical during this period, as we put ourselves under the microscope in order to get to the bottom line: what's wrong with us and with our lifestyle regarding our approach to practical, work-related goals? What can we do to correct whatever is needed to enable us to function smoothly and do the best job we're capable of doing in living a purposeful life? We have serious work ahead of us, but first we'll need to shape up, retrain ourselves to be better problem-solvers, then point ourselves in the direction of relevant employment.

Actually, it's not as easy as that with Pluto. "Getting the job done" sounds more like the favorite motto of the Sixth House. However, Pluto knows that just getting in touch with what truly works for us is a job in itself. Our age and the various life-passages through which we have already traveled make all the difference in how we evaluate this house. Transiting Pluto is first going to break down parts of ourselves that will be of little worth to our future objectives, once we are preoccupied with work that captures our full attention and passion. We especially need to rid ourselves of urges that would have us uselessly scatter the creative energy that we worked so hard to unearth and vitalize during Pluto's Fifth-House transit. It's at this breakdown phase that things can become problematic.

Neither Pluto nor the Sixth are going to baby us as we move through these necessary transitions. We will see our flaws and defects under the cold, clear light of reality. People, or situations themselves, will point out our weaknesses in a matter-of-fact way that can make us feel incompetent, and that's discouraging—yet the intent of this transit is to convince us that we are highly capable of handling the complex tasks required by life. We could end up discovering we've become *very* well put together before this transit is over.

THERAPY SESSION

Some of us might assume that we'll never do certain things well even though they must be done (necessity is often a bigger theme in this house than free choice). In fact, a few of us probably haven't done so hot in coping with life's daily rituals thus far—we've made too many stupid mistakes already, leaving our life at loose ends and vulnerable to failure. None of this helps to boost our confidence or promote a "can do" attitude. If this sounds like us (we claim we can't even boil water), Pluto will probably force us to dissect the hidden reasons behind our continuous ineptitude, and ask why nothing seems to work right in our lives, not even our coffee-maker! It's not going to be easy to survive in an increasingly complicated world when we malfunction repeatedly. Therefore, Pluto will help us to fix the mess we've made of ourselves. That means that we'll have to concentrate energy on a deep, totally honest study of our inner self.

During this period, it's hard to escape the need for practical psychological insight. Therapy is one way to help ourselves solve our dilemma, yet it's probably the route that we dread hearing about the most. *What?*—on top of all this junk we constantly hassle with, we've got to hear that we're nuts as well? Actually, we'd *really* be crazy to continue living our life inadequately. It's true that, when undergoing Plutonian therapy sessions, we'll find out a few things that we wish we never knew or had confirmed. That's because they're so darn painful to relive in our head and heart. However, to really "know" such things in Pluto's profoundly emotional way can unburden us. Although we intensely feel the emotions that arise from within us, that intensity has a special kind of energy that later translates into the drive and motivation to make something of ourselves; to make a relevant contribution to life, even if in only small, but potent, ways.

Many of us are probably going to be drawn to self-help techniques. Life is a hugely interesting puzzle, and we feel driven to interlock the right pieces. Several years of this transit could be spent in search of our deeper purpose for living—or humanity's deeper purpose for being on the planet. We probably will be attracted to tools for self-realization that we find fascinating to use. And, guess what? We often comprehend such matters almost as if we've studied them before. Hmmm, we're not such dumb-dumbs after all; we can learn practically any subject that really intrigues us.

With Pluto, whatever we pursue seems to become more important to us, and to our destiny, as time goes by. It's best to deal with our developing interests in a here-and-now manner and let the future take care of itself. We need to simply immerse ourselves in our interests and see how far we can go with them. We'll know if we're on the right track when we find ourselves feeling stronger about facing up to life's challenges, knowing that we'll learn from our mistakes rather than be overwhelmed by them.

JOB FROM HELL?

This heading may sound negative, but some of us will realize the truth in it. The more we work in an environment where others have unlimited power (including the power to make or break us), the more hellish our job can become. We might not work very well with people's power drives to begin with, but life forces us to do just that now that Pluto is calling the shots—especially during Pluto's conjunction, square, quincunx, or opposition phase. The more we sabotage our own ability to demonstrate power within our hired role or chosen trade, the more unpleasant it becomes to operate on the job. That's partly because others may try to take over and underplay or bypass our authority. Maybe we're just not as convincing a commanding authority figure now as we will be by the time Pluto finishes this transit.

We could harbor unexamined doubts about our skills and talents, robbing us of the total self-assurance we need to make real headway in our Sixth. Much of what is demanded of us can prove exhausting over the long haul, yet we seem driven to conscientiously deliver excellent service. We want to give it all we've got. However, when it comes to getting full support and praise for all our tireless efforts, we may feel cheated. Maybe there's jealousy in the air or a shark mentality at our workplace that intimidates us. All of this could promote a silent anger and brooding resentment that we typically keep to ourselves. We can be very good at stuffing our real feelings.

A lot of people need their jobs, even if they can't stand the atmosphere in which they work. Economic necessity plays a major role, as do the politics of ambition and the long climb up that ladder to success. We may have to endure a lot of subtle and not-so-subtle Plutonian abuse if we are too terrified to quit a position that otherwise gives us desired material security or status. Still, we're well aware that the work environment can be poisonous at times. We can be the target of another's hard-to-fathom hostility or underhandedness. In this case, Pluto will continue to bear down on us until issues erupt that are too aggravating to ignore, or too demeaning to take, without fighting for our rights. At that point we'll be forced to quit, unless we're unfairly fired first. Actually, being fired under these conditions can be a blessing in disguise.

Maybe we work for the boss from hell who has a reputation for scaring everyone in the office—or for keeping key people in the dark about important matters and procedures. This could be a supervisor who has a hard time delegating power to others, or sharing much of anything else. We can be very sensitive to his or her shadow side, because we're the ones projecting a lot of this stuff onto that individual.

Boss figures are usually shown by our Tenth House, but Pluto deals with power themes, so it seems likely that we have our run-ins with authorities as we struggle to find a comfortable level of professional autonomy. We surely don't want a dragon breathing fire down our neck, or some hyper-efficient tyrant who is quick to detail every one of our humiliating errors. That would feel punishing to us, not constructive. Maybe our boss wants us to be a compulsive-obsessive workaholic, just like him or her, and gets steamed up or bent out-of-shape when we admit to having limits (or even a mind of our own). We tend to feel most drained by the intensity of our employer or by certain coworkers, who each can make everything more complicated than it needs to be. We sense that our power is slowly being devoured by people who suffer personality disturbances.

Sometimes it's the physical environment that pointedly shows Pluto's influence. The job itself could be dangerous—such as police work or vice squad activity—but we probably like it that way. Still, it can be grueling to work in these locations—prisons, trauma units, undercover operations, drug enforcement agencies, psychiatry wards, archeological digs, even tax agencies like the IRS. We unconsciously go where trouble goes. The healing profession may especially be a field in which we can do some transformative work by serving physically or psychologically-troubled clients or patients, as long as we don't become fanatical about performing our services.

Work is also hell when ruthless office politics override ethics and justice, especially when we feel pressured or coerced to silently go along with these despicable tactics—if we want to avoid getting the ax ourselves. We usually see the problem slowly but insidiously taking shape, perhaps over several years—misused power takes its time to corrupt. Things can get treacherous if we express our dissatisfaction to the wrong people, who may interpret our remarks as a sign of disloyalty or subversive temperament. When the air grows thick and suffocating, it's time to leave this madness behind and move to higher ground. We'll only compound our problems if we convince ourselves that we must endure such darkness in order to grow or burn off karma. Why torture ourselves like this? Maybe we have hidden reasons that need to be unveiled. Some honest soul-searching may decode this on-the-job mystery.

PRIVATE WORK

The upbeat side of this transit is that we eventually find work to which we can totally devote ourselves, and that empowers us as well as the people affected by our service. We could attract dedicated coworkers who are living examples of the power of transformation and renewal. Hopefully, these are people whose depth and integrity make our job easier. For some of us, a more ideal work set-up would be a job where privacy is underscored and nobody invades our territory. We may wish we could close ourselves off from all needless distractions and put our full, laser-beam focus on the work that we love. We certainly don't need the melodramatics of an undisciplined workplace, where strong but self-centered personalities clash and create tension in our surroundings.

Therefore it would be good to consider what we can do to be our own boss and run our own business. We need to reclaim our power in this area of life. Self-employment can provide a measure of control. Reclaiming power also means having the courage to do everything for ourselves to ensure career survival, although taking such steps could put us in contact with any lingering fears of inadequacy. Still, with Pluto's guidance, we find that we are more resourceful than we ever imagined, and more determined to make a success of any entrepreneurial adventure. Although we may allow this topic to obsess us, what is critically important is to eventually come up a winner while doing work we love. Some of us also want to leave a long-lasting legacy of our work to future generations—especially if what we do already has broad social implications.

HEAL THYSELF

If health problems become recurrent issues during this transit, it's Pluto's way of saying that we've spent years unknowingly polluting our inner self. Now toxins must be released on all levels to restore body-and-soul harmony. Plutonian symptoms—when they are not buried deep within, insidiously undermining proper functioning—can erupt with fury on the skin in the form of angry-looking dermatological problems, or stubborn ones like fungus growth and psoriasis; even scary ones like dreaded melanomas. These symptoms seem to show a willful resistance that make them hard to treat and cure. They resist attack, but that's how you know they're of Plutonian origin. We don't have to go through physical crises to get in touch with our Pluto transit. Yet if we do, a lot of inner soul work urgently needs to be done while doctors and alternative health practitioners work to eradicate our physical ailments. Just medicating the symptoms will do little to cleanse the emotional wounds that are a part of our lack of wellness.

Transiting Pluto gets us to start distrusting medical or psychological authorities. We will want to do our own research, once we become fearful enough about impending consequences. This could be great if we don't go to extremes or reject all conventional remedies. Sometimes, a simple antibiotic does the trick better and quicker than a few weeks of trying to gulp down aloe vera juice! However, strictly allopathic means lack the holistic approach that benefits many Plutonian diseases. Even if the diagnosis is cancer, this transit will magnetize us toward those brave helpers on the planet who will teach us about respect for the body, emotional self-love, and the all-important need to release the hatred and bitterness we've managed to hold on to, perhaps since a traumatic childhood (although this is certainly not the only reason why people develop lethal tumors). We'll probably learn to be mindful of what we eat and how we best can nourish ourselves in many other ways as well.

Even if we are not wracked with aggravating symptoms, Pluto can urge us to learn about what we can do to stay well. Self-help takes the form of exercise, yoga, self-hypnosis, deep sleep techniques, more veggies and fruit in our diet, vitamin and mineral supplements, herbal remedies—and anything else designed to add physical stamina. Most important is learning how to handle whatever happens in our world with the serenity that transforms us, once we tap into our core source of inner strength and power. If we truly each have specific jobs to do on Earth, one job in our Sixth House is to make sure that we remain physically and mentally fit. It's then that our highest goals have much better chances of succeeding. Our Pluto transit helps to make this a living reality.

PLUTO/EARTH MERCURY TRANSITS

GREEK TOUR GUIDE

Mythic Mercury (as Hermes) had an interesting sideline job: he guided the souls of the deceased to the Underworld, although we don't know if he handed out pamphlets clearly explaining that this was a non-refundable, one-way trip! None of the other Olympians dared to set foot in Hades because they thought Pluto was a creep. Besides, they were scared of him. Therefore, Zeus hired curious but neutral Mercury to act as a go-between. When Mercury provided this special service, descending into the realm below with the recently dead, he was known as Infernal Hermes.[1]

Mercury played a recognized role in our soul's transition process: first he negotiated with that death-warmed-over ferryman, Charon, who then transported newly-arrived souls across the River Styx and into the darker regions of Hades—all for a cover charge! My guess is that Mercury probably had to double-check and make sure that each soul of the dead had the requisite coin in his or her mouth, which would be collected by miserly Charon before his ferry took off. Those with no money would be left stranded and "gibbering" at the river's bank.[2] I would bet that clever Mercury brought along a few extra coins—just in case—to stop that dang, nerve-racking gibbering if nothing else! This facet of the Hermes/Mercury mythological profile hints at earth Mercury's function in astrology. This god offered a specialized service—doing "the dirty work"—that the denizens of lofty Mount Olympus would never want to handle themselves.

OH YEAH?...PROVE IT

Earth Mercury represents Virgo-like qualities at work involving traits less speedy and restless than those belonging to air Mercury—but not that much less speedy. Earth Mercury functions in a practical, intelligent way when serving well-defined purposes. It appreciates having "just the facts"—an unvarnished assessment of reality unembellished by emotion, faith, or intuition. It acts as cool, collected, and humorless as a chemical engineer at work. The earthy side of Mercury is as brainy as its airy side, but hardly can be accused of being scattered or distractible. Harnessing mental power is one of its prime talents.

In this transit, we are urged to apply theory sensibly; if we can't, theory becomes useless and discardable. Air Mercury would argue that any unworkable but *interesting* concept is nonetheless valuable, even if only for its thought-provoking stimulation. Ideas don't always have to be grounded in concrete actuality to be worthwhile. Yet earth Mercury insists that its data be backed by solid evidence that can be repeated and made reliably useful. This leads to the development of techniques upon which we can be depend. It also tells us that earth Mercury symbolizes the skeptical side of our mentality, urging us to carefully evaluate information and put it to the test.

Total Focus

During this transit, we desire total focus. We can accomplish much once we realize that we can't afford to waste time and energy on nonsense. We probably don't feel stimulated by casual pursuits, nor do we want to proceed at a leisurely mental pace. Pluto is a hard-driving influence. We're even willing to fix our attention on a central project rather than spread our interests all over the map. This allows us to be single-minded and purposeful. Our ability to concentrate can be awesome. We feel driven to studiously probe matters that are utterly vital to us and, perhaps later, important to the world as well.

Often, with the square or the opposition, we are focused too much and are too ready to shut out environmental distractions, including people. We want to be left alone to intellectually delve into complex issues. Even talking to others on a mundane level may seem to be a nuisance. Silence is more appealing. We seek to remain in uninterrupted, deep thought. This is obviously a great transit for serious research. The sextile can be particularly good for stimulating curiosity and the willingness to organize the information we unearth. With earth Mercury involved, we'll want to put our attention more on external tasks than on inner development. However, some of us will still feel driven to work on ourselves by polishing our mental skills and having deep psychological dialogues with ourselves.

One problem with this transit is that we can become too grim-faced and solemn about everything, giving us a heavy quality that doesn't work well in social situations. We want to compulsively talk about whatever we are studying, even if the subject is too specialized and technical for others to appreciate. Our over-disciplined mind becomes impatient with chit-chat and small talk. We could even come off as aloof. It's probably best not to force ourselves to be gregarious at this time. We are into a "loner" stage and feel the need to isolate ourselves from standard mainstream activities. Privacy becomes more important than ever. Some of us will probably screen every phone call that comes through our answering machine to make sure that we won't be talking to major time-wasters.

SABOTAGE

We all have a capacity to apply logic and reason to our lives so that we can bring order and organization to our daily experience. But let's not overdo it. Pluto's transit tends to emphasize the nit-picky quality of earth Mercury, because Pluto also likes to analyze situations to death and uncover how things actually work. In-depth communication is not our major motivation (that's Pluto/air Mercury's challenge). However, being clear and accurate in our communications is critical at this time—so much so that we could become wary about what we say and to whom, especially if we know we haven't done our homework or researched our subject matter thoroughly, or simply if we don't trust the person to whom we're talking, especially at our workplace.

At this time, deliberately distorted information can be used as a weapon against us—a smear campaign, in some cases (although sometimes we're the ones trying to dig up a little dirt on others).

We can't stop people from being devious, but we can protect our-selves by being precise and factual. We may need to have solid proof of what we wrote or said or did if we wish to avoid misrepresentation. Otherwise, crafty backstabbers may be waiting in the wings to destroy our credibility. At least, we may be suspicious enough to think so. Obviously this is a smart time to keep impeccable tax records and other financial documents (Pluto's domain). Complications can be avoided if we discipline ourselves to be orderly with our business and legal paperwork. It's vital to be organized during this time, because efficiency works in our favor.

Should we give in to the temptation to be untruthful, perhaps by becoming tight-lipped, Pluto has a way of cornering us in an attempt to make us confess (we attract straightforward, intrusive people who "interrogate" us); yet our strategy is to cover up and play dumb. Later, when the facts surface, we can look pretty conniving and untrustworthy if we knew more than we conveyed. At the time we are keeping our lips sealed, it seems as if our self-preservation is at stake—silence is golden and the less said, the better. Pluto is trying to force the facts out of Mercury, but we're afraid that those facts could prove disruptive to the order and control we try so hard to maintain.

By the way, air Mercury probably would never clam up like this. It would either compulsively talk itself into a more convoluted predicament or shrewdly talk itself out of any looming complication. This facet of Mercury is quicker at thinking on its feet than earth Mercury, who needs time to mull things over. Air Mercury is better at spotting readily available escape hatches, while less-impulsive earth Mercury typically gets stuck holding the bag!

X-RAY VISION

With Pluto, it's hard not to turn on our sensory depth-awareness when observing a multitude of things going on around us. Both sides of Mercury excel at scanning the environment and making mental connections. However, earth Mercury is better at retaining details; images sink in and settle there for a while, giving us a better opportunity to analyze situations from all sides. If we have shown a superficial interest in life—knowing just enough to coast on its surface—now's a time when we're more reflective and willing to dig deeper. We feel an urge to penetrate to the core of any condition that captures our attention. We're looking for less obvious meanings and are able to interpret subtleties.

It is unlikely that we can be easily fooled by others during this transit, which is one benefit of being detail conscious. We see through certain people and their manipulation games (Pluto/air Venus transits also share this ability). We probably speak more carefully to those we don't know, if we feel the need to speak at all (such "strangers" could also be family members with whom we've always had trouble relating). In many ways, it's a time to listen, not talk, and to draw information out of others rather than tell them all we know. With a transiting sextile or trine, others will want to unload a few secrets anyway.

This X-ray vision can help us to become uncannily accurate about other people's motivations. Maybe we also are drawn to self-help books and articles that give us clues about how to figure out what makes us and others tick. Some of us may consider going back to school to get a degree in psychology. Studying the criminal mind may intrigue us. Any branch of the medical field is also a possibility. Taking a few classes in mind power and hypnosis might be very appealing. We might even be enthralled exploring the mysteries of science.

Earth Mercury wants us to study subjects that later have practical use, such as in our career. Pluto won't steer us toward interests that ultimately are dead end roads. If the subject matter doesn't arouse real passion in us from the beginning, we won't be giving it our all, anyway. In real life, however, sometimes other people who have control over us can sidetrack us. We can detour from our own path and instead find ourselves stuck following theirs, usually in an aggravating, second-fiddle capacity. We'll need to have a long, hard talk with ourselves about why we let that happen to us, especially if it happens again and again.

TOO STRICT

Even if we do have serious, inner reviews about why we may not feel quite alive and well during this time, we'll need to be careful not to be brutal in our self-analysis. Earth Mercury, like Virgo, can act like an uptight correctional officer, with Pluto ready to play the role of cruel warden. We can come down hard not only on ourselves, but on those who dare to make inconvenient mistakes. We can be peevish and irritable, especially when undergoing the opposition, as we project our hidden mental deficiencies onto others, and then try to control and even punish them. Sometimes we punish others by withholding speech, remaining stone-silent for long periods of time, which they find excruciating (in contrast, Pluto activating our air Mercury side suggests that we punish by spewing words that sting).

Earth Mercury by itself can have a problem with wanting to be right about everything. We can be too eager to pounce on people's ideas that don't match our own or that seem half-baked. We can be a fiend for thoroughness and preparation at this time, egged on by extremist Pluto. This is a sign that the closet dictator in us is coming out, trying to get the upper hand by policing what other people think and say—this trait can become a source of fierce arguments, during which neither side capitulates.

We also may be needlessly strict with ourselves, trying to clamp down on invading thoughts that seem a bit too dark and uncomfortable to entertain. Any form of Principle Six (Virgo, Sixth House, earth Mercury) can try to censor material that it considers objectionable. This is a big mistake with such a Pluto transit. Raunchy sexual images, even those of a hateful, murderous nature that spontaneously surface, may need to be ventilated rather than pushed farther down into our unconscious swamplands, where they become even more deformed and twisted. While such thoughts and images may shock us, especially if we overvalue "living in the universal Light," they could nonetheless represent powerful energies that have been repressed for too long. No healing can occur until our darker creatures of the mind rise from their swamps and break through to our conscious realm.

Actually, this could be a smart time to solicit our air Mercury ability to have an open dialogue with these otherwise revolting mental images. Why wait until we are forced to deal with them in our dream state, where they may act out in even scarier, more dramatic ways? Besides, air Mercury doesn't mind chatting with anybody! Perhaps we find that we are able to adapt to these images, making them seem less horrible and alien. This helps us to own up to and integrate their frightening energy. It's typical of earth Mercury to be obsessive, rejecting certain material outright, but then wanting to review it again and again in order to understand it.

This is the side of Mercury that would worry about how unclean and shameful taboo thoughts can be. But wise Pluto knows that much of what is now erupting was first born of unresolved pain that lead to scars we buried long ago. Maybe we need to engage both sides of our Mercury to find out more about the source of our otherwise troubling imagery. It's a good time to keep an uncensored journal and write down everything that disturbs us.

MIND MAGIC

It would be misleading to talk about Pluto/earth Mercury transits without mentioning the transformative power they can have on our everyday thinking. We may end up feeling uplifted, although not in an idealized, Jupiterian manner. We may have survived mind-altering challenges—or health concerns—that now make each new day special. There's less and less that we take for granted as a result. Our ability to cope with whatever the Universe throws at us is truly remarkable. We become resilient and wisely adaptable to change, keeping our thought patterns in a continuous state of renewal regardless of our true age. Pluto has bestowed treasures that are not to be taken lightly. Our resulting wealth of in-depth awareness is something that can support us, as well as empower those we serve and heal, for many years to come.

NOTES

1. Freda Edis, *The God Between: A Study of Astrological Mercury,* Arkana/Penguin Books, NY, 1995, p. 84.

2. Charles Mills Gayley, *The Classic Myths in English Literature and in Art,* Ginn & Company, Atlanta, 1939, p. 47.

CHAPTER TWELVE

PLUTO TRANSITING THE SEVENTH HOUSE

DEEPEST BOND

When transiting Pluto enters our Seventh House, life creates reasons for us to thoroughly examine our most intimate partnerships. We've spent many years, with Pluto in our Sixth, learning to deepen our observational and analytical powers, with a keen eye toward ridding ourselves of whatever doesn't work. We've zeroed in on the reasons why parts of our life have misfired. Now our attention turns to marriage and to the ideal of sharing ourselves with another. If we are currently married, the underlying strength of our union will be tested—sometimes by tensional external elements that seem beyond our control, but more often by internal pressures that we've kept hidden and unaddressed for many years. How bonded are we to our mate? What is the real substance of our marriage? How do we *really* feel about each other, deep down inside? Could we live without each other if we had to?

If our bond is deep and not based on romantic fantasies or societal expectation, but on the fact that we've candidly revealed our authentic selves to one another as time has passed, Pluto will spend the next several years consolidating the strengths of our marriage, helping us to find empowering ways to pool our resources and make this union an even more enriching experience. Our level of shared honesty and commitment rises to greater heights. We find different ways to re-energize each other. It all sounds like a super "shot in the arm" of vitality for our relationship. The deeper we go with Pluto, the more soul-connected we can feel with one another. We deeply appreciate knowing our mate and sharing our intimate space. However, this is *not* how Pluto unfolds in the beginning for most of us married folk. Ah, we should have known that things could never be that simple with Pluto designing the game plan!

Big Showdown

Some of us, by temperament, are easy-going and have a knack for making the best of any uncomfortable situation in life. We rely on positive thinking and good will to avoid the unpleasant potholes and bumps on life's sometimes rocky road. We've managed, up until this point, to not get side-swiped by Mars or pulled over and fined by Saturn or Pluto for various violations. One would think that this upbeat approach to better living would be our best way to deal with Pluto going through our Seventh (or through any life zone in our chart). That's not the case. Being too cheery about our existing partnership or handing our marital troubles over to the Universe for repair leaves us susceptible to having the ground suddenly split wide open and swallow us whole. If that happens, it's a good bet that we'll be unwillingly heading toward our inner Hades, that dreaded abyss of our personal unconscious.

Why should this happen to us when we've spent so much energy being kind and good to others? Pluto knows that we're clueless about how mean, cruel, or manipulative we can be in our darker moments and wants to destroy our naiveté—our unexamined innocence. By taking inventory of the darker rooms of our depths, Pluto realizes that we've been stockpiling an arsenal of secret weapons for eventual retaliation. We've been getting ready to angrily redress our oldest wounds and pains—perhaps going as far back as the day we were born and found ourselves trapped in flesh, or even back to stormier lives before this one. Maybe this explains why newborns cry so ferociously.

This transit is a matter of facing up to what's going on "down below" inside us when it comes to our marriage partner and even to the concept of marriage itself. We may be forced to confront ourselves in ways that make us squirm. We may also make our partner writhe as we strip our marriage of its major illusions. Pluto compels us to drink truth serum and, after a few sips, we find we can no longer tolerate keeping in feelings that continue to corrode our identity. If it's false, it must be wiped out—that's Pluto's way. It all depends on how awful our marriage has become.

SCENES FROM A ROTTEN MARRIAGE

Many of us may not feel that we are having severe marital problems, even when Pluto is knocking on the door of our Seventh House. Still, there could be one or two sore spots that we'll have to work to resolve during the next several years. These are usually in areas where we diametrically oppose one another and have our strongest bones of contention. The fact that Pluto first makes an opposition to our Ascendant while entering our Seventh suggests that *we,* more than our mate, may stir up things that have had a long and bothersome history in our existing partnership.

Our identity is ready for a revitalizing facelift, or a complete overhaul, if necessary. Such personal, inner changes create reverberations in our marriage that lead to a period of agitation, which could be healthy. This type of friction provokes honest dialogue about the kind of people we've both turned out to be since our relatively innocent newly-wed stage. We'll have to be careful how we handle this sometimes radical phase of self-revelation, because we can go to extremes in our response to the many ways we've outgrown one another.

However, before we get to the point in our union where we're willing to review pressing issues and air our pent-up feelings, some of us may realize that we're living with someone who's making our life miserable. It's rare that we'll be objective enough to admit that we are making our partner unhappy, as well. All that we know is that there's too much awkward silence at inappropriate times, as we project unappealing Plutonian traits onto our mate, making him or her the one who willfully holds back feelings. Yet at times, we may have periodic screaming matches that sound like two outraged eagles in battle. Of course, we'd probably see ourselves as the proud but wounded eagle, while our partner becomes the crafty vulture, forever picking at us!

Each of us is subject to having the touchiest parts of our nature provoked, sometimes resulting in hidden anger and resentment shooting hot gases to the surface that can burn and sting our partner. Grievances over sex or finances may become obsessive for at least one of us. So far, none of this is what I'd consider to be bad news, because we're now less willing to hold back whatever needs to be expressed and shared. However, our internal waters are just starting to boil.

The part of Pluto's volatile transit that screams "rotten marriage" comes when one of us underhandedly betrays the other. We do it, we rationalize, to take control over our life in an attempt to satisfy frustrated desires that have been thwarted by our mate. Hurting another may be more intentional that it seems—the offending partner must pay a price. We could be the culprit here, justifying our actions all the way, maybe because we see ourselves as desperately trapped in a no-win situation with a difficult spouse who drains us like a bloodsucker. Perhaps we've grown to loathe the weaknesses in our mate which make him or her exceedingly unattractive in our eyes. Our partner may disgust us for reasons only our unconscious knows. Yet we feel too entangled by circumstantial complications to just call it quits and make a clean break. We also worry that our partner could penalize us for leaving him or her (especially financially). This, ironically, implies that we sense that our spouse is actually more powerful and threatening than we'd care to admit.

If it's our partner who betrays us, the issue is usually infidelity. It seems that all of the Outer Planets going through our Seventh impel us or our mate to seek out new people who show us different ways of being. They become our agents for the disruption that often triggers our needed transpersonal changes. We act as if under the influence of forces mightier than either our ego or our will. This gives these transits the feeling of fate intervening and messing with our normal life patterns. In this case, our mate could feel a compulsion to explore a union about which we know nothing, because it is kept tightly under wraps. At some dramatic point, the sordid facts are exposed and we find ourselves reeling from the sneaky subplots involved. Our bond is now broken in the deepest way, and it's unlikely that our wounded heart will be repaired. We may find that we now hate our spouse, and inner rage takes the place of our hurt and grief.

Let's say that things break down totally, with no chance of reconciliation. At the time of our potentially nasty divorce, Pluto ensures that one of us can play rough and dirty and be quite unyielding. Attorneys hired use tough strategies designed to ambush the other side. One of us could be afraid that we'll end up weakened by the experience. It's doubtful that this hair-pulling marriage will end in a quick or easy manner. Neither side is willing to give in an inch, especially if transiting Pluto squares or opposes someone's natal Mars or Saturn. It's very Plutonian to have such matters drag on for so long that they force us to deeply feel the transitions through which we're passing. Maybe this is so that we never repeat our mistakes in a future marriage—that is, unless this experience has cured us of the belief that being married is vital to our happiness.

PLUTO TIMES TWO

What if we are not married, and never have been, but are itching to change all that? Just before Pluto enters our Seventh, we may have spent many of our adult years studying other people who are married (a common pastime for single individuals). We've envied the "good" marriages and winced when witnessing the "bad" ones. We may even have read plenty of self-help material on the subject and attended a lecture or workshop here and there—that is, if we are hopeful that we will eventually make this commitment ourselves. Of course, the longer we wait, the scarier the prospect becomes. It's sometimes easier to take the plunge during young adulthood when we know less about who we are. Our innocence at that time makes us bold and filled with hope.

However, now that Pluto is transiting this house, a lot of soul-searching is forcing us to face up to inner realities that may explain how and why we've manage to block all chances for matrimony in the past. Even if weird twists of fate have been partly to blame (our spouse-to-be dies a week before the wedding day), there are also unconscious reasons why things haven't worked out, assuming that we've tried our best to establish serious companionship. A few of us have deliberately avoided intimate relations, allowing powerful fears to keep us from making contacts that could result in marriage or its equivalent. That's really why we have been so alone. However, most of us feel sure that we've searched for our ideal partner and just haven't gotten lucky yet.

This pattern is apt to change due to Pluto's transformational magic. Pluto is willing to work with us if marriage is what we truly want—we must first ask ourselves that profoundly important question—and if we are willing to dig deep to reach the source of our insecurities and hidden problems regarding our trust in others (we may see people as more likely to hurt than heal us). We'll need to go through an alchemical phase, during which the energy that we've been feeding to our hang-ups is transmuted into a surplus of irresistible magnetism, probably after we undergo an emotional period of purging and cleansing. This all sounds good, but it's often difficult to see the naked and sometimes unflattering truth about ourselves. Years of this transit may pass before we enjoy the pay-off that comes when our rigorous inner work is done. Unfortunately, some of us may be tempted to give up too soon after attracting a few "weird" Plutonians during our early transitional stages.

How weird? If we're not on the right track with our death-and-rebirth patterns of self-unfoldment, we can attract someone who possesses the power that we still don't recognize as also dwelling with us. That alone might make our attraction too compelling to resist. Our partner has plenty of charisma and sex appeal, but also is troubled by his or her own shadowy parts. This makes him or her inscrutable at key moments in our relationship and, therefore, emotionally inaccessible. Perhaps our partner is also someone who takes more than gives, and easily trespasses into our psyche to steal our energy and autonomy.

Violence can be an issue. We may discover that we're dealing with a time-bomb temperament, easily triggered to explode over even minor incidences. Pathological lying leading to major betrayal is another possibility, as is being ripped-off in innumerable ways. We'll need to be especially careful of this scenario when Pluto squares or opposes our natal Mars, Saturn, or Uranus (particularly when we already feel that we want little to do with incorporating these three planets into our nature). Altogether, the picture painted here is not healthy and certainly not empowering. It's enough to make us want to crawl back into our hole and forget about wanting a significant other.

Trial and error is the name of the game with Pluto at this stage. Once we realize that no one is to have ultimate power over us, we approach new relationships differently. We send out strong signals from the beginning, informing the other person that we are not going to be abused, we have our own trusty power source, and we will firmly deal with behavior on anyone's part that is dishonorable and demeaning. We will simply abort such a union and make no excuses. Some of us already know exactly how important it is not to surrender too much of our will and ego to another. We have to be accepted by our partner as equally worthy and important. It would help, though, if we stop acting as if we're in constant awe of this person's established power base.

There is a chance that we have tried everything and still can't attract a decent companion. In that case, forcing the issue has gotten us nowhere. So let's quit for a while and go underground to rest. Celibacy is an option for a few of us. Keeping a low social profile helps as well, because the people we currently tend to attract can complicate our lives (even in non-sexual unions). We may need quality time alone to reflect—something we may not have had before—in order to heal from the effects of a turbulent or self-destructive past.

POWER TO THE PEOPLE

While we can go underground to restore our internal balance, we can't stay there forever, isolated from mundane human experience. When we eventually emerge and move out into the day-to-day world, we may find we can be a source of strength and a role model of self-discipline for others, including our closest friends and business partners (Seventh-House people). As we effectively process our Plutonian cycle of renewal, the results spill over into the lives of those close to us and those who seek our advice (how we affect our business clients becomes a Seventh-House matter). People perceive that we are loaded with in-depth understanding of life's more complex issues. No big surprise; we think we know how we got that way!

We'll have to be careful that people don't project onto us the image of an all-knowing one who has unlimited power to help them. Maybe they're a bit too awestruck regarding our perceptive skills. They won't grow from clinging to such an interpretation of us, and besides, we can't be plugging into our Plutonian power all the time (it's too intense). Maybe we need to quietly listen rather than immediately try to fix others with our assortment of potent, surgical psycho-tools. Otherwise, we can appear to be superhuman and above ordinary mortal predicaments. The danger is of becoming a power-freak who knows that we can captivate, even seduce the wills of others much too easily. This transit is therefore a test of our character and integrity in all interpersonal relationships.

PLUTO/AIR VENUS TRANSITS

PHONY BALONEY?

This transit demonstrates how Pluto deals with deepening our values in love and other social relationships. The airy side of Venus is concerned with people more than with coveting possessions or achieving financial security (which are earth Venus interests). Much about this facet of Venus is learned by observing society and conforming to behavior that is considered acceptable, polite, and civilized. There are benefits to be had from such social conduct, because being considerate of others endears us to them and persuades them to assist us in our needs. This Venus operates in a style similar to Libra's approach to life—which can be contrived at times—rather than along more basic Taurean principles, which are grounded in earthier instincts free of social pretenses.

Earth Venus deals with how we relate to the physical world in personal and subjective ways, typically according to our body's direct sensory experience of our immediate environment. Air Venus encourages awareness of the outer appearance of ourselves and others in social settings; it employs less-subjective methods to evaluate our human experience, in addition to our instinctive response to physical stimulation. We learn to cultivate our air Venus mannerisms and are aware of the effect they have on others.

Pluto is harsh in its treatment of phoniness, especially when the source of artificiality can be traced back to cultural programming, unconscious or otherwise. The air Venus part of us is specifically concerned with making a good surface impression in hopes of being well-regarded, approved of, and liked by all. We use our air Venus energy to gain social acceptance and harmonize our relations. However, we sometimes do this with insincerity disguised as cordial diplomacy, which suspicious Pluto interprets as a convenient way to lie for the sake of social advancement. We sell a bit of our soul just to make it in the world. We flatter others, they like it, and we eventually gain clout and accessibility within desirable ranks of society. All of this works as long as we never run into die-hard Plutonians who refuse to play our phony little social-climbing game. Unfortunately, with this transit, Plutonians are the *only* types we seem to encounter. They're also the only types we're interested in, as we will find out.

Pluto knows that we've got as much dirty laundry to hide as anybody else. This planet will disclose our foibles unrelentlessly if we shallowly insist on judging quality and value based on outer packaging. When Pluto transits Venus, one of the things under attack is our hypocrisy (assuming that we are showing a favorable but unsustainable image to the world). We can't live it out because it has little to do with who we really are and what we really desire for ourselves. As a result, this transit could symbolize a time that's ripe for scandal. Maybe some of us are not as squeaky clean as our carefully crafted image. Pluto loves to bring hypocrites down from their lofty perches, especially if they've been sanctimonious. For this to happen, all it takes is involvement with one tantalizing but undermining Plutonian—or even one angry opponent whose power we've underestimated. Public opinion can change drastically, for the worst, when our bad press erupts for the world to learn about.

POWER LOVER

Sometimes falling heavily in love during this transit feels like being possessed by someone who spends a lot of time "down under"—and I don't mean in Sydney, Australia! This is especially common if we're *under*going the opposition—an aspect that brings emotional intensity to the surface due to our enthrallment with a sexy, sizzling-hot somebody. Our secret buttons may be pushed in all the right ways, and we feel turbo-charged and highly aroused. We're alive and well, all right, although feverish with passion and a little concerned that we're losing control. We're willing to throw caution to the wind. We've attracted this Plutonian and cannot get him or her out of our mind, nor do we wish to. Assuming the attraction is mutual (and God forbid if it isn't), we may think that we have met *the* love of our life. Our future possibilities with this person are tremendously important to us. This is not a romance we wish to mangle by showing how psychologically messed up, weak-willed, or fear-based we can be. Our urge is to give it all we've got—and then some.

Who is this extraordinary person we're going gaga over (although "gaga" in a quiet, smoldering way)? He or she could be a highly capable, multi-talented renaissance individualist who oozes self-confidence and delectable sensuality. Later we may discover that we're actually dealing with a moody Phantom of the Opera! Time will tell if this affair's going to be a "magnificent obsession" or a psychological horror story. Inner strength in others will be attractive to us at this time, perhaps because we're learning to develop it for ourselves. Lovers who are cool and self-possessed are appealing, because we are drawn to their air of mystery. We may realize that our special someone has a great sexual appetite; no problem, because we're feeling rather hungry, as well. A conjunction, square, or opposition transit intensifies these traits.

Sexual energy can be the basis for much of what is exchanged in this love affair. However, air Venus begs to differ, claiming that it prefers to take a cerebral, sophisticated approach to the ideal of love. Pluto knows better. Pluto realizes that we need to experience the root power of our sexuality through an all-consuming relationship that goes beyond the dictates of socially approved behavior. Our affair has primal undertones that can both frighten and excite us. This shouldn't imply that there's something immoral about our activities. Pluto sees nothing wrong with a heavy emphasis on the erotic. Lust is just another type of high-grade fuel for Pluto. Some of us—maybe because of our early upbringing—could be in a state of conflict about surrendering to our passions. However, trying to stamp out strong sexual impulses during a Pluto transit usually backfires; we may explode out of control in another life area because of frustrated desire. It's better to learn how to create mutual empowerment in our relationship, both sexually and psychologically, in ways that encourage a non-judgmental openness on our part.

ON THE SKIDS?

What if we're married while Pluto transits Venus, evoking its airy side? If it's a conjunction, trine, or sextile that we're enjoying, we can tap into new veins of love-energy. Life may set up situations in which the expression of love soothes and heals our existing relationships, taking them to new levels of intimacy and mutual caring. Most marriages could benefit from such a depth of loving. We can find one another immensely valuable in ways unacknowledged before. Our partner may even be the one to generate deeper affection, strengthening our mutual commitment and encouraging a profound respect for one another. It would be transformative if we could both use this period to become more accepting of each other's all-too-human flaws and defects. Pluto doesn't always mean tearing things apart just to rebuild; here the lesson could be one of developing a loving tolerance.

With the square or the opposition, we still can experience all of the above, but much more effort, and lots of give-and-take on both parts, is required. The flaws and defects that we criticize in each other seem to bother us too much at this point. Worse, they seem unfixable (maybe because our willful behavior thwarts mutual cooperation). If we have any ideas about playing the make-over artist who totally remodels our mate, we could encounter tremendous resistance and a heap of resentment. While the urge to improve our marriage is commendable, the tactics we or our spouse use can be coercive. When we push too hard and disregard fair play, and our efforts arouse a combative response. We also could engage in "cold war" strategies, in which both of us defensively freeze over to emotionally shut each other out—behavior that can be followed by underground blasts of rage brought about by seemingly minor triggers.

Love can be on the skids when one of us starts to hate—not just dislike—things about the other. Compulsive and unfulfilling sex may replace the love-making we once freely shared. After a point, sex itself becomes the source of our power struggles. Withdrawal from physical contact altogether is another way to punish our partner, and vice versa. None of this is ultimately satisfying as a revenge tactic, because we are left feeling empty inside. Pluto's double-edged sword wounds us as we wound others. Reason is bypassed in favor of complex emotional release. One of us has become uncontrollable at the expense of the other, but once we're at this point, nobody's interested in damage control.

Another area where conflict abounds can be that of joint financial holdings. We may not like the current situation in our marriage regarding how money is spent or who controls the purse strings. Air Venus advocates democratic treatment. However, with Pluto involved, one of us could exhibit a take-over mentality and forcefully try to manage the way income is saved or spent (it's hard not to have a few earth-Venus issues creep into the picture). Pluto itself deals with pooled resources and the battles that they create. Money can be used as a bargaining chip or as that which financially holds another person hostage in a relationship.

The square, quincunx, or opposition can symbolize financial feuds that turn ugly during divorce proceedings. If evolutionary growth means anything to us, we'll need to make sure that greed and spite don't undermine our integrity, no matter how far downward our marriage has spiraled. Ivana Trump was having transiting Pluto squaring her Venus during the thick of her marital troubles with "the Donald." She was already born with a natal Pluto/Venus opposition, meaning that she'd be attracted to a mate with significant money or power, but also with a capacity for betrayal. She apparently handled her difficult transition well, once she realized that she *had* to let go of this relationship and get on with her life.

'TIL DEATH DO US PART

It's usually not good form for astrologers to dwell on predicting physical death based on transits (or on any other forecasting technique). This is not just because a death prediction is a "bummer" for any client who wasn't asking to hear it, but because "death" operates on many levels—especially with Pluto in action. Astrologers feel on safer ground discussing the many psychological deaths that people can undergo, but sometimes that's not the only manifestation of this transit. During this period, we need to consider the fact that loved ones will some day die, and we can't do anything to stop it. What is our perspective on death, especially the death of those we personally know? This transit is a good time to explore this issue and examine ourselves to determine if we are psychologically braced to handle such a reality. This doesn't mean that transiting Pluto spells the death of one near and dear to us. However, it could, and we'll need to do some inner work at this time to emotionally prepare ourselves for such an experience.

Some of us may know this to be a distinct possibility because we are aware of a loved one who is already very sick and not expected to improve. Such Plutonian periods as this are great times to learn about the stages of the human dying process, brought to the world's attention by Plutonian pioneer Elisabeth Kübler-Ross.[1] It's Pluto's nature to make us deal squarely with conditions that are terminal and rarely subject to overnight miracles (although Pluto can be associated with the amazing but short-lived rallies undergone by people's bodies at critical times).

Many previously unspoken feelings can be revealed to our loved one during a Pluto/Venus transit. We can mutually forgive each other for past mistakes and hurts in our relationship. This transit provides cathartic relief. It urges us to connect with a loved one on a soul-to-soul level, which can have a tremendous impact on everyone involved. It's too bad that we wait until someone is near death's door to do this, but perhaps the impending finality of our relationship triggers this deep response. Understanding more about death rewards us with a greater appreciation of life and improves the quality we bring to all of our relationships.

COUNSELING THE WOUNDED

One excellent way to use any Pluto transit to our air Venus is to work with people who have been caught up in the turbulent waters of outraged emotion. Many of us have had at least a few things done to us in childhood that were terribly unfair—even unforgivable—yet those events don't tear us to pieces and destroy us in adulthood. For some, however, it's a different story, depending on the severity of the harm done. Pluto has a knack for ferreting out the dark secrets harbored by troubled people. Now we have a chance to help others feel alive and well, once they understand the source of their wounds. They may have pain in areas that are familiar to us. If we show an increased interest in human psychology during this transit, it's usually because we would like to know what makes those close to us behave the way they do; we may seek to heal certain parts of our existing relationships as a result.

Some of us feel an urge to become involved in whatever it takes to heal society, or at least our community. We could provide help involving grief counseling, hospice work, shelters for the battered, detoxification centers, gang violence, animal abuse, or similar worthy causes. People in crises may be moved by us, sensing our depth of commitment to heal and make whole broken members of society. Our honesty and human reality is evident to them, especially if we're experiencing the transiting trine or sextile.

We can find the intricacies of the human psyche fascinating at this time. However, rather than just read stacks of books on the subject (an air/earth Mercury option), we may attract people who teach us, first hand, about human complexity. Sometimes these people scare us, because their emotionality is so raw. Still, we're ready for them, even if, initially, we think we aren't. Before this transit is over, we may find that we simply cannot stand being around shallow people or those who have no burning interest in remedying human suffering.

More than just helping people help themselves, a few of us could feel that we're on a mission to make sure society transforms itself in ways that protect human dignity. It probably would take a conjunct, square, or opposition to get us involved in passing legislation that ensures the rights of the socially abused. The air side of Venus represents how balanced we are in our social expression, but Pluto can go to extremes. It's important not to get fanatical in our attitudes regarding the folks in our lives—those we love and those whose lives we help to improve.

NOTE

1. Elisabeth Kübler-Ross' birth chart can be found on page 130 in Donna Cunningham's *Healing Pluto Problems* (see Bibliography). Note Kübler-Ross' natal Pluto/Sun conjunction, with Pluto ruling her Eighth House, and squared her gutsy, pioneering Mars in Aries in her First. In addition, her Tenth-House ruler, Saturn, is in Scorpio in her Eighth, trining her Pluto.

CHAPTER THIRTEEN

PLUTO TRANSITING THE EIGHTH HOUSE

DARK ROAD HOME

It's homecoming time for Pluto, because the Eighth House is where the most profoundly life-altering themes of this planet are to be confronted. In this house, we have little choice but to visit our underworld to investigate any embedded thoughts and feelings that we've had trouble consciously accepting. We're highly susceptible to projecting shadow qualities onto others—we unconsciously pick them to play out our darker, unexamined side. We then struggle with these people when they effectively mirror back those qualities all too well.

There is a raw and primal reality about us in the Eighth that we've customarily learned to suppress and with which, therefore, we have failed to come to terms. Either we regard these facets of ourselves as being "bad" or else we're afraid they would overwhelm us, and others, if openly expressed. Yet true inner peace eludes us until we allow ourselves free access to these potent subterranean energies. The less we willingly recognize their existence, the more we jeopardize our psychological welfare.

What concerns us at the deeper layers of our Eighth contradicts the more presentable, sanitized image we display to the world and even to our Seventh-House partner. Pluto's transit puts pressure on all parties involved to uncover these guarded, private traits and validate their existence. Just being able to say, "Yes, this is a real part of what I am!" without the intervention of harsh self-judgment can start a process of internal healing that's been long overdue for some of us. Keeping vital facets of our inner nature disowned gives them great, destructive power over us, in a mysterious way that invites the unsettling workings of fate. Transiting Pluto here exposes, for the sake of our own well-being, much of what has dwelled too long in a state of darkness and ignorance.

What might we find here? If we have natal Eighth-House planets, this transit is a demonstration of Pluto's infamous tearing-down-and-rebuilding process. Each planet contacted will never be the same, once the transit is over. Change becomes permanent (which neither transiting Uranus nor Neptune guarantee). What we have to do to achieve a successful transformation is not going to be easy. It's not a simple matter of undergoing a few "positive" attitude adjustments. Pluto makes sure that we thoroughly and dramatically feel our transformations. Some of us are not prepared for that. Pluto takes us down haunted emotional paths that we've repeatedly avoided in the past. It's very likely that we'll have to examine hurtful material that we had hoped was buried for good. Yet Pluto knows that such buried hurts and pains, when unresolved, have a ghoulish life of their own that drains our psychic vitality. The energy trapped by such unventilated feelings is precisely what Pluto aims to release and recycle.

We can get a head start on this transit by admitting that we may still harbor grudges about harsh or traumatic incidences of our past—subconsciously, we don't forgive the people who have made life difficult for us, even if some of those people are now dead or otherwise out of our life. Our parents and our ex-partners become ready targets for our previously unaddressed fury. Now's the time to come clean with our true feelings.

We don't have to go berserk with rage upon discovering that we still have to attend to unfinished business, but a phase of moody introspection followed by dramatic spurts of outraged emotionalism is justified. As when swallowing a caustic poison, we must induce purging to release toxic psychological material. Pluto is the perfect planet for that. The rest of our chart will determine if we can endure this experience, or whether we'll be taken aback by it. Rational air and earth don't do as well expressing eruptive feelings as do volatile fire and water, two elements that could win awards in this area! However, Pluto loves awesome challenges and will not let up on us. In the long run, it will be for our own good to release whatever conflictive energies we've internalized.

EXPOSING MARITAL SECRETS

The strength of a marriage's intimacy is put to the acid test when Pluto transits this house. Marital situations or committed intimate relationships associated with our Eighth trigger deep needs that are not easily met. Shared financial concerns and the sexual dynamics of our union are two typical issues that demand sharper focus. Pluto is most interested in provoking that in which we have invested strong emotional energy. Our secret feelings about one another surface during this transit. However, despite our fears, these feelings don't have to destroy our partnership. Revealing important truths can clear the stagnant air and oxygenate our union to robust levels. What's so good about Pluto transiting our Eighth is the promise of new beginnings based on deep insights regarding past relationship problems.

If our marriage has been long frozen on some level, Pluto can thaw the ice. Raging fury expressed during no-holds-barred confrontations is not every couple's way to resolve matters, so other methods of getting our hidden material out in the open will need to be explored. In fact, if the transit forms a trine or sextile to a natal planet, we may discover creative ways to further empower our bond. We'll want to experience an intensity level that is reasonably manageable. A greater spirit of cooperation in unraveling what has bothered us about our union is also suggested. We can fortify what has already proven valuable to the integrity of our relationship.

If both of us are intellectually oriented (in other words, we like to read about how we're feeling), this could be a time when at least one of us stocks up on self-help books geared to facilitating a

clear exchange of emotions. This is our Pluto transit, not our partner's, so it would be good if *we* started to research the matter.
This is a non-threatening way to broach shared emotional concerns. If Pluto is undergoing tensional aspects, then our need to
be aware of the unhealthy parts of our union becomes more
urgent. However, talk and theorizing about matters that need to
be felt with instinctual passion and gut realism may not do the
trick. Marriage counseling might help, if *both* of us are ready to
heal our pain by first recognizing our capacity to hurt the ones we
love. We also need to realize that emotionally injured people can
be unconsciously vicious when provoked.

SEXUAL SABOTAGE

Sex becomes an easy way to manipulate or punish one another
during this time. It's also a way to indirectly attack someone who
has wounded us. Our Plutonian frustrations can lead to underhanded strategies. It's hard to tell who's being the most sexually
coercive in this case—the aggressor who wants to take pleasure
without first asking, or the withholder who refuses to give pleasure without ever explaining why. Both partners play a willful
game that becomes self-defeating in the long run. As an aggressor,
we give in to predatory instincts that can make us exceedingly
selfish in our compulsions to satisfy ourselves. As a withholder, we
can use chilliness and emotional distancing as a control tactic to
mask our build-up of lava-hot anger. The aggressor may not realize that making further wrong moves at this point could blow up
in his or her face, because the withholder is now ready to explode
and attack. Also, the attack is not necessarily physical.

We who withhold sexual energy are in trouble as well, because
too much deliberate self-restraint can damage intimacy beyond
repair. This transit could suggest the onset of sexual dysfunction
based on unexamined control issues. If we are not willing to talk
about why we're feeling cold or seemingly indifferent to sexual
contact, nobody will learn much in this marriage except how to
prolong mutual suffering. Pluto can penalize us for our dishonesty as well as for any cruelty we've shown. Sometimes, hidden

medical problems may affect our sexual functioning (assuming that we've not feeling cold or angry about our partner). The Plutonian rebirth that awaits us during this transit involves a rekindling of mutual passion—now based on newfound understanding and compassion—that helps to breathe new life into our approach to emotional intimacy. Now we can better tap into our regenerative powers within.

THE SINGLE SCENE

So far, our examples have been geared toward married people or others already seriously involved in a relationship. What if we are single, unattached adults during this transit? It becomes a time of sexual exploration, made more complicated than ever in today's world by the perils of transmittable diseases. AIDS has made us realize that sex can equal death (a very Plutonian death, at that). Preaching "safe" sex has made many of us more conscious of what we're doing while in the throes of heated passion, but it has also put a damper on erotic spontaneity. Still, sex has become a potentially life-or-death issue, and it's better to be safe than sorry.

Pluto's transit prompts us to be more thoughtful about sharing this personal experience of our body and emotions. Therefore, sexual irresponsibility (such as mindless promiscuity) must take a back seat. We are to ponder the meaning of sex means on its many levels. Pluto doesn't want us to be enslaved by driving, hormonal urges. However, any pressure to control our sexual appetite is not necessarily coming from a Saturnian point of view, which would introduce elements of guilt and shame. Transiting Pluto just wants us to exercise self-control to ensure that we'll be more in charge of our sexual energy (because discipline equals empowerment), and that's why being conscious and aware of what we're doing in the name of sex is so important at this time.

This advice sounds wise and mature, but our hormones can possess a defiant will of their own. Sex may be more appealing to some of us if certain expressions of it are deemed off-limits by society, or if an element of danger or risk is involved. This is where our Pluto transit has much work to do as we probe our sexual underground. This transit can help us to dig into the root causes of personal complexes and fixations that, when left unchecked, can create emotional difficulties later in our committed relationships. This is especially true when Pluto makes a transiting square, quincunx, or opposition. Some of us get to know about this darker side of ourselves by studying those we attract as our sexual partners—particularly the few of us who only pick married lovers, a situation that typically forces our romance to hide behind the scenes, away from the threat of unwanted exposure (making it a real Eighth-House experience).

We may literally get hot for those who are undergoing difficult transitions, because this gives us a excuse to help others reform their past and rebuild their future by making personality adjustments that allow for a new life. But Pluto also ushers in those with shady backgrounds or health crises, often due to self-abuse (compulsive behavior). We also may unconsciously be drawn to the intrigue offered by hidden affairs, knowing that we're engaging in something that's our delicious secret. Perhaps we deliberately pick those who are married as our way of controlling the situation: if they end up aggravating us too much—and they probably will—we can tell them in no uncertain terms to go back home to their spouse! We know that our lover is not exclusively ours, so this spares us from making a total commitment (something we have problems doing).

When our romantic interests become too complicated, especially when we end up feeling paranoid and untrusting, it's a sure sign that we are mishandling our Pluto transit. The degree of mutual manipulation and dishonesty involved in our relationship should tell us how poorly we've managed this transit. We need to keep things simple from the start, although Pluto doesn't appreciate simplicity and tranquillity, even in the best scenarios. It is advisable to read up on psychological material that specifically helps us to get a handle on various possible Plutonian issues before they crop up and make our life difficult (as well as the lives of people mysteriously drawn to us).

DEALINGS WITH DEATH

Pluto knows that the thought of loved ones—or ourselves—dying is not comfortable, yet these are years when we can develop the wisdom and inner strength we will need to handle periods when people (and pets) inevitably die. Perhaps someone important to us is already getting close to this transition, and we're very upset and conflicted about it. People born with Pluto in the Seventh or Eighth may have had time during their youth to "feel out" this issue. Therefore, when death visits them later in life, they seem more inwardly prepared to cope with it than the rest of us. They've had a greater opportunity to contemplate this final chapter of earthly life. Thoughts of death have likely been with natal Seventh- and Eighth-House Plutonians since childhood, perhaps backed by family traumas that made us face this reality at a tender age. This could include a nasty divorce that destroyed our family bond and made us a sought-after possession in a bitter custody battle.

Yet for many of us in the here-and-now, death is a dark intruder who completely shakes up our world and makes us rage against a seemingly heartless and unjust Universe. We can sink to the bottom of black despair and Plutonian depression when a loved one dies—especially if the circumstances are tragic—or we can do our proper mourning, then resurrect ourselves from our sorrow, sensing that no one we really love is dead, merely departed. If a good friend decides to visit a faraway land for a while, do we get hysterical about it and think we'll never see them again? No. Although we may miss them terribly, we feel assured we one day we will be reunited. Adopting this same attitude can empower us when a loved one dies, but we must embrace it emotionally, not just intellectually. A physical death experience is often the best way for this to occur. Our grief has to be real and come from our depths. A "near-death" experience, maybe during Eighth-House Plutonian surgery, can also be transformative.

One prediction here is that, yes, someone we're close to may indeed die during this transit. We shouldn't be too quick to view this as a "negative" experience to foresee, much less undergo. Of course, we can also encounter many other symbolic "deaths," such as the death of bitter feelings or unspoken resentments that have infiltrated our emotional system from long ago. To continue to attach ourselves to such poisoned attitudes can damage our physical well-being, so we'll need to interpret any disturbing bodily symptoms with this in mind. Maybe a personal health crisis is what the most fixated of us needs to open our eyes to this psychological reality.

Pluto passing through our Eighth is an excellent time to study the world's different concepts of death and the afterlife—from comparative religious to mythological or metaphysical beliefs. We will need to be armed with enlightenment to fight off our all-too-human fears and dreads. Plutonians don't waste too many tears at funerals, because they know that the essence of their loved one is not to be found with his or her physical remains in the cold ground. Who knows, if we work with Plutonian energy instead of fighting it, *we* could end up feeling quite alive and well, even after we die!

Sharing the Wealth

Both Pluto and the Eighth deal with the tricky issue of learning to share power and resources without resorting to dirty tactics. This is especially important for the Eighth House, where our challenge is to co-manage the material goods of close partnerships, marital and business alike. Pluto knows about the temptation of wealth and how it tests our character. We will be confronted with experiences that reveal our position on give-and-take situations. Are we greedy and self-serving? Or do we play fair and share freely? If some of us are chronic users, this becomes the transit that brings out that character flaw for others to see and condemn. Pluto means that it's time for major penalties to be meted out to those who have abusively ripped off others on some level, or tried to manipulate and control someone else's possessions with an iron fist. Cheating others, no matter how, will not go unnoticed at this time. Life will find a way to clamp down on dishonest and unethical practices, and that can refer to our partner or partners as well as ourselves.

In business relationships, we can have a driving urge to make big bucks by turning on our energy for productivity like never before. We can also network with those who have clout and resources to strengthen us. Risk-taking decisions are made in hopes of serious profits, assuming that we are not wasting energy and talent by embroiling ourselves in power struggles. We also need to avoid shady deals. Is transiting Pluto making a tensional aspect to our natal Saturn or Uranus? If so, typically someone in this financial partnership gets a little dictatorial and wants to take over the show. This person may especially want to be in total charge of the money flow. The remaining partners feel threatened and can put up a good fight to prevent being undermined or bullied. The results may get ugly. Somebody may threaten to walk out on the arrangement or plot to oust the power-freak who is causing the trouble. Cooler heads need to prevail during no-nonsense negotiations. Putting our cards on the table and being totally honest at this time is very important.

In this scenario, we can play the role of psychological counselor, trying to prevent battles from breaking out. This especially true if Pluto is making a trine or a sextile while it's also in hard angle formation to the planet that's being affected. A degree of detachment is needed to avoid getting caught up in the thick of hostilities. We also could provide savvy insights that might help to mastermind better business strategies that satisfy all parties involved. Our ability to analyze and to solve problems can be greater than usual during this time. It would also be good to use this gift when negotiating a settlement and divvying up the assets of the business. Many of the above statements can be modified to fit a dissolving marital scenario, as well. Dirty legal maneuvers in the name of controlling money and possessions pose problems for a healthy closure. Remember, Pluto tests an individual's character and integrity at this time.

PLUTO/PLUTO TRANSITS

ONE UNIQUE TRANSIT

This is one of those Outer Planet "life cycles" that large numbers of people undergo at the same time. In this case, much depends on when we were born during the century. All of us will have major Saturn/Saturn cycles every seven years or so, like clockwork. That makes pinpointing these times a neat and tidy task. Similarly, we can expect our Uranus opposing Uranus and our Neptune square Neptune cycles to visit us sometime during our "mid-life crisis" years (ages thirty-seven to forty-six). However, because Pluto's orbit is so elliptical, its passage through the signs is variable—it can spend around thirty-one years in Taurus (a change-resistant sign that forces Pluto to work overtime) or as little as twelve years in Scorpio (a self-probing, elimination-ready sign that's right up Pluto's dark alley).

Those born in the early part of the twentieth century have experienced all of their major Pluto/Pluto cycles late in life, hopefully when maturity was gained after undergoing pivotal adult experiences. For example, people born in 1900 had Pluto squaring their Pluto when they were around sixty-five years old—a reflective period initiating the retirement years, when most of their life passages had been experienced, for better or worse. These folks had the Plutonian challenge of finding purposeful, self-focused activity during their remaining years to offset the wear and tear of decades of soul-grinding material pursuit. A few malcontents unable to adjust may have succumbed to depressive states from feeling useless when stripped of the identity structures supplied by their careers and social roles.

Those born from the middle of the twentieth century to its end will undergo the same Pluto/Pluto cycles much earlier in their lives, maybe sooner than they can wisely assimilate their effects. Still, such a quickening likely serves an evolutionary purpose that is probably better understood at a soul level. If we were born from the mid-1950s to the early 1970s, Pluto can square Pluto as soon as age thirty-seven. That makes it part of our mid-life crisis years, which older generations didn't get to experience (although I'm sure they didn't feel that they "missed out" on anything at the time). It may be an intensely reflective period for this younger crowd, but certainly not a retiring one. During this group's early forties, all of the Outer Planets are in a state of uproar. They are determined to destabilize any rigid elements that support the status quo and keep us stuck in ruts.

In fact, ever since Pluto was discovered, and particularly after the A-bomb was dropped—when total human extinction became a dark possibility—the generations to follow have had a Plutonian speed-up process in their lives. Astronomically, Pluto is closer to us on its orbital path whenever it's traveling quickly through a sign. It seems to always transit most rapidly when in Scorpio, probably because Scorpio already "gets" Pluto's energy. Thus, this planet doesn't have to waste too much time convincing this sign that certain collective social issues urgently need the old "death-and-rebirth" routine. Scorpio on a collective level has also been linked to revolutionary shifts of social power.

Pluto's last tour through Scorpio (1983 to 1995) universally forced people to think a lot about death issues (the concept of dying with dignity began to be advocated by "right-to-die" movements; living wills were strongly promoted; and assisted suicide became a phenomenon open to hot debate). Those who were single and/or non-monogamous felt pressured to take responsible, life-protective measures during sexual activity due to the worldwide devastation resulting from the AIDS epidemic. In addition, the stunning fall of communism created much power-shifting among nations formerly under the Soviet Union's rule. (Pluto seems to only mess around with life's heaviest issues!)

Leave it to Pluto to complicate matters regarding the timing of its own life cycle transits. We'll need to acquire ephemerides (books of planetary tables, also found on software programs) for the twentieth and the twenty-first centuries to figure out exactly when transiting Pluto aspects itself during our life span. Those born during the final sixty years or so of the twentieth century will experience the opposition phase when it occurs for them during their mid-eighties.

Although Pluto/Pluto aspects are felt by many people at once, giving the appearance that they are less personal in influence, we still can experience them individually in terms of the overall atmosphere of our inner lives, whether outer symbolic Plutonian events occur or not. Our personal unconscious seems as much like an "outer" influence to the ego as the external world does. Each one of us has an individualized relationship with our unconscious and its outpourings; therefore, Pluto can work here in very personalized ways.

Pluto Sextile Pluto

Notice that I'm not including the age ranges of this or any other Pluto/Pluto transit because so much depends on the decade during which we were born in this century. Pluto encourages us to do our own research in this matter. However, let's say, for the sake of perspective, that if we were born in January 1900, our Pluto/Pluto sextile would occur near our forty-ninth birthday. Maybe for some people of this generation, Pluto opened up a few doors of perception and renewed opportunity *after* their mid-life crisis.

This would have been a time when society was really starting to modernize day-to-day living. As the 1950s unfolded, the world was revolutionizing in many mundane ways. Maybe the Pluto sextile tied in with individuals in that group buying TVs for the first time. We forget how radical it was to own a TV in the early post-World War II years—radical, very exciting, a big financial investment, and a whole new way of being exposed to American culture, whether one lived in a busy metropolis like New York City or in a small rural town in the Midwest.

Yet for those born in January 1950—a half-century later—this transiting Pluto/Pluto sextile occurred around age twenty-eight or twenty-nine, just before that generation's first Saturn Return. Perhaps this cycle provided (at least on a soul level) the motivation to breathe vitality into emerging constructive qualities needed to make one's mark in society (something also supported by the Saturn Return). Just how connected we are to our core self may determine the extent to which we can take advantage of this transit, whenever it takes place. Our outer environment plays a guiding role in providing opportunities to forge ahead with life-altering plans (made more real if also coinciding with transiting Saturn's conjunction of our natal Saturn). Not all social environments will facilitate Pluto's revolutionizing intentions, but in today's world, it's easier to relocate to wherever the cultural climate offers more options to be ourselves.

This sextile cycle, whenever it occurs, can become a not-so-pushy but still relevant underground force helping to rid us of non-essentials in our life. It can clear the way for new starts, like a gentle sweep of a big broom rather than a bulldozer mowing down whatever's in its path. We feel encouraged to let go of parts of our past that have short-changed our potential. While this phase may not carry the weightiness and drama of the Pluto/Pluto square, it nevertheless becomes one factor that helps us to purposefully individualize. Here, we're catching Pluto in a good mood! Better try to make something personally valuable come out of this user-friendly transit. The sextile aspect itself always encourages us to make smart moves, which is good, because anything we do under a Pluto transit can endure and grow stronger.

PLUTO SQUARE PLUTO

People born in the 1890s had the transiting square as late as age seventy. This probably proved to be a self-reflective transit for some at that age, perhaps brought on by strained life circumstances—mainly health, I'd imagine. However, everyone born in the second half of this century gets to go through the square cycle during their mid-life crisis years. No other planet does this—that is, presenting similar challenges in consciousness to people at radically different ages! The Pluto/Pluto square phase is probably at its most intense when operating during one's forties, due to the simultaneous critical phases of the other Outer Planets. Whenever it occurs, Pluto square Pluto shares many themes common with our Neptune-square-Neptune life cycle.

How so? Both planetary cycles push for a deeper self-confrontation of dark, hidden facets of personality that we've failed to understand or acknowledge while growing up. Typically, we've neglected such matters by putting more energy into worldly interests and living as much as possible on the surface of life. Pluto square Pluto and Neptune square Neptune both represent the need to review the past with an emotional focus that allows us to contact our real nature, our core self. We're pressured to seek some degree of creative and spiritual renewal. With Pluto, however, changes can be both permanent and far-reaching.

At this time, many structures in our current life have outgrown their purpose and are ready to be broken down and swept away. We just need to make sure that *we* don't get swept away with them. Anything non-functional to our total growth pattern must go; usually, areas in which our desires have been repeatedly thwarted. The more we resist giving up all energy-trapping attachments, especially those that put us in no-win situations, the more life attempts to destroy them. The inevitability of Plutonian change will make its presence known through sometimes harsh and drastic circumstances.

Some of us might feel alienated from our environment at this time. However, our withdrawal can be so subtle that it goes unnoticed as we move our attention toward our inner world in order to dig at the source of any discontent. Meanwhile, our calm, outside demeanor can fool others. Inwardly, we could be feeling anxieties that have much to do with our sense of mortality: our allotted time on Earth is starting to run out, and we know it. Our aging body makes that clear. Although we may function as usual in the world, our inner reality is less orderly and secure.

How deeply we internalize in an effort to decode life's meaning cannot be predicted by our chart alone. The nature of Pluto's subterranean operations within our psyche is typically unfathomable. If we consciously work with this life cycle, we can wind up at a new place within ourselves. We can enjoy a total renewal of self-concept and a newborn sense of power—not the power to manipulate outer affairs, but the power to recreate our character. This results in having the fortitude to cope with anything and everything that life places in our path. Depth of self-understanding provides the ability to approach our remaining years with the integrity and courage that comes with precisely knowing what we are all about, and loving it!

PLUTO TRINE PLUTO

People born in 1890 experienced this trine phase when they were in their mid-eighties, around the time of their Uranus Return. Succeeding generations had or have it earlier and earlier. If Pluto's life cycle is ever to experience a mellow stage, this is it. Some of us may feel that we have a wider perspective now regarding the human experience, especially if we are having or have had our Uranus/Uranus and Neptune/Neptune trine life cycles as well, give or take a couple of years. We'll need to see what's happening with transits in our chart during our fifties (if we were born from the 1940s onward). That's the age-decade when these multiple trine cycles occur.

At this time, we could be very sensitive to progressive situations in the larger world that instill within us a sense of hope for deeper human understanding and global unity. Technology may excite us as never before with its promise of a revolutionized tomorrow. We also will live in times when more is known about the mysteries of the Universe and the human mind's potential. On a more personal level, Pluto trine Pluto suggests heightened self-awareness as we happily tap into latent inner resources. We are now comfortable with experiencing our own self-generated power, and we feel confident that we can creatively channel this power.

It's easier now to shed old, outgrown roles without first undergoing the traumatizing intensities more common to our Pluto/Pluto square phase. If anything, our efforts to break down whatever was non-functional in our life during that self-renovating Pluto-square-Pluto phase determines the fruits of renewal to be picked during this highly rejuvenating period. We can attract people and conditions in our social structure that facilitate the constructive expression of our power drive and social conscience. This is also a great time to open doors of spiritual perception, especially if we have never before taken full responsibility for our soul-development. It's also good to follow any burning visions about the life we truly feel we deserve to live!

PLUTO OPPOSING PLUTO

People born in the fall of 1937, when Pluto first entered 0° Leo, will have this transiting opposition no earlier than early spring of 2023 at the age of eighty-six, relatively soon after their Uranus Return, and after the transiting Neptune/Neptune opposition. This could be a heck of a decade for such folks! Remember, those born in 1890 had the Pluto/Pluto trine right after their Uranus Return, not the opposition—only in very rare instances did some live long enough to experience that cycle, but never during the same decade when each of the other Outer Planets also formed a major transit to itself. In addition, Pluto wasn't even discovered yet. However, those born during the last sixty years of the twentieth century are going to experience this Pluto/Pluto transit at this momentous time, a cycle that's not common to every century—only those in which Pluto mostly passes through its "fast" signs.

What does it mean? Here, Pluto forms an aspect noted, at best, for granting us a fuller perspective regarding the planets in question—in this case, a double-emphasis on Pluto. This allows us the ability to deeply evaluate the societal framework in which we were born (natal Pluto), compared to the complex social pattern in which we find ourselves now (at the time of Pluto's transit). We may reflect on the many decades in between during which we were forced to learn to deal with our Plutonian passions (strong loves and strong hates). We saw social eras die as new ones were born. We witnessed collective upheavals and marveled at technological breakthroughs. And maybe those living long enough to have this opposition get to cheat death a little longer—because, by then, medical science may be able to regenerate vital body organs, and being reborn may take on a literal, biological meaning.

For those who've seen enough of this world and are ready for the spiritual freedom of the afterlife, this period could be a time to burn off any residual negativity that would only weigh our soul down. We probably need to forgive those who have been rotten to us (something we hopefully began to do during our Neptune/Neptune opposition)—and besides, many of those folks are dead anyway, so why hold a grudge against them? Now, we can let go of our insecure grip on this physical world and prepare to passionately embrace our new birth to come on the Other Side, once our tired body expires!

CHAPTER FOURTEEN

PLUTO TRANSITING THE NINTH HOUSE

A WIDER SCOPE

Any Outer Planet moving through our Ninth House prompts us to question the broad and sweeping concepts that we or others have about the true nature of the Divine and how our Universe operates. What do we believe will provide everyone with a real sense of life purpose in relation to their moral conviction or spiritual growth? Our approach to the Big Truth can also be scientific, devoid of religious undertones, whereby we seek to discover and understand the mechanics of existence solely based on the laws of the physical plane. Any deep, subjective meaning behind everything that science critically measures and "objectively" evaluates is deemed irrelevant, even non-existent. Still, both pathways to discerning what's real and true lead us to expansive understandings of this puzzling phenomenon called Life. These paths take sharp turns and strange twists when an Outer Planet is involved. However, they often explain more of the puzzle than expected.

The Ninth House is also where we participate in helping our society to function in better ways. Its focus is on building an ideal community. Here, various social mind-sets impact on our individual frame of thought, with mixed results. This house inspires us to behave as model citizens, ethically driven to make worthy contributions that benefit the whole. We must have faith in humanity's potential before we even bother trying to improve social conditions, which explains why cynics are rarely the do-gooders of the world. Any questions and answers to be found in our Ninth are generalized to include the concerns and welfare of large numbers of people. Individual needs become less important than those of the collective mind—the growth of the many comes first. The Outer Planets are willing to inspire us by widening life's ongoing possibilities in our quest for global and universal understanding. If we are truth-seekers, our philosophy tells us that, while yesterday is history of an educational sort, a fresher tomorrow awaits us with open arms and gifts of enlightenment.

This is also a house of long journeys of the intellect, inspiring us to wonder where the human race is heading—could it be nuclear oblivion or the colonization of Mars? Perhaps an eventual eternity spent in Heaven or Hell? Strong Ninth-House stimuli make us eager to know what the next evolutionary steps for humankind might be. The future becomes stimulating, especially if it includes an uplifting vision of fuller potential. It would be a very Ninth-House thing for some of us to impatiently want to know when angelic space-beings will finally land and show us better ways to live in peace! We're not expecting these aliens to have evil intentions, of course, because we hope that they'll be our wise teachers who'll show us a whole new galactic way of being. Behind the belief in UFOs may be a desire to feel part of vast, interstellar communities. *Any* sense of community is very important to the Ninth-House approach to life.

In this house, we are curious about the rules (universal laws) that guide the whole, unfolding process of existence, as well as who or what determines these rules. How does the Cosmos connect and work with us on personal levels of consciousness—our expansive realm of "inner" space? Big questions demand big answers, plus a lot of breathing room to explore at will without being tied down by narrow, intellectual restrictions imposed by others.

THE POWER OF FAITH

Transiting Uranus in our Ninth surprises us with brand new ideas and ideals to explore regarding all-encompassing, ageless truths. Transiting Neptune in this house at first disillusions us but then offers rays of hope in other inspirational areas that reveal the deep unity of all life. However, with transiting Pluto passing through this life-zone, we could initially find ourselves repelled by a guiding, glorified belief that once provided our total foundation for living. For us, it was pretty much "the last word"— an unshakable security system that explained "the way things really are," leaving us with little to doubt. The more sold we were on the rightness of our beliefs, the more apt we also were to shut out any other options for viewing reality. We didn't wish to handle valid criticisms that were thrown our way. We may also have felt the need to defend our belief system from being invaded by challenging and seemingly incompatible concepts. All in all, these staunch, unquestioned articles of faith become Pluto's prime targets. Life is ready to slay a few of our sacred cows.

Getting into "know-it-all" or "holier-than-thou" mind frames are commonly a part of what makes any "true believer" so fervently assured and unappealingly dogmatic (let's not forget that diehard skeptics and professional debunkers are also true believers of a sort). Zealousness can eventually turn into unconditionally justified fanaticism, even if these beliefs are more political than religious, and more society-based than otherworldly. What if we were born with frictional Pluto/Jupiter aspects involving our Ninth in some fashion, such as having Scorpio or Sagittarius on the cusp? In that case, some of us may have already gravitated toward extremist beliefs that we've fiercely advocated, typically polarizing others in the process. This is especially so if we have attempted to convert them using strong-armed mental tactics or propaganda. We could become an inflexible enforcer of moral standards, a dictator when it comes to the rules of social conduct.

A few of us may not only shut out challenging viewpoints, we may even pray for their destruction, because they threaten to pollute the clear, pure waters of God's or science's revelations. On the other hand, we may have lived a lifetime thus far believing that nothing can be considered an ultimate, universal truth; nor do we have faith in any continuation of life and consciousness beyond this physical existence. Thus, when Pluto enters this house, destruction becomes a theme. What are to be destroyed are those rigid concepts that have limited our extended vision of life's possibilities. With this transit, both the Holy Roller and the pragmatic atheist may find it hard to sustain their beliefs as the years go by. Pluto first eliminates totally before rebuilding from the ground up. It could take years of Plutonian transit activity before we will ourselves to let go of what no longer works for us. Once we do, there is no returning to former beliefs. They're dead, and we've taken great pains to kill them off.

While we're going through this transition, we become aware of the power of belief and the abuses that blind faith can engender. Life probably brings people into our path who are too intense in their theories about God or their philosophies about reality's meaning or lack of meaning. They seem utterly convinced, and their absolutism enthralls us, scares us, or turns us off in disgust. Still, this is how Pluto demonstrates the problem of thinking one knows everything about issues that might truly be unknowable, at least while one's mind is still operating on the third-dimensional plane. Let's face it, the Ninth House is not as transcendental as the Twelfth. It still wants to wrap its spirituality in forms that sometimes satisfy the intellect more than the soul, and then inspires us to spread "the word" far and wide. Therefore, we should welcome both fanatics and disbelievers, up to a point, because they're revealing paths we are *not* to take if inner growth is our number one concern.

THE DEPTHS OF TRUST

It's a hard pill to swallow, knowing that we may have to divest ourselves of beliefs that once made perfect sense out of our Universe and gave us a special kind of internal security. Such beliefs made our life less rocky and uncertain. But now, clinging to them only keeps us stagnant, unfulfilled, and angry—angry because we feel that we've been duped and are once again vulnerable to life's random chaos and quirks of fate. Actually, this Pluto transit will convince us that we have the power to recreate our universal visions with greater self-honesty than ever before. We are going to have a new relationship with the Cosmos, without third-party interpreters getting in the way. We can now play an active and energizing role in our future soul-unfoldment.

The fact that we've survived Pluto's transit through our Eighth House helps this process along. Much has already died in our Eighth that would have been heavy, needless baggage to carry on our journeys in the Ninth. Hopefully, what died for good was our fear to live out our own truth—our authentic self. The thought of now taking on new handicaps and crutches goes against all that we had to learn the hard way in our Eighth. Therefore, our sense of being an independent agent in search of spiritual wholeness is emphasized. Resourceful Pluto urges us to take bits and pieces of wisdom wherever we can find them, but we are learning to be careful not to become addicted to one single source of truth-seeking.

The Universe is also helping us to work out issues of trust. Maybe we've ripped ourselves to pieces with brutal self-analysis in the Eighth (or we've torn apart others in our intimate circle). Restoring trust will therefore be very important. This is not the time to give away our power to another, who then tries to determine the right way for us to live. We'd do better trusting our Higher Self to make such decisions. Similar to Uranus in this house, transiting Pluto takes guts and courage to live out its theme of empowerment.

In some way, we may not feel ourselves to be a part of the social scene, even on a civic or activist community level. Older astrology texts like to make us sound like we're eagerly spearheading social reforms left and right when a powerhouse like Pluto is moving through our Ninth. Yet very few folks seem to take the crusader's route. If anything, we probably will withdraw from too much group involvement in favor of a more private quest for universal meaning. We realize the power of silence and stillness, not hustle and bustle. Trust here also means not worrying whether or not seeking solitude is the "right" way to respond to our spiritual needs. However, if we've been isolated for too long, maybe it is time to dynamically emerge in a collective or communal way, offering our talents to help a group cause. Whatever we decide to do, we must not force ourselves to do things that go against our sincere desires during this period, just to please the crowd.

LUSTY ADVENTURE

Not everyone is well-suited to read volumes of esoteric literature or sit in sweat lodges chanting and meditating (two Ninth-House Plutonian options). Some feel Spirit can be discovered and experienced while exploring the fascinating variety offered by Nature. Pluto can empower the fearless explorer who wants to experience the most intense and impossible-to-reach spots on the planet. If a destination has volcanoes, gorges, steep cliffs, or underground caverns, we may be interested in paying a visit. Danger and Pluto often go hand in hand. Although Neptune is swept away by unearthly beauty, Pluto goes for the raw and the primal, or the awesome and the eerily ancient. Anything Incan or Mayan may appeal. Deserted areas become intriguing, such as ghost towns or places that were nearly wiped off the map by some destructive, natural force. When we think of taking a vacation, the last thing on our mind is frequenting popular tourist attractions.

In today's volatile world, however, we'll need to carefully study our destination before we arrive. We may unconsciously choose areas that are ripe for civil unrest or other explosive circumstances beyond our control. This is especially so if we've been struggling with this transit for a while, fighting and resisting the overthrow of our personal status quo. Pluto becomes projected onto a foreign environment and is mirrored back to us during our trip. We'd better play by the rules and not defy customs when abroad, because life will let us know that we're not above the law!

Only a few of us will have to concern ourselves with the consequences of breaking the social rules of another country. If we are going to have problems overseas, it's usually because we attract heavy-handed people who show little warmth and cooperation.

Let's not argue or stubbornly try to enforce our will with these folks. It's also wise to figure out how we can best safeguard our money and possessions from possible theft or loss—is Pluto making a tensional aspect to our natal Mercury or Venus? Things associated with those planets may become damaged, or may mysteriously disappear. Yet if we truly have deepened our trust in the Universe, it won't crust us to part with a few possessions on our travels, should calamity strike. We know that the Cosmos will provide even better replacements later. This is not a time to let such travel mishaps devastate us or fill us with resentment, but maybe it's best not to bring along anything of value on our trip.

We should instead thoroughly enjoy the rewards of exploring new places and seeing new faces. This transit can be a period of the most remarkable, memorable trips of our entire life. Our journeys take us to places deep within us. They stir our emotions in ways that nothing else has before, and we can return home feeling like a totally changed person (Pluto's influence can be deeply life-altering). Let our Plutonian adventures far away from home profoundly show us how varied the planet and its inhabitants really are, and enable us to feel how vibrantly alive and well this big world is.

Insatiable Intellect

What if deep soul exploration is currently not our thing— maybe some of us have been doing it since our hippie communal-farm days—and traveling to Iceland during a time of major volcanic activity is less than appealing? Another path we can take in our Ninth is an academic one. It's a suitable option because any degrees we seek to attain may take years of schooling, giving Pluto the long-term focus that it needs. Usually we want to feed our mind tremendous amounts of knowledge during this transit, even if only in specialized areas of intellectual interest. We want to concentrate our mental energies and delve deeply into our subject matter. It's helpful if we first commit ourselves to a disciplined course of study and then give it all we've got. We can't afford to scatter our attention and lose our concentration.

If we feel compelled to return to college, yet insist that we really don't know what we wish to tackle, our problem is deeper than just having too many academic choices. We haven't recognized and claimed our power resources, probably because of unresolved psychological complexes that continue to erode our confidence. Pluto's trying to tell us that our life challenges can be mastered by applying steady, unstoppable effort. Maybe we are at a loss as to where to direct ourselves because we are flat-out afraid to fail, or to follow our dream all the way just to watch it crash and burn in the end. Yet, what makes us think that this is what will happen? We'll need to explore the origins of our self-distrust and why we unwittingly hold back our power when we show a lack of decisive enterprise.

What about those of us who have never doubted our intellectual strengths? We still need something that intensely grabs our interest, so Pluto will provide us with studies that will arouse our passion. They could involve tackling social or ecological problems that have plagued the world for a long time. Restoring things to vibrant health is always a Plutonian concern; here, the suffering patient is society itself.

Going back to school will not be a breeze with Pluto here, because complications often crop up and interfere with our progress. We may even be forced to drop out for a while, only to return later, with a vengeance, to complete our studies and nail that degree! Once committed, our motto should be "Never give up." Let's not put a time limit on our education; that's the sensible way to go with Pluto. Just realize that someday we will have our B.A., B.S., M.A., or Ph.D. Then the doors of professional opportunity can open, getting us psyched up for our ambitious Pluto in the Tenth transit.

PLUTO/JUPITER TRANSITS
HUGE APPETITE

When these two planets join forces, forming a natal or transiting aspect, we may feel urged to extract a lot out of life in big and sometimes indulgent ways. We are hungry for vital, robust experience and don't wish to be held back from having our grand adventures satisfied—those of the mind, body, and soul. We may also feel impelled to pour a lot of ourselves into the world in an effort to make expansive, relevant socio-cultural changes, although we can become tireless crusaders with a Plutonian bone of contention to pick regarding the System. This Pluto transit tries to elevate our natal Jupiterian aspirations to greater heights of fulfillment than we ever dreamed possible (which is impressive, considering that Jupiter already believes that anything is possible). We can be uplifted by powerful surges of inspiration that fire us to actualize our ideals. However, Pluto also demands that Jupiter know about life's potential depths, a subject with which the eternal optimist in Jupiter is less comfortable.

The squeaky-clean side of Jupiter wants to do good works and shows a lot of heart when dealing with people, but this planet can also be superficial and too easily impressed with the image-enhancing trappings of social success. This is often a worldly planet, with a big appetite for having and enjoying life's luxuries (it's Neptune, the martyred one, who glorifies the sacrifice of creature comforts). Jupiter doesn't solely focus on that which gets our spirit soaring (unless winning the lottery or making a killing on the stock market is considered spiritually uplifting). However, in this regard, Jupiter avoids getting its hands dirty in life's darker, seamier soil. Too much direct encounter with humanity's sordid miseries becomes disheartening and overwhelmingly downbeat— but gee, that's Pluto's natural stomping ground, isn't it? Therefore, it's hard to avoid unsettling territory with this planetary mix in motion. That's right, Jupiter, you're not in Neiman Marcus anymore!

Theoretically, some Jupiterians could launch a successful charity or "big cause" fund-raiser to assuage the plight of the suffering poor abroad, then go shopping for a new Jaguar the next day and think nothing of the dichotomy. For them, abundance in life is taken for granted, and they seldom sense when they're wasting resources on shallow, material pursuits. Maybe Jupiter simply believes that we can "have it all" in life if we just open up to the

Universe's bounty while never doubting our worthiness. After all, the Universe has so much to give, why not reward relatively "good" souls like us? Such a positive philosophical spin can be a fine thing if it doesn't lead to snobbery, arrogance, or attitude problems created by feeling divinely privileged. If we start hyping ourselves, though, transiting Pluto would love to knock us off our high horse and shut down our bank account. More on this soon.

Jupiter can be as outer-involved as Pluto is inner-focused. Here we have an extroverted, gregarious fire planet that's now being transited by a notoriously introspective, solitude-embracing water planet who tends to regard too much social engagement as a complication. (Paradoxically, Pluto is driven to impact the masses in areas of reform and social enterprise—but always at a safe emotional distance.) We will therefore need to strike a workable balance. If we are having a sextile or trine, we feel less driven by both our Pluto and Jupiter urges, so we probably won't over-emphasize appetite fulfillment. Pluto's ambition is less ruthless and Jupiter is able to enjoy a few perks without being piggish about it.

However, with the conjunction, square, quincunx, or opposition, Jupiter can go overboard when seduced by Pluto's extremism. We know no bounds in striving to claim something that we desperately desire—but we'll need to be aware of the big bellyache that awaits us when we gorge ourselves beyond reason on anything too delectable! But don't blame Pluto, a planet more than willing to exert forces of self-control—it's Jupiter that has a hard time accepting the restraint of discipline.

Microsoft's Bill Gates has a natal Third House Pluto/Jupiter conjunction in Leo, and really started to step up the pace of his fiery ambition when transiting Pluto squared that conjunction in the summer of 1995. Around that time, he discovered the potential of a whole new universe of communication to master—the Internet. It didn't hurt that he also released Windows 95 amidst an unprecedented frenzy of worldwide consumer interest. It seems that, in his case, doors opening to future opportunity are fated for profound success—or are they? The enormous appetite potential of Pluto/Jupiter needs to be carefully monitored during this transit—in Gates' case, an appetite for tremendous financial profit and the ongoing domination of the software market. We can similarly want to win big when Pluto transits our Jupiter.

LETTING BELIEFS DIE

What we believe about the better tomorrows that may await us, as well as how we approach all issues of hope for life improvement, is symbolized by our natal Jupiter. What do we put our faith in these days? Pluto wants to know what we hope will enter and upgrade the quality of our life in the future. Do our beliefs represent what we are all about, or are they merely what we were taught to blindly trust at an early age, regardless of whether they conflict with our real nature? One's family religion is usually a good example of this dilemma. Many of us feel that we've outgrown the religious doctrines of our childhood, although we may have retained the essential values of that training and found ways to incorporate them into personalized forms of spirituality.

For folks like us, Pluto's transit can deepen our faith by the addition of supportive viewpoints that current opportunities allow us to explore. We probably also find ourselves connecting with wisdom-givers who help to open our eyes wide to lines of spiritual understanding, according to Pluto's no-nonsense way of learning. This is a time when we can learn more about the hidden roots of our childhood faith in ways that enable us to adapt this faith's tenets to our existing philosophical framework. All of this is done with great seriousness and reverence (the "hallelujah...joy to the world" side of spirit-filled Jupiter often takes a back pew when Pluto is at the pulpit). Still, this period can feel like a time of urgent metaphysical renewal, typically after many years of non-seeking. If we've abandoned spiritual practices in the past after becoming too caught up in the daily grind of material survival, Pluto impassions us again and allows us to find ways to confidently reconnect to our soul.

But what if some of us are struggling with our existing religious values and are feeling a deep void that makes our current lifestyle seem hypocritical or meaningless? What if we have lost faith in the goodness of living? What if hope is dying on the vine? This scenario is ripe for Pluto's rejuvenating process. Pluto often comes into our lives to infuse us with needed vitality when we are down to our last "whatever," or when we're running on empty and all the odds are against our making it through a dark night of despair. It's at these most intense moments of soul-exhaustion that Pluto springs to action and vows to rejuvenate our spirits.

During this transit, some of us start out feeling deflated or trapped in a slump, perhaps as we agonize over life's meaning even while we're not getting much joy out of our worldly successes. Undergoing a lack of purpose in life can make people crazy and bitter. Pluto, nevertheless, is preparing us for a resurgence of vision, a confirmation of future promise. No matter how down we are, we should think twice before giving up and ending it all if we're having a Pluto/Jupiter transit. Our ability to make a comeback—after which we feel like a vibrant part of the world again—is more powerful now than we realize. Still, we may have to let go of something or someone we've over-glorified. This permits us to feel the temporary pain of separation, rather than to self-defeatingly hang on too long, and end up feeling nothing but dead inside.

With Jupiter, what we are pressured to let go of might be a religion or a political affiliation that we've treated as gospel, the ultimate path to Truth. Sometimes issues revolve around devastating realizations that the teachings or social guidelines into which we've put so much faith (and the teachers or leaders we've revered) are now false and worthless. This becomes a reason to be both disillusioned and furious. Pluto's transit can be a heartbreaker for chronic "guru-chasers" and for those who've longed to be at the foot of charismatic individuals who claim to be Ascended Masters or Evolved Beings from higher spiritual dimensions. Similar to Pluto's transit to Neptune, this is a time when Jupiterian illusions are crushed under the weight of Pluto's harsh, penetrating analysis. Our beliefs die a hard death, and we go through a palpable mourning period, grieving over the loss of what was once a beautiful collective dream that fired up an illusionary personal vision.

Within due time, we wake up feeling wiser than ever (and hopefully less gullible). We'll tell ourselves that no belief system will ever have such power over us again—and no person on Earth is to be our sole guide into the sublime realm of Spirit. Pluto/Jupiter can be a transit full of such rude awakenings, but heck, naiveté can be a dangerous thing in today's world. Why subject ourselves to harmful mind manipulation disguised as comforting food for the soul? It would be understandable if some of us abandon any further spiritual seeking while we heal, take stock of ourselves, and start to listen to our own inner voice for self-guidance for a change. Jupiter is forced to seek its enlightenment from within (which actually means it starts to function more according to its traditional Piscean nature).

SALES PITCH

Whenever our Jupiter is aspected, it's a time to see how close we can get to becoming our ideal self—that is, "ideal" in a sociable sense rather than striving for saintly perfection. Jupiter is a lenient planet, unlike Saturn or Pluto, and it realizes that we will make a few errors in judgment in the real world while we try to raise our consciousness. Jupiter's sign, Sagittarius, is half-horse and thus symbolic of animal instincts that work against the elevated part of us that shoots arrows of less worldly desire into the heavens. We could say that Jupiter shows us where we want to both look good and make a great overall impression on others (it's a bit like Leo in this regard).

Pluto's transit can promote our willingness to shape up by smoothing out our character's rougher edges. We polish our personality assets and find better opportunities to market them. In short, we learn powerful ways to package and sell ourselves to the world. And we don't have to feel phony in doing this, because we are recreating ourselves in a new, improved fashion that meets our sincere approval. A well-handled Pluto transit means that we remain self-honest in our presentation, not manipulative.

Jupiter's not a "health-nut" planet *per se* (aside from its abstract-sounding "health of the soul" concerns), but it does play a role in encouraging those dissipating vices and excesses that result in an inefficient use of our body's fuel. Pluto prefers the lean-and-mean look. We'll need to cut the fat on many levels of our being to satisfy Pluto. A good start is to work on our body image. Getting enthused about some sort of exercise ritual would be a great way to burn up Jupiter's fire and flab, while keeping our metabolic rate from slowing down. However, we can't afford to unwisely choose exercises that bore us to death!

Walking is a natural Jupiter thing to do, because the simple act of walking can lead to wandering, and thus to exploring the distant reaches of our environment. With Pluto, daily walks can coincide with an ability to unclutter our minds and solve problems. We also may notice the strangest Plutonian things in our environment as we make our rounds (like a used condom in a church parking lot). However, if Pluto's opposing or squaring our Jupiter, let's not get too nosy or too friendly with the strangers we meet on our walks. Simply observe, take mental notes, and move on. Random encounters can otherwise invite complications with Plutonian people we would rather avoid.

Survival of the Fittest

Gluttony can be a problem with out-of-touch responses to Pluto/Jupiter transits (both planets can symbolize doing "too much" of something that we find hard to resist). If we are carrying extra body weight, Pluto helps us to knock off unwanted pounds by getting us involved in vibrant, energy-releasing activities. Sports become a great way to melt away the fat and keep us feeling alive and well energized. With Jupiter, having fun is the key to motivating this planet to do anything. Therefore, the advice here is to stay active and realize that Pluto is eager to have our bodies match the exuberant vitality we may be feeling on our inner levels. If we stick with our self-improvement campaign, people take notice. It could open up a new world of social activity, if that's what we desire. Otherwise, we at least feel healthier and more fit than we have in a long time. When it comes to quality living, let's give it our best shot during this time. We need to enthusiastically adopt a new lifestyle (Jupiter) where robust physical activity plays a role in our self-renewal (Pluto).

THE DEATH OF DEBT

Well, now that the above motivational pep talk is over, there's another sensitive matter to consider: living beyond our means. Jupiter's really good at buying now and paying later, and even doing whatever fast-talking it takes to bump up its credit card limit whenever and however possible. Some of us know that we have lifelong problems with impulsive, irresponsible spending sprees, while others among us respect our financial limits and refuse to abuse our Jupiter—hmmm, what does our natal Saturn look like? Jupiter likes to pretend that it will someday be happily rich, usually due a major stroke of luck on the day its ship comes in. Yet its habitual handling of money matters almost ensures that it won't be able to sustain wealth for long. Saturn-challenged types seldom save money for a rainy day, because Jupiter doesn't want us to even think that day might come!

On the other hand, Pluto's wealth is secure and solid, well-protected, and shrewdly managed. Pluto sees an out-of-control, over-extended Jupiterian as a walking fiscal disaster waiting to happen. If we show that we're willing to work with Pluto during this time, we could still be in trouble with the economics of life that seem beyond our control, but things are more fixable. However, fixing things—Pluto-style—takes time and self-discipline, depending on whether or not the situation is salvageable. We typically already have more than we need (check those over-stuffed closets). This might be a good time to shed a few seldom-used possessions, giving them to charity or trying our luck with a few weekend yard sales. However, we can't afford to then turn around and buy more needless junk—that's not something we can slip by old Pluto, who's watching our addiction to mindless spending like a hawk. Some of us may have to stop purchasing goods altogether for a while, as if going cold turkey. We'll simply have to endure the withdrawal symptoms that follow.

Should a few of us particularly stubborn types willfully ignore the writing on the wall (and the pile of bills accumulating on the table), Pluto can get quite nasty during its stress-aspect stages. The environment will bring out its strongest ammo in the form of hostile creditors and not-so-amused authority figures who press for severe legal charges. They may fine and penalize us to death, until we come to our senses and fork over what we owe them. We certainly don't want to play cat-and-mouse with tax collection agencies at this time! Sometimes the matter is more complicated than just being a shopaholic or an occasional tax cheat. We could pool large resources with others in a major business venture that ends up sabotaging us. Someone else's unscrupulous ways can get us in a heap of trouble, because we're usually left holding the bag in the midst of a war zone.

It's not unreasonable to think that bankruptcy may be our only option in some cases. Once we're nearly wiped out, our road back to financial redemption can be long and grueling (there will then be so much that we have to do without that we currently take for granted). Yet what choice do we have? Next to none. At this point in our sad saga, our Jupiter wings have been clipped, and we have many years ahead of us to try to rebuild our credit-worthiness. Life is not hopeless—just very strained. Before things get this drastic, let's get a grip now. Pay off any small debts before they multiply and loom to gargantuan proportions, and think before buying anything costly that will be rarely used. Keep Pluto happy!

CHAPTER FIFTEEN

PLUTO TRANSITING THE TENTH HOUSE

THE PRICE OF AMBITION

It seems that any major planet going through our Tenth House has a better chance of being smartly handled the older we get, because what makes this house work well is a seasoned understanding of worldly reality, afforded by maturity and real-life experience. It also helps to have a sense of realism regarding the contributions we feasibly can make to society. Maybe that's why pragmatic Saturn—a planet that improves with age—loves to call the Tenth "home sweet home." Yet Saturn's way is slow and thorough, and its wisdom doesn't come without first paying its dues in hard work and the steady application of ambition. It certainly helps to have clear-minded professional objectives to begin with, plus a humble acceptance that we'll have to start our climb at the bottom of the mountain. Still, time is on our side. We can't rush such integrity-building Tenth-House matters.

Astrologers realize that, if an Outer Planet moved through our Tenth when we were just a kid—perhaps only a first-grader—our options to willingly act out such a planet's energies were few. That is, unless we were a child prodigy like Mozart, or we lucked out in some form of show business at a tender age and gained

early "career" experience—the kind that could directly invite pre-
cocious Outer-Planet challenges. Think of a "mega" child-star
(along with his/her parents) playing Plutonian hardball at age
seven when negotiating a contract with a top movie studio.

Having this Pluto transit as a child suggests that we were
born with it in either our natal Ninth or Tenth House. Assuming
that we had "normal" childhoods, our parents most likely lived
out much of that typically unsettling energy for us, while we in
turn became a pawn of their fate. Our parents' moves totally con-
trolled our destiny, and with Uranus, Neptune, or Pluto passing
through our Tenth, parental actions may have been disruptive to
our status quo at a time when stability and consistency meant so
much to our well-being.

In contrast, being a full-fledged adult—on our own and independently determining our social role in life—allows us to evoke a
wider range of Tenth-House possibilities. With transiting Pluto,
our freedom to choose our niche in society may not be nearly as
great as when "don't fence me in" Uranus moves through our
Tenth. Even Neptune, in its starry-eyed pursuit of a Big Dream,
has periodic immunity from situational barriers and obstacles in
this house. It's one planet that benefits by flowing with the collective tides of the moment and being ever-attuned to the public's
thirst for idealism. Yet with Pluto, as always, we first get to find
ourselves in a power struggle with our hidden, inner elements,
which we deny and yet compulsively project onto the outer world.
In this case, it's the world of authority figures, most of whom echo
back the early control themes we once experienced in the guise of
parental dynamics. This typically involves our image of our father
or subsequent father figures.

Professional matters, if they have been a source of personal
frustration and closeted anger, can now come to a head in the
form of a crisis requiring decisive action—decisive but not impulsive, because Pluto demands that we probe the heart of the matter and think things through (even if we don't like what we discover). We may have shown keen ambition in the past to make it
to the top in our field, or at least entrench ourselves in a solid,
secure position—yet we may have been driven to climb the ladder

for all the wrong reasons (the glamour of status, power, and glory). Now we may discover that our position is not what it's cracked up to be, and that the way we got here has taken its toll on our spirit. Maybe it's even hardened our character in less-than-admirable ways. If this describes our situation, Pluto is "ready to rumble" and take a few well-aimed potshots at the professional setup we've quasi-unconsciously created for ourselves.

Up to this point, some of us may not even be paying attention to the warning signs of an impending career burn-out—one of the prices we pay for our single-minded ambition and status-seeking. We may be feeling a hard-to-articulate dissatisfaction with the current results of our strivings compared to what we expected would happen by now. Perhaps we've won the coveted prize—the prestigious title, the power to command authority, or the social privileges that come with such success—yet feel a strange emptiness inside. Winning the prize apparently is not enough. Pluto intensifies this kind of anguish in the early throes of this transit; especially when we're also having to deal with the opposition from the Midheaven that Pluto forms to our Nadir. Whenever our Nadir point is triggered, we get to inspect our "bottom line" security needs. We check to see how grounded in reality are our expectations of safety and psychological shelter. Don't expect Pluto to shield us from the weaknesses hiding at our roots. To handle what transiting Pluto in our Tenth brings our way, we'll need to be well-anchored within. Weaknesses in the form of blind spots involving insecurity must be weeded out.

CAREER REBIRTHING

It's so characteristic of Pluto to present us with situational hassles that complicate matters before the momentum of a life-altering renewal of outlook takes shape. Our career or social position as we know it may be on its way out. It's dying a slow death, and the more we resist this likelihood, the more unrelentingly Pluto shows us the evidence of decay and deterioration. Situations that seem unjustly stacked against us may force us out of the picture. We could be unceremoniously given the boot from the powers that be! Our loyalty may have been betrayed by those in high positions who have ulterior motives. Sometimes, the cold impersonality of a huge company doing business for profit plays a role in our dismissal. Our reputation or credibility may not have been personally attacked; instead, we're the victim of a major downsizing brought on by economic forces beyond our company's control.

This may leave us more sad than shocked, more angry than confused. Such a Pluto experience can make us deeply uncertain about our future prospects and a tad too paranoid to trust anyone professionally again (at least that's our initial reaction, especially if we were let go under questionable circumstances). We may even feel unwilling to further follow the rigid rules of the System—our newfound defiance won't permit us to ever play that thankless game again. Of course, while we may blame fate for any devastating turn of events, we'll need to also examine our responsibility for this outcome. What could we have done differently to sidetrack this scenario? Self-examination hopefully leads not to useless guilt, but to a clearer understanding of how we can better fulfill future goals in our career pattern. We'll need to pick a profession that rings true to our real nature, not just one that supports society's expectation of what we should be. We'll only suffer with Pluto in our Tenth when we betray *ourselves* and go against our inner grain, our core reality.

Time for some good news: if we are on the right track with our professional focus because we have chosen a path that suits our inner being, our career doesn't die but undergoes a metamorphosis. This can give us a tremendous recharge. It may happen gradually, as we find ourselves ready to tackle challenging tasks that further empower us. Pluto is very protective of those dedicated folks on the planet who feel that theirs is a calling, not just a career. As we plod on, situations unfold in ways that smack of a special destiny at work. We are handed a power role that we're ready for, a position often solidly supported by those who are well-established in their fields.

In other instances, there may be little about our career that deserves to be salvaged. We're stuck in a position that is going nowhere but down. A few of us don't wish to face this, and self-destructively hang on to our role (power-addicted politicians seem to do this, even when their popularity is sliding in the polls). We feel that our survival's at stake when Pluto is bearing down on us, so the temptation is to tighten our grip. Life, however, is telling us to let go of this ego-draining way of making it in the world; it's no longer working for us, and no worthy contribution will come of it.

Perhaps we simply have outgrown this role and are feeling as if our greater, untapped talents have been put on hold for too long. Pluto doesn't have to spell professional disaster, but it often makes us feel as if we're wasting precious resources that will disappear altogether if we don't take effective action soon. Do we remain in an unfulfilling job and slowly lose our soul, or will we show some guts and bravely move out into a world where our creative juices can flow? Obviously, being young and single can help us to make bolder moves at this time, because we feel responsible for only ourselves should our boldness prove foolhardy. We don't mess up other people's lives as we would if we were married with a kid about to enter college. Being older when this transit stirs us requires different, less-dramatic strategies for change that still feel transformative.

Brave New World

If we're fresh out of school and just starting to test our professional strength, this can be an overwhelming transit in the beginning—especially because of our relative immaturity and inexperience. We are starting to plug into an internal power drive at a time when, unfortunately, we have little or no knowledge of the cut-and-dried ways of business. Our first hurdle will be learning how to deal with uncompromising bosses or with the authoritative structures of established companies. Here is a hierarchy complete with set rules of conduct that we may find absurd (for instance, if we're born with our Sun conjunct Pluto and with Saturn in Aries quincunxing that Sun).[1]

With Pluto moving through our Tenth, our impulse is to buck the system and persistently keep doing things our way, defying procedures or ignoring policies that don't suit us whenever we can slyly get away with it. Yet it won't be long before someone of rank is breathing down our neck or quietly observing us and taking detailed mental notes to share with the boss about our performance. It sounds devious and it is. You just never know where the company spies are planted when Pluto is at the workplace!

Should we get into trouble, our inclination is to fully justify ourselves and our actions, detailing our grievances loud and clear to our employer in hopes that justice and truth will prevail (*our* subjective brand of justice and truth). Maybe if transiting Pluto sextiles or trines our Venus, Mercury, or even Jupiter, we might be heard with more sympathy—but don't count on it. Pluto can be a strict and punishing force, nailing it to those who try to turn the tables on authority and act as if they're above the law. We'll probably get harshly chewed-out that first time we try to defy the rules, but be fired on the spot the next time we show similar insubordination. Or we throw our tedious paperwork down on our desk one stormy day and quit in an eruptive manner, leaving zero room for future negotiation. This is how a few of us can behave when we are young and too full of Pluto's spit and fire.

Still, perhaps after a rocky start with a few more tension-building jobs, we realize that we need to show our courage and real strength to the world rather than indulge in that futile chip-on-the-shoulder routine. Unless we are determined to be self-employed, a rotten attitude toward authority gets us in hot water time and time again (and with transiting Pluto in the Tenth, even our boss can be more uptight than usual about any challenges to his/her authority). We eventually, for survival's sake, learn to temper our passion for confrontation with supervisors and other authority figures. Pluto's telling us to work on ourselves, instead, and strengthen anything about us that could prove valuable in a career sense. Therefore, we'll need to eliminate the more problematic features of our professional temperament.

With Pluto, getting to where we want to go can be profoundly slow. Yet when we're consciously tuned in to the calls of our destiny, we won't give up the pursuit no matter how many obstacles await us. If anything, we'll learn to defy the nagging insecurities often fostered by repeated delays. We can't give up the struggle to be what we know is within our reach. Something big out there in the world is waiting for our brave and forthright involvement. It requires our total commitment to excellence and the engagement of our power base.

HEALING WITH DAD

For some of us, this transit coincides with an opportunity to reflect long and hard about our father. We may find ourselves needing to deal with areas in which we felt attacked and hurt by him on some level in the past. For a few of us, there may have been early experiences of parental wounding that we now recall (perhaps as Pluto opposes our Nadir). However, Pluto knows that it's hard for any child to remain emotionally unscathed deep inside while growing up with parents who are imperfect. High divorce rates show that marriage can be a battlefield, and the children can be held hostage in such a negatively charged, bitter atmosphere.

In the best Plutonian scenarios, we find that we are strengthening bonds of love and loyalty with our dad. Maybe we can get more closely involved during a meaningful period in his life, such as a time of personal fruition along some line of deep interest to him. It's great to see a parent like this in the midst of such (re)constructive focus in life. He becomes a renaissance man in our eyes, or a true survivor who won't let any previous failures bring him down. Mutual misunderstandings in the past are cleared away as we both feel fresh new starts energizing our relationship. It's hard to expect more than this from such a transit. Sometimes our father is even receptive to our intuitive guidance and respects our savvy awareness of his life, and of life itself.

In other, sadder, instances, when we've established dark patterns of relating to our father for years on end, this transit can either make or break the relationship. With much hard work and with a spirit of true cooperation, we could end up blessed by the scenario mentioned above (given time for wounds to heal). Still, Pluto brings touchy issues of pride and self-will to the surface, where one or both of us feel that we cannot give in to the other without the fear of ego-annihilation. Destructive power-plays can create a rupture in our relationship.

Yet by refusing to come together in loving understanding and with the will to forgive both of our trespasses from long ago, the union dies on some level. Perhaps our father dies in a heart-wrenching way just before we get to work out our psychological complications with him. The result can be great remorse and guilt, mingled with waves of rage and hatred. Our battle with him when he was alive internalizes for us after his death. We surely can't feel alive and well until this dilemma is inwardly resolved. Meanwhile, we'll keep running into symbolic variations of our dad in the outer world, whenever we display our ambition and social strivings. It's better to make peace now with this difficult parent rather than withhold our love and respect as a form of ongoing punishment. In the end, we only punish ourselves in that particularly cruel way demanded by a thwarted Pluto.

PLUTO/SATURN TRANSITS
GETTING TOUGH

Here we have two heavy-handed planets that seek to rid us of our human weaknesses. Saturn, however, is more patient and pragmatic than Pluto when it comes to helping us build inner strength. The Ringed One acknowledges that any weak links in our psychological chain, once examined and understood, can be used to better fortify our entire being (Saturn is key to how we develop inner security and self-sufficiency). We've seen how people with various social and physical handicaps work harder to improve themselves so that, in the end, they're more accomplished than they or anyone else ever expected. They've turned personal vulnerabilities and liabilities into character assets earned the hard way, and they remain true to their authentic selves.

Expect Saturn to slowly but steadily guide us through its process of learning to fix whatever is malfunctioning. If it's worth repairing, Saturn is interested. If it's going to bring sanity back into our lives, Saturn is *really* interested! With this planet, we'll typically struggle with a nagging lack of confidence, but we nonetheless make a steady effort to develop sound capabilities and masterful skills. Perhaps such uncertainty keeps us on our toes, alert to what we're doing step-by-step, while realizing that nothing is to be taken for granted.

Pluto takes a more drastic approach to human weakness: it wants to smash it like a bug and eliminate it entirely if possible! In Pluto's fantasy, we can all become superhuman with tremendous inner resources and unlimited energy at our disposal. Any lack of ego-strength and the whining that often goes with it are less sympathetically understood by Pluto, who instead advocates the total destruction of whatever impedes self-empowerment or keeps us feeling puny and insignificant.

Pluto doesn't tolerate lame excuses that begin with the phrase, "I can't because..." It flatly figures, "You can and you *will!*" Pluto can be the screaming Drill Sergeant of the Cosmos, bearing down on us and stripping us of our defenses. However, there is nothing traditionally parental about Pluto (mythic Pluto never had offspring). Unlike Saturn, Pluto won't caution us in advance when we're heading in the wrong direction, at least not in any clear-cut manner. This makes us wonder if Pluto is perversely curious to see how out-of-kilter we can get—how deep a pit might we dig for ourselves before we are stopped in our tracks? With transiting Pluto, we can make a sharp emotional turn around the bend and suddenly slam into a brick wall, at a moment in life when it feels as if the Universe has unfairly singled us out for special punishment. Heavy karma indeed!

Saturn is willing to take time to teach us to cope effectively with reality's limits. We learn to apply discipline to our advantage and make full, practical use of the here-and-now. What Saturn teaches us about ourselves is always useful information. Whether we apply what we've learned or not is our responsibility. When well-handled, Saturn can teach us to toughen up and not give in to escapist urges.

In contrast, Pluto won't waste much time trying to get us back on track when we've made an unfortunate or untimely detour (unless we're worth it). Instead, we're apt to encounter fateful crises designed to break our will before we further mess up our life affairs, if that's what it takes. Pluto knows that things can always get worse when we don't have a clue as to why they're already pretty bad. With Pluto, we often are forced to start all over again, picking up the few salvageable pieces of what's left of the faulty structure on which we've been leaning. Maybe nothing's left, and we're back to the basics of putting a new life together. To do this will require, with Saturn's blessings, that we get tough, adopt a survivor mentality, and become more resourceful. Pluto knows that life must and will go on for us, so let the past go!

RENOVATION PROJECT

Pluto and Saturn terminate that which no longer works for us. That's what they're really good at. With Saturn alone, we aren't as quick to rush what might turn out to be an inevitable ending when it comes to letting something or someone go. We'll try this and that to get the darn "whatever" working again, before we realize that there's no choice but to dump the blasted thing! For Saturn, that's the sensible way to go—not releasing our tight hold until we've tried everything to get the situation ticking once more. Yet with Pluto involved, we're going to need a bullet-proof reason to keep things going after a certain point. Pluto's way of eliminating something is more brutal than Saturn's—sometimes as swift as a bird of prey—and seemingly senseless, at times. Pluto does a thorough job of shredding our past when that's the only way to ensure a meaningful future.

A few minutes of a wild brush fire on a windy day enables an outraged Pluto to destroy all of our worldly attachments. We don't get to even say goodbye properly as we witness our past tragically go up in flame and smoke. It's hard to say why this would have to happen to us, but if it occurs during a Pluto/Saturn tensional transit, this is not just a freak accident, randomly and impersonally claiming its victims. These two planets are more focused and deliberate in their action than that. Tragedy becomes a dramatic method of forcing us to confront issues involving our loss of control and power. Out of the ashes we are compelled to build a new life that is more expansive and rewarding than anything we've known before. Remember, Pluto has hidden wealth to offer. However, during our period of immediate loss, we certainly can't imagine that to be true. At this juncture, fate seems cruel and obscene.

During this transit, we have the option to make things easier for ourselves by being willing to tear down security structures that have seen better days (and we know it). Heavy drama need not be part of this scenario. With a transiting sextile or trine, or even a well-handled conjunction, we should be looking around at things we own that are candidates for permanent removal. Check closets, tour the attic, prowl around the basement, and go through drawers to see what's dispensable. If we've been dedicated consumers through the years, there's going to be a lot of underused stuff that has been out of sight and out of mind for a long time.

Pluto transiting Saturn is a great time to actually clean house on all levels, but it's easier to start with the world of tangible attachments. Our effort to lighten our material load becomes a symbolic act of the inner relinquishment required by Pluto for soul growth. Our next step is to rebuild our reality foundation based on a new meaning of security, the kind that comes from being constructively self-possessed and clear about our identity. From this moment on, security is never to come from impermanent, outside sources; it is to come from deep within our core being.

NO BED OF ROSES

During Pluto/Saturn transits, we have a good reason to take a sober look at our personal world. Reality demands our undivided attention as life takes an uncompromisingly serious tone. Major tasks at hand can be taxing, especially regarding matters associated with Saturn's natal house and the house it rules. With the conjunction, sextile, and trine, we may feel an urge to be industrious and focused on how we utilize energy. We learn to conserve vitality so that it can last longer and help us accomplish more. We can't afford to scatter our resources at this time. We'll just have to make sure that pessimism doesn't set in and convince us that we'll never finish the jobs that we know we must complete. Both planets deal with closure themes, so certain issues may come to an end—not necessarily in a satisfying way.

Pluto seems to always bring along a few extra complications that sidetrack us and, even when things are progressing steadily, time drags on. Nothing is allowed to be rushed. Our patience is really put to the test. We could feel that we're stuck in this place in our lives, forced to resolve difficult issues under strain and anxiety. Saturn is aware of Pluto's inner rumblings and wonders if trouble is brewing. We fear that the accustomed structure of our lives may require an overhaul, and that means a phase of instability that we cannot control or avoid. From Pluto's perspective, this is a creative and empowering time to get out of any major ruts.

On the plus side, our staying power is getting stronger and our determination can see us through nearly anything that life throws at us. It's normally good to have a demanding but not impossible personal project to sink our teeth into. Nothing grueling, but household chores and yard sales may not be sufficiently compelling. Most routine, daily activities won't accommodate Pluto/Saturn energy, unless perhaps we work the night shift at a nuclear power plant. Therefore, what can we do to bring new life into tired social structures in our community? How can we give our world a burst of Plutonian vitality?

Groups of volunteers who pick up trash and debris along highways and secondary roads—in a campaign to clean up the environment—demonstrate civic responsibility of a Pluto/Saturn nature (even if few of them are actually undergoing this transit). The activity itself fits the tone of this planetary combo. What can we do to help clean up messes due to neglect that have made our locale cluttered or ugly? What dirty work needs to be done for the good of all? Renovating the scenery is something Pluto could enjoy, and Saturn likes to keep things tidy and in order. Heck, we could at least make sure we get to a recycling center twice a month—but do it like we mean it, because both planets abhor laziness and procrastination.

Another way to use this transit is to provide service on a more personal level, dealing with people caught up in life emergencies: the homeless, addicted, terminally ill, poor, and disenfranchised people in society—all of whom need a measure of security to help them through their grim passages. Maybe this becomes our professional concern. Here we can involve ourselves in doing what it takes to alleviate society's most troubling elements. Pluto is trying to make Saturn not just see, but *feel* the darkness of human conditions co-created by an uncaring society. Perhaps then we may become determined to push for long-lasting progressive changes in any way we can.

While Neptune/Saturn transits also give us the urge to aid and comfort society's most vulnerable citizens, Pluto is no Mother Teresa out on the teeming streets rescuing the unfortunates of the world. Rather than just putting in a few hours at a soup kitchen or volunteering at a nursing home, Pluto wants us to get to the heart of the matter at a socio-political level and go straight to where the power to transform society on a mass scale lies. What can be done on federal and state levels with government resources to help eradicate the plight of any otherwise forgotten group of suffering people? Pluto would rather help pass controversial but timely legislation than simply attend a protest march and chant fiery slogans (leave that to rabble-rousing Uranus).

Pluto is a radical mover-and-shaker who'll demand drastic action. Saturn is more cautious about the consequences set into motion by rash actions. Saturn is the careful social planner. Therefore, we'll have to feel things out and determine the smartest course of commitment. But it will be hard to ignore society's problems if we're already politically active in our community. Perhaps it takes a transit like this to prompt us to be a first-time activist. We could target one social issue that needs reform, and bring that issue to the attention of authorities who could get the ball rolling. We need to pick one that particularly riles us regarding injustice, because Pluto works best for those who are passionately involved and more than just a little ticked off.

HEAD-ON COLLISION

If we're undergoing the conjunction, square, quincunx, or opposition, we could be feeling stormy about power abuse from those in authority—the mighty (and arrogant) rule-makers. We may feel that we're being pushed around and over-controlled by someone who's not to be trusted. The opposition particularly warns us against butting heads with the guardians of the System. We're susceptible to having Pluto come at us through others in ways that pile on Saturnian limitations and intensify our sense of inadequacy. Our response could be to put up a steel wall of resistance. This is another one of those important times to not inflame our boss, tax auditors, or the entire highway patrol! We'll need to remain calm, which helps to reinforce self-control while we're struggling with forces that could undermine our security. The "Force" *is* with us if don't give in to the temptation to bulldoze others with the might of our will—that would be a losing game.

We don't want interference from anybody, especially with the transiting conjunction in play, but if we think that Pluto is not able to shake up an inflexible planet like Saturn, we're dead wrong. The more unyielding we are regarding deep change, the higher on Pluto's hit list we go! Rigidity is to be eliminated, because it stunts our spiritual development in the long run. Pluto knows this and, therefore, starts taking a sledgehammer to Saturn's fortress of defense. We're not gong to be able to keep up any stiff upper lip routine if we're hiding a lot of repressed pain and resentment. The Universe wants us to realize how wounded inside we are really are and how it sours our experience of life's more joyous parts—not that Pluto truly understands joy and bliss, but it does hate to see energy trapped and unable to surge. A mismanaged Saturn is, to Pluto, like a blood clot stopping an artery's vital flow.

FRESH START

This is a time to streamline our life, get rid of needless excess, live within our means, and maybe save enough—but not hoard—for rainy days, efforts that are all signs of greater maturity and character development. We don't have to experience tragedy to jolt us into this awareness. We shouldn't waste time forcing people and things to stay put when it's best that they leave. We need a little breathing space and a chance for a fresh start. By working with Saturn, using our common sense and a respect for sensible timing, we can impress on Pluto that we're ready for high-quality transformations—although perhaps not coming at us all at once. We've got some psychological trash to take out, one big bagful at a time. So it's best to approach this transit with this philosophical attitude: what manages to stay, we fortify; what goes, we no longer need for our true security. Pluto is trying to unburden Saturn of whatever has kept us down and limited by frustrating restrictions, even needlessly self-imposed ones.

NOTE

1. To better understand Saturn in Aries or Saturn in any natal sign, please read my Llewellyn book: *Twelve Faces of Saturn: Your Guardian Angel Planet* (published in 1997). Saturn's natal house position as well as Saturn's natal and transiting aspects are covered in detail.

CHAPTER SIXTEEN

PLUTO TRANSITING THE ELEVENTH HOUSE

GROUP POWER

Hopefully, we revamped our career priorities by the time Pluto left our Tenth House. We've learned that we don't need authoritative structures to cramp our style or dictate our professional performance. We also paid close attention to power on a large scale and how it can be abused to manipulate society—especially when the boundless ambitions of the few people in charge override fair and ethical treatment of the many they are supposed to serve (remember, Pluto often has us first view the dark side of a situation). We recognize the responsibility entailed by having power to alter society's quality of living, especially the long-range impact of creating and upholding laws that the masses are expected to obey. All of this pervasively affects citizens' lives in ways that they cannot control; nor do they necessarily find the laws to be of personal benefit.

Pluto transiting our Tenth has given us a sometimes unflattering view of the real world, where the strong survive not always by virtue of their sterling character or true merit, but by the way they skillfully work the System, maneuvering cleverly in business and taking advantage of legal loopholes and the weaknesses of competitors. These people seem shrewd about timing and often end up amazingly successful in a worldly sense. Yet we may now despise how some of them got to the top, knowing all of the dirty tricks and social ploys they may have unethically used. Our assessment of their success may sound overly critical, but that's a typical Plutonian reaction whenever we sense corruption at work—especially corruption that has gone unpunished.

Watching governmental affairs and the power strategies at work between rival political parties gave us an eye-opening Tenth-House education. Our reaction may have been acute: we now know the pitfalls of having power factions take control of society. Where is the voice of everyday people? Are we being heard? Is our central leadership being honest and straightforward with us, or just playing the role of a domineering parent who seeks to keep us in an ignorant, childlike state? It's not uncommon for us to take a dim view of traditional authority by the time we're finished with our Tenth-House Pluto transit. We may end up wanting nothing to do with politics or social hierarchies—but if so, aren't we just adding to the problem? After all, being stubbornly cynical about such matters is, in itself, a Plutonian abuse of this transit.

Pluto moving through our Tenth also demonstrated that people in high positions can show great integrity in their attempts to heal collective wounds and clean up social and environmental complications made by the government and big business. After all, Pluto rules deadly pit vipers, but it rules soaring eagles as well. We need to trust that light-bearers with high principles will gravitate toward governmental service and work to transform our lives for the better. It's in this spirit of hope that we now turn our focus to loftier, Eleventh-House ideals. In this sector, the rights of everyday people *do* matter, and humanitarian solutions are given a high priority. In the Eleventh, a democratic vision of society takes the place of the Tenth House's caste system, where class and rank alone determine one's social worthiness, not the individual's creative contribution to the whole.

REVOLUTIONARY TIMES

There's a little bit of the anthropologist turned archaeologist in an Eleventh-House transiting Pluto, a planet that can dig up and analyze the bones of a previous culture's values in order to pinpoint current patterns needing broad reform. We get to see a fuller picture of humanity's potential in our Eleventh. Pluto, an excellent researcher willing to study this matter deeply, doesn't take long to figure out why certain institutional dinosaurs must become extinct in order for society to grow by leaps and bounds. An Eleventh House transiting Pluto can help us to see far ahead and intuit what the next big wave of human progress might entail. Its focus is certainly not narrow or immediate.

We may not actually be so prophetic as to know the trends of tomorrow's brave new world, but we can easily find fault today with the way certain social conventions idiotically limit human potential. Why are there so many stupid rules and regulations devised to keep people in line? Why is no one allowed to step out of line and be different in ways that make the stiff-lipped fuddy-duddies of the world uncomfortable? Are these restrictions designed solely to keep power-trippers happily in charge of the rest of us?

Actually, if you think about our last Pluto/Uranus conjunction,[1] during 1965–1966 (another example of Pluto and Principle Eleven), it's simple to see how that period was the symbolic start of a radical breakdown of conservative social behavior. Blame the hippie movement and the war protesters, if you must, for the looser and less-obedient societal patterns that were set into motion. Those patterns haven't peaked yet. These planets, when combined, want to kill off the stuffiest parts of our social conditioning, the fear-based way in which many of us approach things that are offbeat and unfamiliar. An Eleventh-House Pluto transit is on a similar mission.

There is much about other cultures around the globe that we would find alien and bizarre if we were exposed to them on a first-hand basis (as if Los Angeles motorcycle gangs of tattooed body-piercers with shaved heads weren't enough). But how will there ever be a lasting degree of universal tolerance while we still put down or suppress people and things that are very different from us? Interestingly, some of us never think how abnormal we would look (with our corporate power suit and attaché case) to isolated Amazon native tribes. It just shows how short-sighted people can be when objectivity flies out the window.

NOT SO WEIRD

This Pluto transit forces us to confront strangeness: life's peculiarities and oddities—those "freaky" people and things that exist beyond the fringe of mainstream, Tenth-House normalcy. We're apt to run into unusual social elements (local color?) more often when Pluto or any other Outer Planet moves through this house, particularly if, in the past, we've tried our darndest to avoid such "weirdness." Fate has a way of setting up impromptu encounters with people from all walks of life at this time. This theme carries into our Twelfth House, as well. However, we are to discover—much to our surprise—how not-so-strange other humans are once we get past a few obstacles: their nose rings, radical theories, or counter-culture lifestyles, and *our* programmed social biases that condition us to fear and distrust the non-traditional elements of culture.

As the years go by, we find ourselves sensitized to the dilemma of society's scapegoats, eccentric individuals callously labeled as "undesirable"; offbeat folks who never quite got with the social program. Pluto will make sure that we rub shoulders with a few of these underdogs from the other side of the tracks. Our unlikely association with such people becomes just the eye-opener we need to deepen our humanity. Neither Pluto nor the Eleventh will let us get away with rejecting others merely because they are so different from us. It's the many ways in which they are just like us that is a surprising discovery.

While sometimes showing us the extremes of the human condition, Pluto works to attack prejudices by removing the blinders and barriers that come with being too class-conscious. It's easy to separate groups of people into distinct social categories,

Tenth-House style, and then rate them according to status. Too much mismanaged Tenth-House emphasis results in snobby social-climbing if our ambitious power drive is not balanced by humane, non-material values such as empathy and compassion. In the Eleventh, class distinctions begin to break down. The right of all individuals to be respected and allowed freedom of expression gains greater support. Each individual is evaluated according to his or her own merits rather than on the basis of family background, ethnic origin, religious affiliation, or financial standing. This house is less concerned about our station in life and more interested in our idealism and uprightness, and how broad-mindedly we deal with society.

Our Pluto transit slowly works to transform the ways in which we view a wide range of people who collectively play an essential part in our education of the human race. Our Eleventh House can speed up our evolving humanistic outlook, an awareness deepened and made more real by Pluto. We confront the dark nature of our intolerance toward others (especially those biases developed during early childhood exposure to bigotry). Sometimes, the least that can be hoped for is that we take on a "live and let live" policy regarding other people, even when we don't understand or agree with their lifestyles. However, Pluto is more interested in getting us to investigate the root causes of *why* some of us are so bothered and threatened by how others colorfully live out their truths and express their individualistic identities.

DARKER VISION?

Pluto in the Eleventh may help to revolutionize "group consciousness," reforming the way large numbers of people perceive life and create collective reality. Yet Pluto itself does not care to hand over its power to any group or group leader. It has a tough enough time temporarily sharing power in good faith. We may have a problem with trusting others when working together for common causes in situations where large numbers of people network. Ironically, we are nonetheless drawn to the power that only mass participation can generate.

Some of us wonder whether or not we should belong to any organization that might make heavy demands on us. Actually, *we* could make great demands on a group at some point, the result of our no-nonsense attitude toward social participation—we want everyone else to be equally loyal and dedicated to the great cause at hand. Still, the Eleventh House encourages us to volunteer time and energy to construct community projects that can only succeed with effective teamwork. Therefore, even when in doubt about collaborating with others, we sense that we're eventually headed toward such activities, almost as if fate is steering us in this direction.

There's strength in numbers in the Eleventh, especially when highly progressive minds get together and pool their brain power and expertise (which may be considerable). The ideal of group cooperation—even if only implemented until a project or mission is completed—becomes very appealing. In reality, it's not easily accomplished, especially by an unusual mix of individualistic thinkers of strong will and great courage. Pluto is teaching some of us to be single-mindedly involved without trying to take over operations, because that could prove alienating and counterproductive to the group dynamic (after all, this is *not* the Eighth House). Manipulative or undermining actions on our part can be met with antagonism. We could be expelled from membership, although we may not understand why everyone's turning their backs on us and acting "so mean" and unfair. Perhaps it's because we tried to push our weight around once too often and didn't know how to treat others as equals. If so, this is no way to feel alive and well with Pluto.

Transiting Pluto in our Eleventh can magnetize us to groups that are trying to use joint effort and shared resources to foster new visions for society that often demand the elimination of targeted current social policies that seem unjust or immoral. The spirit of activism can be intense. The will to break down an old order may capture our full attention. We can get obsessed about some social wrongdoing based on the fiery rhetoric we hear from those ready to fight for total change. If our group is spiritually directed, our leader may become fanatically sold on his or her visionary "truths" about a punishing future of retribution. He or she may sound downright apocalyptic, preaching about global destruction and humanity's deserved punishment for acting... well...human! Beware of such ominous scare-talk; it represents a shadow side of Pluto that can keep us too paranoid and anxious to fully live in the here-and-now. Sin, guilt, and blame have no place in the enlightenment-seeking Eleventh House, except to underscore how *not* to straightjacket our consciousness. Our mental freedom is at stake.

If we are undergoing the square or opposition, we may gravitate toward people who are emotionally fired up and on a passionate crusade to wipe out the evils of society, usually by pushing a political or religious agenda to the extreme. We're strongly attracted because their shared outrage at the status quo resonates with a similar anger to which we may be awakening, concerning the threat to real meaning in our lives. This is most likely if we have tried to survive in the material world by going against our ideals. We've conformed in ways that sabotage our true self and rob our life of authenticity. If our chosen group is loud and visible, it represents an extension of an internal facet of our psyche that has had enough of social repression and being boxed in by the limiting agents of our culture.

AT A DISTANCE

Although some of us will find ourselves swept up in causes made more relevant and urgent by charismatic leadership, this transit usually manifests with less large-scale drama—that is, unless it occurred during those high-flying mid-1960s when Pluto brought Uranus along for the wild ride. Those of us who had both of them transiting our Eleventh at that time must have felt like the times, indeed, were a-changing!

More often, this transit will teach us about nonpossessive camaraderie. Eleventh-House contacts have a casual friendliness about them, not necessarily superficial, but not filled with the depth of focus and commitment evident in our Seventh-House bosom-buddy relationships. It's hard to have just one best friend in our Eleventh, because that would exclude all of the other interesting pals and associates that this house wants us to befriend. Hanging out with the same few people in a lifetime seems like a social disadvantage from an Eleventh House perspective, because there are so many fascinating folks out there who could help our mind to expand in exciting ways. Like Uranus, the Eleventh loves to share brilliant mental explosions that light up the dark sky of ignorance!

The trouble here is that loner Pluto doesn't encourage a lot of company. It can't handle chit-chat and happy talk, unlike those gabby Mercury/Jupiter types who can make the rounds and spread cheer at large social gatherings. Pluto and Saturn, even when they are officially in charge of events, don't know how to handle situations where too many people are having too good of a time. We just finished a profound Plutonian assignment in our Tenth, so we may now hunger for others who can look at life with a similar profundity. Perhaps we will join a group to meet equally heavy thinkers and intuitive social analysts. However, the setting doesn't have to be a structured one for us to find the right companionship. Leave it to fate to introduce us to the Plutonians who can teach us about Eleventh-House values.

Part of that lesson will involve detachment. We may be non-romantically attracted to someone fascinating and constantly want to be around that person (it feels obsessive), only to find that he or she needs space and already has more exciting social connections than it seems we'll ever have in a lifetime. Our "friend" constantly circulates among a wide range of interesting people. This leaves us little time to get closer and more attached to this energizing person. If we have had trouble in the past with letting people claim their needed space in relationships, this transit will intensify our problem.

On the other hand, our new friend might be involved in us to the point that *we* need a breather. Maybe he or she is too intense, a bit troubled, and a magnet for complicated life scenarios. Perhaps this strong-willed individual wants to monopolize us, and wonders why we'd need any other friends. This sounds like scary stuff. It would be good to study new people who enter our lives before we try to involve them further in our world. Freedom of self-expression is one of our big lessons, yet that becomes hard when we are dealing with someone whose dark compulsions suck the life out of us. This transit will require skillful balance. At best, we can learn much from others who energize us and teach us about self-sufficiency and the power to follow our vision. They offer their insights without wanting something in return, other than the joy of our stimulating friendship.

There will be strange but necessary times when we'll want to be around no one. We'll feel a strong urge to pull away from all active social participation. No need to be alarmed—Pluto is just keeping us from engaging in time-wasting affairs that could divert us from the new goals we're formulating. Besides, with Pluto, we can learn plenty, from a safe distance, by impersonally observing human interactions. To force friendships with the wrong Plutonians, or let ourselves be so pressured, could blow up in our face as these volatile types transform into personalities that both enrage and terrify us. That's not what our Eleventh House had in mind.

FARSIGHTED

In general, this transit helps us to look far ahead to determine how empowerment might play a role in our future. We become less concerned with material security and more driven to attain less-tangible goals. With Pluto, our "hopes and wishes" are not just for a better world of tomorrow, but also for a fuller release from those elements of our past that have trapped our potential to be more than we currently are. Both Pluto and the Eleventh seek to shatter and destroy whatever has held us back for all the wrong reasons, although Pluto's raw emotional power can prove unsettling to the cerebral atmosphere of the Eleventh House. It's hard to stay intellectually cool and detached when Pluto's coming at us from our environment.

As time unfolds, we may get better at defining the human race in terms of life's broader evolutionary challenges rather than from strictly historical perspectives. We'll learn to under-stand how humanity's up and downs happen for reasons that often defy ordinary, logical analysis. We can start to develop true transpersonal consciousness as we pull back to witness larger societal patterns working slowly but progressively. All of this helps us to make more sense out of Pluto's upcoming transit in our Twelfth House—a time when we become even less identified with worldly experience.

PLUTO/URANUS TRANSITS
AMAZING ENCOUNTERS

We'll only have a few major Pluto/Uranus transits to experiment with in a lifetime, which is a blessing, because we probably couldn't handle more than that, anyway. At least we'll have many years between each transit to adjust to the results of any sweeping changes, whether made by us or forced on us by an environment in transition (considering that these are two Outer Planets, we don't always get to choose from life's menu—instead, we're stuck with the Cosmos' "Special of the Day"). Still, our unconscious is working seamlessly with our environment to magnetize just the right experiences that we need, even if we don't agree at the time that this could possibly be happening. In some cases, we could be too young to even be paying attention to our surroundings.

Just to get some idea of how often these transits occur, folks born in June 1934 with 0° Uranus in Taurus had a natal out-of-sign Pluto/Uranus square that became exact by transit when Pluto entered 0° Leo in October 1937. Being only a bit more than three years old at this time, they certainly were too young and innocent to remember changes through which their family and society passed. (In contrast, I had the transiting square in my early twenties when I began doing astrology professionally, with Pluto moving through my Sixth; this just goes to show that, with Pluto involved, everyone is not in the same boat when it comes to transit timing.)

For that same Uranus at 0° Taurus crowd, their next transit would have been Pluto trine Uranus in late October 1956, at age twenty-two or so. (This was probably when they became excited about the conveniences of modern technology, energized by thoughts of flying saucers, and were soon to be thrilled by the potential of early space exploration—Sputnik was launched in 1957. Meanwhile, they probably loved wearing 3-D glasses at sci-fi and monster movies.) The lower/waxing quincunx that followed was in October 1971 (age thirty-seven) and the opposition challenged them in November 1983 (age forty-nine); the upper/waning quincunx to follow occurred when Pluto entered Sagittarius in January 1995 (age sixty).

BIG SHAKEUP

What happens when a planet of volcanoes (Pluto) joins forces with a planet of earthquakes (Uranus)? There's a whole lotta shakin' going on, that's what! This is an unsettling mix of energies. Stable patterns of habit and behavior that have provided comforting rhythms of security are now altered by circumstantial and psychological forces that deviate from anything orderly and predictable. One minute we're watching nostalgic re-runs of Lawrence Welk, and the next minute a freak tornado has ripped off our roof and moved our house off its foundation. And the TV has gone flying out the window to parts unknown! This dramatic scenario is not likely to be ours (besides, during this transit we'd ideally be watching re-runs of *Star Trek,* instead). Yet our sudden disorientation from being tornado-struck symbolizes our situation on mental and emotional levels.

Pluto's transit makes it plain that we can't stay stuck in the past, especially if it's a cozy way to avoid the challenges to growth best provided by an unknown future. Once a sense of monotony takes the place of what was once simple routine, our creative spark begins to diminish, forfeiting some of its vitality, and we feel trapped. Something within us begins to die as we lose spiritual muscle tone. Too much passivity leads to dull, soul-suffocating patterns of repetition. We've "been there, done that" too many times to count. Pluto, as keeper of the eternal life-force, wants us to avoid the consequences of unchallenged tedium. Even during the sextile and trine phases, Pluto's mission seems to threaten those natal planets (such as our Moon, Venus, and Saturn) that would rather keep things intact or flowing steadily, without interruption. However, fire planets like Mars and Jupiter sometimes enjoy the major changes that Pluto evokes (as long as Mars doesn't get pushed around or given orders, and clumsy Jupiter doesn't hurt itself tripping over unanticipated obstacles).

But Uranus, of all the planets, seems the most ready for anything that adventurous Pluto has in mind. Being a mad scientist with the reflexes of a race car driver, Uranus finds getting tossed around fun for a while, and worries little about not playing it safe in life. Ups and downs are part of the thrill of the roller coaster ride. Instability is exciting. Besides, Uranus figures that it can always come up with brilliant ways to use Pluto's power. If things get too intense, Uranus can simply drop out (although no planet is actually allowed to just turn and walk out the door on Pluto). Pluto provides the basic transformative material, while Uranus has the technology to make something mind-blowing out of it. The friction these two planets generate can result in awesome illumination. The power to destroy is equally evident.

When Pluto transits Uranus, our ability to free ourselves from restrictive social and family conditioning can be awakened, maybe for the first time. This is not a period when we can tolerate feeling boxed in, held back, or denied access to something we badly want—especially if we are having the square or opposition, which suggest that we're very insistent. It takes great courage to live out Uranian energy in Saturn-dominated societies (those that are tightly organized according to time-honored traditions and set rules of conduct), so many of us don't nurture our expression of creative freedom. Yet for our entertainment needs, we depend on brave souls who do. Thus, our approach to fulfilling our Uranian needs is a passive-receptive one for the most part, suggesting that these needs are underdeveloped.

Transiting Pluto now signals a time when something deep within us—perhaps some angry, heat-producing energy—is ready to flip the switch and get our Uranian electro-magneto waves strobing. Suddenly we find that we can no longer endure the status quo of our lives. Our Uranus house position offers big clues as to where we are fed up with predictability. Indirectly, Saturn's house, where we seldom rock the boat or alter our patterns, could get a jolt as well. Both Uranus and Pluto would love to gang up on old Saturn and fling his ridiculous black book of rules out the window. Actually, Pluto suggests using a blow-torch!

These energies all may sound psychologically and spiritually liberating, yet this combination can be a "touchy" one—not in the hypersensitive lunar sense of hurt feelings and sulking for days, but in a vivid, "you tick me off one more time and I'll smash this place to smithereens" kind of way! It's like a quick bite from a rattlesnake, even though you didn't mean to step on it. Pluto provides a level of irrational fury that catches excitable but never really hateful Uranus off guard. Some of us can become agitated about how slow or stupid others can be. We may snap at those who aren't telepathic enough to quickly know what we want or need. We may also want to forcefully push away people who make the mistake of crowding our space.

Pluto intensifies the mental impatience of Uranus, but by doing so it also underscores where we tend to be unreasonably self-willed. Pluto demands self-examination, because disruptive ways of handling frustration are not going to help us to truly feel free. We could attract someone who overreacts to our rudeness by pitching a fit at a most inappropriate time or place; we may think that he or she is going nuts, but we partly brought on this response ourselves.

My Way or the Highway

Uranus is not a planet that calmly discusses situations the way Mercury or Saturn can. It doesn't want to waste precious time yakking about that which it "knows" to be a hopeless cause. It sizes things up quickly, then urges us to emotionally detach, split the scene, and not look back. Cooperation and common sense are not part of this picture. We may make little attempt to work things out. In some instances, a partner who might play out the

Plutonian role could try to force us back in line in order to keep the union from being destroyed. Our conflict is partly due to a stubborn refusal on someone else's part to allow this union to break up (especially with an opposition, whether in marriage or business partnerships). When Uranus feels manipulative energy coming at it, it gets even more contrary and uncontrollable than ever. Violent confrontation is not out of the question, even for those known for being mild-mannered up until now.

A few of us have been quite good at this "explode and run away" routine in past partnerships, when the pressure was on to get real with our intimate feelings. We'd unconsciously set up a scenario in which we'd allow someone else to take control and suffocate us, then have little choice but to pull away loud and clear. If that's the case now, Pluto indicates that it will be harder to make a clean break this time around. Complications detour our last minute plans, particularly with the quincunx and opposition. What if we are about to slap a spouse with divorce papers the same week he or she has a near-fatal car crash? Now we're unexpectedly caught up in a state of inner turmoil (guilt as well as anger), as we realize that this relationship will drag on. Is the Universe telling us to think again before letting our partner go, and that maybe such a tragic mishap could be what brings us closer together? Maybe yes and maybe no. The problem is that we're suddenly not sure of anything, except that we're caught between a rock and a hard place!

It's usually a bad time for others to give us ultimatums in the heat of the moment (mostly because we are highly tempted to walk out the door for good, with no regrets). Of course, the tables could turn on us if we're the one acting like a tyrant in a state of unresolved, infantile rage. Neither Pluto nor Uranus will apply the brakes once the bulldozers get rolling. In fact, things can escalate with the unstoppable force of an avalanche. Actually, Pluto might prompt us to slow down and analyze the bigger picture if we're taking too many foolish risks for the sake of freedom, especially if long-term financial security is at stake (Pluto deals with financial complications). We may not stay in a bad marriage at this time for money alone, but we'll make sure that we're financially in good shape when we leave this union, especially if we're not the one itching for a divorce. Pluto's shrewdness combined with Uranus' intuitive power to read future trends gives us an uncanny sense of timing regarding these matters.

WHEN THE DUST CLEARS

Whether our shake-ups are major and disorienting or minor and refreshingly exciting, Pluto aspecting our Uranus means that we can be alive and well in ways that do more than just recharge our batteries—our ego's engine gets rebuilt as well. It's time for a total renovation of our spirit. We can develop a deeper trust of our intuitive abilities, while granting skeptics their right to remain in the dark if that makes them feel safer. Well-handled Pluto/Uranus energy means that we feel no urge to push enlightenment onto others, because any sense of power gained is used in areas where our ego becomes the servant of a big social cause worthy of our time and effort. Power struggles won't feed us the energy we need at this point. Instead, they short-circuit us and drain our soul.

If we are determined to walk a spiritual path during these periods, let's not forget about potent virtues such as kindness, tolerance, and forgiveness. It's too easy to put punishing pressure on ourselves and others in an effort to powerfully tune in to higher levels of Spirit. Worse, we might do so with a grimness and an emotional impersonality that we assume all dedicated shamans, magicians, and energy-alchemists must achieve in order to be taken seriously by the Universe. It's a harsh view that may be coming more from our own state of ignorance than from direct, transcendental experience. Let's be careful not to universalize our current obsessive-compulsive tendencies or our desire to dominate others. Neptune and Jupiter know that the loving Cosmos likes to smile and give big bear hugs a lot more often than we realize!

NOTE

1. The Pluto/Uranus message of revolt from social constraints is especially powerful when these planets conjunct one another every 127 years or so.

CHAPTER SEVENTEEN

PLUTO TRANSITING THE TWELFTH HOUSE

PRISON OR SANCTUARY?

Astrologers view the Twelfth House in contrasting terms. On one hand, it has been dubbed the "dustbin" of the chart, where mental and emotional "trash" collects in the darker corners of our psyche. Jungian astrologers would agree that the "undesirable" traits that we suppress find a safe hideaway in our Twelfth. From this asylum, they quietly exert unconscious power and influence. The more we neglect or reject these misunderstood qualities—perhaps we had childhood trauma related to them that resulted in our distortion of their true value—the more subversively they take root in the least-accessible parts of our psychological make-up.

Some of us may be convinced that these internal forces don't exist and never did. That's how invisible (and threatening) they may be to us, an attitude that later sets us up for adult patterns of confusion, delusion, and slow self-destruction. We find troubling, outside sources to blame for our internal problems. It's easy to see how the Twelfth eventually became associated with "self-undoing" and "hidden enemies."

What we refuse to see within us, whether creative or destructive characteristics, can later hurt us. We typically find subtle ways to sabotage our needs; the Twelfth has many tools in its grab bag that can work to undermine us. All it takes is a self-defeatist attitude to open the door to the abyss. Yet this unhealthy dynamic intrigues Pluto who, with sleeves rolled up, will enter this house carrying an emergency toolbox. Pluto knows that there is dirty work to be done to repair past damage to our inner world. This work typically revolves around themes of abandonment and alienation.

Another concept associated with the Twelfth is that it symbolizes a vast repository of images, desires, ideas, anxieties, fears, and sufferings of the human race, accumulated since psychological time began. This entire spectrum of human information is the essence of the Collective Unconscious. We each are able to plug into this awesome reservoir under certain "transcendent" conditions, including moments as ephemeral as daydreaming. Access is hardwired into our psyche. The Collective Unconscious also plugs into us, often spontaneously and unexpectedly, surfacing from the depths to alter our waking perceptions of life. This accounts for our occasional strange moods—waves of unexplained nostalgia, tears, deep joy, and crazy fears triggered by inner feelings and outer stimuli—even odd twinges of deja vú, during which we eerily sense that we know something from a soul level that otherwise should be completely alien to us.

During our Pluto transit, we may feel a compulsion to dig deep in order to understand this phenomenon, because its random occurrences can haunt us. Some of us will feel a strong urge to do some detective work along these lines. This can lead to satisfying metaphysical research. Getting more acquainted with Jungian depth-psychology could also fascinate us. In the Twelfth, we can tap into seemingly limitless resources of humanity's past experience and draw inspiration from our sense of belonging to something bigger and more complete than just our ego's world in the here-and-now.

Pluto knows that this terrain is ripe for plowing, in terms of offering us a breadth of universal understanding. We can develop a growing urge to render global service, even if contributing in only the smallest of ways (as in supporting charities). It's also a ripe time for putting energy into artistic/musical visions of sublime beauty and harmony, and encouraging soul-excursions into realms beyond the physical. Pluto wants us to realize the empowerment to be had in these areas of our Twelfth House, as well as the degree of ego-surrender required (rather than the ego-annihilation that takes the form of severe mental breakdown—which would be devastating).

In time, we'll learn to appreciate that this house is much more than a garbage dump, dark prison, or psycho-jungle of confusion and dysfunction. Self-forgiveness helps to turn our Twelfth-House energies around for the better, although redeeming ourselves this way is often easier said than done. Still, once we stop struggling with our humanness and accept the fact that we'll only heal when we're ready, our Twelfth House can expand and become a fertile breeding ground for creating a little heaven on Earth (not Heaven in place of Earth). No aspect of our being is to be forever rejected in the Twelfth, not even our earthy but often misguidedly selfish ways of surviving. The unification of our inner parts—leading to true psychological integration—becomes our spiritual quest.

ALL ENCOMPASSING

It's good to welcome Pluto's passage as an opportunity to become a source of light for the world. We may have a special illuminating fire to offer those who dwell in darkness and misery—and that may include ourselves. If so, it's time to fix within us that which has secretly been broken and left in poor shape. Our Twelfth is an orphanage that houses our wounded parts.

Hopefully, our aspiration to use Pluto's transit to heal and renew the environment was given wings when Pluto transited our Eleventh—a time that taught us how social transformations can come true when courageous people work together to build a better future for all. Our dedication and patience may have moved mountains and raised social consciousness in this house of idealistic networking. Now we are to begin to change gears and focus our big dreams on internal, even transpersonal levels of human experience.

Attempting to be a Twelfth-House Plutonian light-bearer is not, however, without its difficulties. This is a sector where energy can quickly become inflationary. We may ignore practical limits in favor of impossible utopian ideals that we then expect everyone to devotedly uphold. We're tempted to force such a state of unification onto others, because the merging of the many into the One is a theme of this house. If our ego is attached to a boundless desire for importance and dominance, a few of us could envision ourselves as *the* only source of light the world needs! Our vision becomes the ultimate salvation for a sick and troubled world and, sadly, we obsessively seek to fulfill this "revelation" at any cost—sometimes by dutifully serving a hypnotic, all-knowing leader whom we worship without question (such a projection of omniscience onto another human in authority almost guarantees our victimization).

Pluto here can add a disturbing element of power-seeking, made even more dangerous by our blindness to the social conse-quences of our beliefs. Actually, in today's world, there exist enough checks and balances to make it harder—though not impossible—for anyone with evil intent to get this far with Pluto. The bad press that detractors are able to rapidly spread through the Internet alone makes it difficult for anyone to mentally enslave people on mass levels. Word gets around electronically in a way that can be formidable in its global reach. Still, all that it takes is a handful of mesmerizing fanatics working on the minds of the ignorant and isolated to cause needless human destruc-tion. I doubt if you or I would traffic in such manipulation. What will keep us safe and sound in our Twelfth House is the desire to nurture a reasonable degree of humility and a love of serving humankind wisely (the real key to Twelfth-House success). We can still wield power behind the scenes, if that's what we want, in ways that truly aid the underdog rather than dangerously inflate our ego.

Pluto in this house intensifies our need for soul-examination. We are being shown signs that say we first must deal squarely with matters we've avoided facing for a long time, especially if we have natal planets in our Twelfth. We'll need to resolve or dissolve our personal hurts and pains before giving vital attention to all-encompassing Twelfth-House ideals that impact the upliftment of many. Some of us may be on a big mission that might invite social controversy and the cynicism of skeptics, but we'll listen to our heart and follow our dream. We sense that ours is a universal calling that requires us to stay inwardly focused and psychologically healthy during this period. A lot of people are to benefit from our enlightenment. However, Pluto suggests that a few traditional social patterns must be shaken up in the process.

Realize that most of us having this transit started out with natal Pluto no more than six houses away. Thus, Pluto has basically transited areas of our chart known for human involvement on worldly, societal levels. None of these houses support strictly self-focused activities in which our ego's needs override those of others. These houses (especially from the Seventh through the Eleventh) become increasingly people-concerned, broader in scope, and more demanding of social cooperation. We center ourselves on one special "other" for significant exchanges of intimacy in our Seventh and Eighth Houses. However, by the time Pluto enters our Eleventh, we are challenged to deal with large groups of cause-committed comrades and strangers who show us what humanity is all about. If we've grown with Pluto from house to house and shed many layers of egocentricity, we're probably at the point where we realize that the bigger world around us needs the best we can offer. We can probe into our dormant, hidden Twelfth-House treasures with that ideal in mind.

BURNOUT CASE

There's another theme common to Twelfth-House transits, and that deals with retiring or cutting back on hectic, worldly activity. Semi-hibernating for a while allows us the psychological rest and quality time that we need to spiritually recharge. We are actually at the end of a long cycle of life experience that theoretically began at the Ascendant (of course, with slow-moving Pluto, not in this incarnation, unless we're talking about a brief and forgettable period as a baby, when our retrograde First-House Pluto dipped into the Twelfth for a few months).

The thought of now winding down may sound like the kiss of death to some, especially to strongly cardinal types who live for action. Even semi-retirement would be something we'd dread if it meant fading away forever and becoming forgotten by a busy world. Nonetheless, if we are at a certain age and most of our life's drama has been played out, the pressure is on to slow down the pace, maybe drastically so, when Pluto enters this house. This is not to be confused with punishment or karmic payback time.

It's best to cooperate with this trend, show some maturity, and not push our limits if we wish to avoid a trip to the hospital or a stay at the mental ward (two not-so-hot Twelfth-House options). Frustrated anger and ignoring physical reality can get us in trouble with our body. (We could transform into a defiant Plutonian patient who refuses to go along with procedures that our doctors have in mind for us.) Some degree of surrender to the needs of our spirit is required. It's time to stop putting up such a fight. Are we afraid that we'll get so relaxed, we'll bore ourselves to death? Maybe, but there's still a lot to explore about life in the Twelfth. Let's view this transit as an intriguing adventure into the dimensions of the soul. It's time for some of us to delve into mystical worlds firsthand, or commune with Nature, or revitalize ourselves in secluded places far from hectic worldly activity.

QUIET MOMENTS

Even if we are not near the age of retirement, we can gain a little wisdom and realize that self-reflection is just as vital to our growth as is being in continuous motion and performing a variety of challenging tasks. If we've been burning the candles at both ends—and our mantra is "go, go go!"—now it's time to enjoy quiet moments, such as walking the beach at dawn or going down a nature trail at dusk, and feel the presence of the Divine all around us. Pluto signals the end of certain lifestyles when in this house. We've usually been overdoing it in some demanding social area rather than taking the time to kick back. Maybe we're still trying to tackle too many larger-than-life Eleventh-House projects. Perhaps we had superhuman strengths then, showing endless stamina in reaching our group-related goals. But now Pluto is teaching us to take time to deepen our knowledge of our spiritual self.

Meditation might be a good activity to pursue, provided we're not forcing it on ourselves or being pressured by others who'd love to see us undergo a cosmic make-over. Heck, it's hard enough just going from being a meat-eater to a total vegetarian! Any efforts here to self-improve have to come from the heart. Sometimes, just finding the peaceful space to read books that delve into deep subjects like the meaning of life (and death) can do wonders for our soul. If some of us think that we're fascinating enough, we may wish to try writing our autobiography. At least we can keep a journal (or a dream journal) in which we record our emotional responses to life on pages that we later can review. However, we'll have to be willing to be unflinchingly honest with ourselves in such private writings (Pluto-style), otherwise the results will not be therapeutic in the ways we need.

Eventually, we'll appreciate the power we learn to claim from within, whose presence has always been with us but has remained untapped for whatever reason. It is very important that we accept being alone during much of this transit without feeling lonely and deserted by others. Some of us may get a little too good at solitude and become fanatical about living a hermit's life. That may not lead to the inner peace we crave, but each person's path is individual. It's important that, whatever we do, we don't lose touch with humanity. Bitter, resentful attitudes can lead to an increasingly paranoid slant on life, a distrust of people's intentions. If we've already been hurt by a cold, impersonal world, Pluto magnifies, in our mind, the threat of evil from without. The results are destructive to our soul. Therefore, we'll need to keep a sane balance between our social involvement with others and our serious, passionate desire to be alone. (Hey, we can at least e-mail the world and still maintain our private inner space!)

Pluto/Neptune Transits
Sextile of the Century

For much of the twentieth century (starting in 1942) Pluto has sextiled Neptune. It continues to do so into the next few decades of the twenty-first century. This is a natal aspect found in the chart of everyone who will be age fifty-nine or younger by the year 2001. This sextile also becomes a factor in every event chart, solar return, or electional chart (a chart calculated to pick the right time for an specific event). Pluto exactly semi-sextiled Neptune in September 1916, but then went out of orb for the next few decades, until the sextile phase was reached during the Second World War.

Those few of us still alive who were born in early January 1900, when Neptune was at 25° Gemini, had transiting Pluto quincunx our Neptune in 1993. The quincunx can be a health-oriented aspect. Perhaps at that age, some degree of disorientation or bodily malfunction interfered with our daily routines, and we may have felt an urge to withdraw from external social/family activities in favor of a more contemplative life (something we richly deserve at age ninety-three). Perhaps seclusion was forced upon us due to a complexity of circumstances. However, that doesn't have to mean lying in bed and waiting for our final transition! We can still be peppy and inquisitive in our nineties, although choosy about how we wish to expend our energies (quincunxes can also deal with learning to be selective by making sensible choices). We also may review much of our emotional past, trying to understand our disappointments and losses (our Neptunian pain) without being bitter about it all (a wonderful sign of a well-managed Pluto).

The rest of us have an excellent chance of living long enough to experience transiting Pluto square our natal Neptune (at around our mid-sixties). Before that, we'll have a "resurrection" sextile period to pump us up and renew our hopes. Then, from the square phase, it's on to the trine for those blessed with the best genes (Pluto pushes for the survival of the fittest). However, our first major transit will be Pluto's conjunction to Neptune. This happened at an early age—grammar school years—for those born in the first decade of the twentieth century. By the time the 1940s rolled around, some of us born then met the challenge of this conjunction when we were in our late twenties, just before our Saturn Return. That age gap makes a big difference!

Our natal Pluto/Neptune sextile has turned out more influential than expected, considering that we're talking about "only" a sextile between two planets representing the more mysterious parts of our collective psyche. However, these two Outer Planets form a natal aspect in the birth charts of the great majority of humans today. Pluto and Neptune belong to the water element—that is, water in its transpersonal, boundary-dissolving sense (unlike the very personal Moon which works securely within the ego's structure). The water element emphasizes less conscious usage by the masses of these compelling energies. However, the results have been strikingly visible regarding how societies have shaped themselves since mid-century.

It is obvious that radio, TV, the film industry, the news industry, and now the Internet all have allowed the world to come together and link diverse segments of the human race. This has given us the sense that we are connected as a family of people sharing Earth, our home. Without these social inventions, various nations would have remained in relative isolation and obscurity for a long time, keeping many of us ignorant about or disinterested in their cultures. International news would have traveled very slowly, in a manner having less immediate impact on us. There is something detached about the printed page in newspapers compared to live TV coverage of history-making world events. Now we have communication satellites in orbit (since 1958) used for the transmission of television images, which gives us an instantaneous feeling that we are there while global news is breaking! If we missed anything, there are replays to watch later if someone thought to tape it on one's VCR (another great Neptune-inspired invention).

This is Plutonian/Neptunian magic of a high order, because much of what's being transmitted is traveling invisibly through the air, covering vast territory, penetrating international borders, and even passing through our bodies daily without our knowledge. Receiving TV-like images on our computers—in the case of cyberspace—is equally amazing. Such wizardry would have astounded our medieval ancestors (although we'd be in hot water or worse with the Church). The world that was so large and exotic just a hundred years ago now seems smaller and more familiar. Best of all, it's accessible from the comfort of our living rooms (giving us the Neptunian illusion, perhaps, that we've been to Tibet, or New Guinea, or Calcutta, India just because we watched a TV special about it).

Pluto has infused these Neptunian images with great potency as they circulate rapidly around the world (ad agencies rely on this fact). The industries that make this possible are financially powerful (Pluto) and able to exert a pervasive influence in developing modern society. Much of what we know about our broader social environment (our country at large) comes through TV, for the most part, rather than direct experience. We may barely know our neighbors, but we do get to observe a bigger societal picture from many perspectives with the click of our remote control.

Even our fantasies, fears, and yearnings are projected onto the silver screen in movie theaters worldwide, playing to enthralled audiences, some of whom then turn around and try to emulate what they've seen in real life. That's how style and glamour evolve in today's world. I attribute these unique sociological phenomena to the ongoing Pluto/Neptune sextile of the twentieth century, a pattern whose seeds began with the Pluto/Neptune conjunction of 1892.

THE FAR REACHES

This sextile phase also suggests that we're learning how to create opportunities to make our dreams equally powerful and available to us as those created by the media. We were born with all of the right equipment. We just need to be open to and unafraid of the untapped potential of "consciousness expansion" of a non-intellectual kind. Pluto/Neptune can take us to the far reaches of our mind, yet self-doubt and fear can lock the doors of perception and deny us entrance to this non-linear dimension. LSD and mysticism, sampled by some in the 1960s as one way to explore these realms, are now replaced by mind-bending excursions into virtual reality that amaze those computer-savvy pioneers on the Pluto/Neptune cutting edge of digital technology. Pluto also can put a lot of vital energy into Neptune's belief in miracles, not from divine sources necessarily, but brought about due to collective human effort and a mass application of will. People coming together in good faith for a hope-filled cause (Neptune) can evoke the transformative energies of Pluto.

Remember Woodstock '69—that historic mega love-and-light music festival in upstate New York? It began with Richie Havens performing late afternoon on Friday at around 5:07 P.M. on August 15, 1969 (Woodstock, New York)[1], and continued until the mid-morning of Monday, August 18. If you do a chart for that time, you'll see that Pluto (accompanied by Uranus conjunct Jupiter) was in the Ninth House sextile Neptune in the Eleventh. Both the Ninth and Eleventh Houses deal with progressive movements embracing futurist social trends. Woodstock was a vivid example of mass faith and will, working hand in hand. It was certainly a landmark social event of the times, yet one that had a great potential for Neptunian failure due to the logistics involved (the moody weather alone). Still, the will of the people prevailed and a miracle not only manifested but set a precedent.

In later years, big humanitarian events on an international scale involving charity causes or disaster relief have benefited immensely from huge gatherings of people brought together by the power of music. In this regard, Neptune on a societal level has much to gain from Pluto's ability to bring vibrant energy and a creative commitment to ideals that help to make for a more compassionate world. All art forms, including musical and theatrical (Neptune), play a dynamic role here that goes far beyond mere entertainment. Pluto helps Neptunian musicians to crusade for causes in ways that reach the heart and soul of the masses; and it's a trend that still continues.

WOUNDED DREAMS

For those of us born with the sextile throughout the 1940s, transiting Pluto had conjunct our Neptune when we were about twenty-nine. That was around the time of our Saturn Return, or close enough to it. Check the ephemeris (folks born in 1900 had the conjunction around age eight or nine, suggesting different psychological dynamics at work; those born in the 1970s had the conjunction by age twenty-five). Saturn Returns alone bring us down to earth and forces us to deal with the rules of real world, like it or not. This first Saturn Return may have been extra-tough on all escapists, as bubble-bursting Pluto simultaneously shook Neptune out of its trance and forced dreamers and schemers to take a cold, hard look at their illusions.

Our emotional blind spots and spiritual assumptions were up for harsh review. It was a time of disenchantment, but also a time to face the facts about earthly life. Many "flower children" during this transit in the mid-to-late 1970s probably left their rural communes, hung up their love beads, and went looking for regular jobs in the big cities—and they probably did so with much sadness. For them, their beautiful Neptunian dream was wounded by a few stark truths that Pluto forced them to admit. No matter what generation we're a member of, this is Pluto's intent: self-deceptive idealism must be destroyed.

Every generation manages to escape in different ways (maybe it's workaholism by glorifying busyness for the Neptune-in-Virgo group; or maybe it's seeking the perfect partner and avoiding interpersonal conflict for the Neptune-in-Libra bunch). During this transit, we need to determine if we have been feeding ourselves fantasies that barely enable us to get through the drudgeries of life, and may hold us back from developing our potential. If so, Pluto says that we can't afford to take another bite without getting sick, or sicker. Addictions to drugs, alcohol, and even sex ensnared a large number of people in the hedonistic '70s. Most of us didn't feel dysfunctional then, just passionately alive and bursting with energy to squander!

By the late 1970s, more than a few baby boomers were showing signs of burn-out (which can be a typical Plutonian symptom before we begin to rebuild ourselves). For many, patterns of alcoholism were well-developed, the drugs of choice started getting harder (cocaine), and the very first life-threatening cases of HIV transmission were insidiously developing, without advance warning, in Western cultures. There were darn good reasons why Pluto was more than ready for certain dangerous lifestyles to come to an uncompromising halt during this planet's passage through Scorpio (1983 to 1995).

Those who didn't wake up and begin to clean up their act by the start of the 1980s continued on a Neptunian downward spiral of slow suffering, psychological as well as physical. There was also, for some, the disillusionment of not being able to sustain the innocent and seemingly light-filled spiritual highs of earlier years. Some of the "gurus" in whom a few of us put our total faith eventually proved to be false prophets, interested in mind-control and all-too-earthbound forms of material power. The group born with Saturn conjunct Neptune (from late 1952 to the beginning of 1954) were particularly susceptible.

However, for those who never partied the nights away, or went hog-wild during the sexual revolution, or even sought bliss in the cocoon of an ashram, Pluto conjuncting Neptune still brought personal reality into sharper and sometimes painful focus. Wherever we show a talent for fooling ourselves, that's where our Neptune is actively at work, usually in collusion with other planets that refuse to grow up. The better we get at self-deception, the more lost or further out-of-touch we are with our real self. As new generations experience Pluto's conjunction to Neptune, the lifestyle challenges will be quite different—but the theme is the same. Pluto wants Neptune to expand consciousness without resorting to short-cuts that sabotage us and destroy our beautiful vision of collective harmony.

RESURRECTION TIME

If we stay psychologically healthy while we learn to balance our practical needs with our spiritual yearnings (no matter how non-ritualized our spirituality has become), some of us will be ready for the "resurrection" sextile in our early fifties. This could start off as a slump period for those of us too young to retire, but also too bored to carry on with the same old routine. Pluto is willing to give a few of our dreams a shot of vitality, as long as we're on the right track. We can get our second wind in life (or is it our third by now?) and let our imagination design viable and valuable life solutions.

This resurgence of creative power is probably also happening because transiting Pluto is trining itself for the natal Pluto-sextile-Neptune crowd. This could be a marvelous time to immerse ourselves once again in spiritual practices, for all the right reasons. We're less zealous about our beliefs (we have less energy to go down that route again) and better able to find sound ways to incorporate our spirituality into our material realities. We now possess a grounded maturity that we probably did not have in our twenties.

If we still are not getting the message, and are floundering in our life direction on all counts, then a decade later, transiting Pluto's square to Neptune bears down on us in less "creatively flowing" ways. Depression and emotionally related illness could be one way to realize the authenticity crisis that we are in, and have been in for decades. We're not all that alive and definitely not so well! Sometimes with Pluto (and most of the time with Neptune), when we're not willing to heal ourselves (and raise the dead that we've become), suffering has to play out its own cycle. Self-pity will not make us feel like we can lick our fate. It's very discouraging to be caught up in such a mind-trap. If we need to have faith to restore our sense of our own goodness and worth, let's give it our all during the resurrection sextile period, because a stronger and more self-content future awaits us!

Well, I hope that you have enjoyed reading *Alive and Well with Pluto,* volume three of my *Alive and Well* trilogy. If you haven't by now, I strongly advise you to read volume one—*Alive and Well with Uranus*—in which we discover how truly one-of-a-kind we can be if we just allow ourselves needed breakthroughs in self-discovery. And don't forget volume two—*Alive and Well with Neptune*—in which we learn about our imagination's power to assist us in envisioning an ideal sense of self that is lovingly guided by our soul's wiser ways.

NOTE

1. I got Woodstock's 5:07 P.M. starting time from *The Woodstock '69 Page* on the Internet (http://www.netwalk.com/~ailes/woodstock.html). This page may have moved or might no longer exist by the time you read this book.

BIBLIOGRAPHY

I am listing the titles of some books that either contain information about Pluto transits, or describe the nature of Pluto at length. This is certainly not a complete list of what's available; I tried to mostly select books that are not out-of-print and hard to find. Happy reading!

PLUTO

Cunningham, Donna. *Healing Pluto Problems.* York Beach, ME: Samuel Weiser, Inc. 1986.

Green, Jeff Wolf. *Pluto: The Evolutionary Journey of the Soul.* St. Paul, MN: Llewellyn Worldwide, 1985.

———. *Pluto, Vol.II: The Soul's Evolution Through Relationships.* St. Paul, MN: Llewellyn Worldwide, 1997.

Greene, Liz. *The Astrology of Fate.* York Beach, ME: Samuel Weiser, Inc., 1984.

Forrest, Steven. *The Book of Pluto.* San Diego, CA: ACS Publications, 1994.

Paul, Haydyn. *Phoenix Rising: Exploring the Astrological Pluto*. Dorset, England: Element Books Limited, 1988.

ALL OUTER PLANETS

Ashman, Bernie. *Roadmap to Your Future*. San Diego, CA: ACS Publications, 1994.

Arroyo, Stephen. *Astrology, Karma, and Transformation*. 2nd Revised/Expanded Edition. Sebastopol, CA: CRCS Publications, 1993.

Forrest, Steven. *The Changing Sky*. 2nd Revised Edition. San Diego, CA: ACS Publications, 1998.

Greene, Liz. *The Outer Planets and Their Cycles*. 2nd Edition. Sebastopol, CA: CRCS Publications, 1996.

Hand, Rob. *Planets in Transit*. Atglen PA: Schiffer Publishing, Ltd., 1980.

Marks, Tracy. *The Astrology of Self-Discovery*. Sebastopol, CA: CRCS Publications, 1985.

Rodden, Lois. *Modern Transits*. Tempe, AZ: AFA, 1978.

Rudhyar, Dane. *The Sun Is Also a Star—The Galactic Dimension of Astrology*. New York, NY: E.P. Dutton & Co., 1975. (Hard to find.)

Sasportas, Howard. *The Gods of Change: Pain, Crisis and the Transits of Uranus, Neptune, and Pluto*. New York, NY: Arkana—Viking Penguin, Inc., 1989. (This is the only book I'm aware of that gives an in-depth coverage of all three planets in a single volume; I definitely recommend that you have this book on your library shelf.)

Thorton, Penny. *Divine Encounters*. London, England: The Aquarian Press, 1991.

Tompkins, Sue. *Aspects in Astrology*. Dorset, England: Element Books Limited, 1989.

Tyl, Noel, ed. *How to Personalize the Outer Planets: The Astrology of Uranus, Neptune, and Pluto*. St. Paul, MN: Llewellyn Publications, 1992. (This is an anthology presenting the works of seven astrologers.)

MYTHOLOGY

Aldington, Richard and Delano Ames. *New Larousse Enclyclopedia of Mythology.* New York, NY: The Hamlyn Publishing Group Limited, 1978. (Hard to find.)

Bolen, Jean Shinoda. *Goddesses in Everywoman.* New York, NY: HarperCollins Publishers, 1989.

———. *Gods in Everyman.* HarperCollins Publishers, 1989.

Clark, Brian. *Hades as Place: The Underworld in Myth and Antiquity.* Abbotsford, Victoria, Australia: Astro*Synthesis Publications, 1998.

Gayley, Charles Mills. *The Classic Myths in English Literature and in Art.* Atlanta, GA: Ginn & Company, 1939; Cheshire, CT: Biblo - Moser, 1991 (paperback edition).

Morford, Mark P. O. and Robert J. Lenardon. *Classical Mythology.* New York, NY: Longman, Inc., 1977.

Richardson, Donald. *Greek Mythology for Everyone: Legends of the Gods and Heroes.* New York, NY: Avenel Books, 1989.

TWELVE FACES OF SATURN
Your Guardian Angel Planet
Bil Tierney

Astrological Saturn. It's usually associated with personal limitations, material obstacles, psychological roadblocks and restriction. We observe Saturn's symbolism in our natal chart with uneasiness and anxiety, while intellectually proclaiming its higher purpose as our "wise teacher."

But now it's time to throw out the portrait of the creepy looking, scythe-wielding Saturn of centuries ago. Bil Tierney offers a refreshing new picture of a this planet as friend, not foe. Saturn is actually key to liberating us from a life handicapped by lack of clear self definition. It is indispensable to psychological maturity and material stability—it is your guardian angel planet.

Explore Saturn from the perspective of your natal sign and house. Uncover another layer of Saturnian themes at work in Saturn's aspects. Look at Saturn through each element and modality, as well as through astronomy, mythology and metaphysics.

1–56718–711–0, 6 x 9, 360 pp.   **$16.95**

THE HOUSE BOOK
The Influence of the Planets in the Houses
Stephanie Camilleri

What gave Marilyn Monroe, John Lennon, John F. Kennedy, and Joan of Arc their compelling charisma—could it be that they all had planets in the Eighth House? Find out why someone with Venus in the Fifth may be a good marriage partner, and why you may want to stay away from a suitor with Uranus in the Second.

Now you can probe the inner meaning of the planets in your chart through their placement in the houses. *The House Book* provides a solid base for students of astrology, and gives advanced astrologers new ways of looking at planet placement.

The author culled the similarities of house qualities from 1,500 different charts in as intensive and as scientific a method as possible. The most important feature of this book is that each description was written from the perspective of real charts with that location, without referencing preconceived ideas from other books. In some places, the common wisdom is confirmed, but in others the results can be very surprising.

1-56718-108-2, 5 ³/₁₆ x 8, 288 pp., softcover   **$12.95**

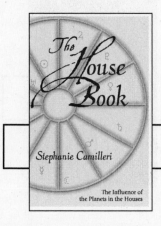

To order call 1–800–THE MOON
Prices subject to change without notice.

PLUTO, VOL. II
The Soul's Evolution Through Relationships
Jeffrey Wolf Green

From the great mass of people on the planet we all choose certain ones with whom to be intimate. *Pluto, Vol II* shows the evolutionary and karmic causes, reasons, and prior life background that determines whom we relate to and how.

This is the first book to explore the astrological Pluto model that embraces the evolutionary development and progression of the Soul from life to life. It offers a unique, original paradigm that allows for a total understanding of the past life dynamics that exist between two people. You will find a precise astrological methodology to determine the prior life orientation, where the relationship left off, where the relationship picked up in this lifetime, and what the current evolutionary next step is: the specific reasons or intentions for being together again.

In addition, there are chapters devoted to Mars and Venus in the signs, Mars and Venus in relationship, Mars and Pluto in relationship, and Pluto through the Composite Houses.

1–56718–333–6, 6 x 9, 432 pp., softcover　　　　**$17.95**

ASTROLOGY: WOMAN TO WOMAN
Gloria Star

Women are the primary users and readers of astrology, yet most astrological books approach individual charts from an androgynous point of view. *Astrology: Woman to Woman* is written specifically for women, by a woman, and shows that there *is* a difference in the way men and women express and use their energy. It covers every facet of a woman's life: home, family, lovers, career, and personal power.

Whether the reader is new to astrology or an old pro, there are new insights throughout. Those of you who don't know what sign their Moon is in or which planets are in their seventh house can order a free natal chart from Llewellyn that will tell you everything you need to know to use this book.

Discover what's at the heart of your need to find a meaningful career, understand your inner feminine power, own up to your masculine self, uncover your hidden agendas, and much more.

1–56718–686–6, 7 x 10, 464 pp.   **$19.95**